JOHN CROFT, ... D

CW01660899

LEE B. CROFT

SPHYNX PUBLICATIONS

MMXXIII
2023

Dear Cousin Tony & Val & Family—
Best wishes for 2024!
Lee B. Croft
1/22/24

© COPYRIGHT Lee B. Croft, 2023
ALL RIGHTS RESERVED WORLD WIDE

No part of this book may be reproduced, stored in a retrieval system, or transmitted by any means without the written permission of the author.

Sphynx Publications is located at 11622 S. Tusayan Ct., Phoenix, Arizona, 85044, USA. The author is Sphynx Publications' Editor-in-Chief, and Agent for all transactions, sales, and advertising purposes. His cell phone number is 480-567-4501 and his email is leecroft333@gmail.com. **ISBN** is **978-0-9884768-9-9**.

The author, Lee B. Croft (1946—), is a teacher, scholar, and Professor Emeritus of the Russian Language and Culture at Arizona State University (ASU), where he taught and administered foreign language programs for 38 years (1973-2011). He is the author of 25 books and over 330 scholarly texts, articles, translations and reviews… "Google" him at "Lee B. Croft."

INTRODUCTION:

This is a work of "faction" about the life of my own great great grandfather, John Croft (1807-1883), meaning that I have recorded in my relation all the known facts about his life, but have filled in the gaps with fiction, plausibly based on his life as I see it. This is the THIRD of THREE books of this nature about him, being preceded as paperbacks in the Sphynx Publications biography series by *John Croft in Burma* (2018, ISBN 9781790872336) and by *John Croft, Aussie Tycoon (2020, ISBN 9798565973303)* and their respective Kindle editions all available at amazon.com.

Here I point out to the reader that the special dedication, the "Table of Contents" and the "List of Illustrations" are to be found AT THE REAR OF THE BOOK on pp. 427, 428, and 429. Cover by Fiverr Designer David Montalbo.

ACKNOWLEDGEMENTS:

I owe a debt of gratitude to many people in my own life whose contributions to this as well as my other literary creations are profound. First is my wife, Dr. Lesley Hoyt Croft, who has read and edited my works with a sharp and competent eye for many years. Also, I have to mention my father, William Sydney "Bill" Croft (1919-2003), who encouraged my research into our family. And my mother, Norma Rose Dingeldein Croft (1927-2022), who inspired me to read, get well educated, and make positive contributions to the lives of others. My English cousin, Margaret Craig Young, whom I regard as the family's leading genealogical researcher and records keeper, has been wonderfully helpful and insightful in her aid to me. The further list into family, friends, and professional colleagues, beyond Margaret's husband, Dr. Stewart Young, is long and is also to be seen in the two preceding books of this series. I dedicate this work to all of them and remind them yet again of the Croft family motto: "**Esse Quam Videri**" ("To be rather than to seem").

JOHN CROFT, BACK IN ENGLAND

By: Lee B. Croft

CHAPTER ONE: Synopses of the Two Previous Books.

Briefly synopsizing content from the preceding books in this series, I relate here that John William Croft was born in a Craven Street house in Shoreditch, Middlesex County, London, at "45 minutes to 1 a.m." on July 16, 1807. He was baptized at St. Leonard's Church there that August 16th. But his family…father Nicholas, mother Mary, brother John James and sister Surrey Martha then moved to Hitchin and then to Hoddesdon in Hertfordshire, where his father Nicholas founded a successful cooperage business and his mother had more children, sons Edmund and Nicholas. John William grew up there in a small house on the outskirts of Hoddesdon.

In my first book about him, *John Croft in Burma* (Sphynx Publications, 2018), John William, an 1823 graduate of the Addiscombe Military Seminary in the London, England, borough of Croyden, became an officer in the British Honourable East India Company's (HEIC) army during the First Anglo-Burmese War of 1824-1826, achieving even at a quite young age both a military medal for gallantry under fire in which he was wounded and his early promotion to the rank of Captain.

In his first battle he took from a killed Burmese soldier's clothing a bag of large cut diamonds and rubies which had decorated the top spire of the historic Schwedagon Pagoda in Rangoon (now Yangon). On February 20, 1825, he married Burma's first woman convert to Christianity, Mah Men Le (b. 9 Jan., 1799—d. 16 Sept., 1827), whom he called "Mena." He adopted and gave the surname "Croft" to her daughter, Mi Kaw Le (b. 25 May, 1815—d. 5 Aug., 1827) whom he called "Mi Mi." And John and Mena had a son of their own, John Edmund Croft (b. 3 Feb., 1827—d. 3 Sept., 1827).

In the course of related events, John offered the Burmese King Bagyidaw a fortune in diamonds to diminish the lethality of his imprisonment of Mena's mentors, the American Baptist missionaries, Adoniram and Anne Hasseltine Judson, who played a large role in Mena's and John's lives.

As an infantry officer in many close combat battles in Burma, John, though wounded severely once, survived. And, exposed with his fellow soldiers to all manner and type of disease…killing more soldiers than the combat even…he somehow survived. But family misfortune haunted young John Croft's time in Burma. His beloved wife Mena died of both fever and grief after her daughter Mi Mi was killed by Burmese agents of King Bagyidaw, and infant son John Edmund died of illness and possibly opiate medications at 7 months of age. John's wife Mena and children Mi Mi and John Edmund are buried in Amherst (now Kyaikkhami) in the Mon State of Burma (now Myanmar). Before he left Burma in November of 1827, John entered into an agreement with Rev. Adoniram Judson to "broker" the confiscated diamonds so as to enrich John in British pounds and financially benefit the struggling American Baptist mission in Burma as well.

John returned to England a widower and was honourably discharged from the HEIC army by October of 1828 when he was only 21 years old. He worked for a time at his father Nicholas Croft's (1768-1837) cooperage business in Hoddesdon, Hertfordshire…CROFT CASK, KEG, and BARREL COMPANY.

In my second book on John Croft's life, *John Croft, Aussie Tycoon* (Sphynx Publications, 2020), I relate that when he was once again settled in Hoddesdon with his parents' family, John was 6 feet 2 inches tall and weighed 13 stone (186 lbs.). He won admiration from his peers for his physical strength and ability to run long distances at speed. He was locally renowned as a wrestler and could beat almost anyone at arm-wrestling and doing his style of "chins" on an elevated horizontal bar. He could swing a heavy sledge hammer for hours in the heat without tiring. No one could match his records for single-handed loading of the oaken barrels onto transport carts. He could throw a barrel twelve yards.

It was his physical prowess that earned John Croft the local magistrate's appointment as an "apparitor," a constable responsible for serving court warrants and eviction orders and for making sure litigants and defendants showed up to court as scheduled. John later told his relatives that his apparitor's job caused him to be engaged in some kind of dangerous chase or physical fight "at least weekly" for the two years he worked in that position. He had to become practiced at submission holds and knockout punches to keep himself "in one piece." The "only thing positive about it," he said, "was that it gave me a real interest in the law."

John's parents, Nicholas and Mary, had not reacted well to their son John's news to them by letter of his marriage in Burma. They told him they had so disapproved of his marrying so young at age 17 without their consent and having children with a woman of a foreign race that they had ceased writing to him in Burma. Upon his return to them in 1828 they asked him not to tell others about his marrying there at all…this to spare the family embarrassment and possible ostracization.

But in the close family itself, that including his older sister Surrey Martha Croft Metcalf and her husband Thomas, who lived nearby, and his younger brother Nicholas who was then still in his teens, John was resolute, stressing that his Burmese wife Mena and their children were "such beautiful Christians as God himself would exalt, and that anyone who would come to know them would realize what a boon and a source of pride to his young life they certainly were."

After his "Burmese diamonds money" was deposited in pounds in his personal C. Hoare London bank account in October of 1830, about which he told nobody (not even his parents), John ceased working and moved to a London apartment to enroll in the initial class of the law faculty of King's College London in 1831. He applied for and received a British Solicitor's License in June of 1834, but, instead of beginning an independent law practice, he took a salaried legal advisor's position with the London-based international mercantile firm of Day, Son and Hewitson Ltd., which specialized in the sales of sailing ship equipment (e.g. hemp and jute rope, cordage, and canvas sailcloth).

In 1836, John's younger brother Nicholas, then a promising young businessman of 23 (b. 14 Jan., 1813) in his father's Croft Cask, Keg, and Barrel (CCKB) cooperage left England to travel to Moscow, Russia, as a representative for the sale of mechanized agricultural implements on behalf of Richard Garrett and Sons, Ltd. of Leiston in Suffolk. The Head of that company at that time was Richard Garrett III (1807-1866), who, at the "Leiston Works," had provided CCKB with heavy-duty carts and carriages to transport their products through the manufacturing process and for delivery to customers. At his father's request, John Croft had traveled to Leiston and consulted personally with Richard Garrett III about the legal requirements of conducting international sales of this nature…as he was then doing for Day, Son, and Hewitson. He and Richard Garrett III, who were the same age and had much else in common personally, got along quite well, so that John's recommendation of his younger brother for the Garretts' lucrative new business opportunity in Russia was positively accepted.

In September of 1837, John received a letter from his mother, Mary Mann Croft (1770-1840), saying that his father Nicholas had taken seriously ill in Hoxton, New Town, Shoreditch. John hurried there by rented carriage and was at his father's bedside for four days until he passed away on September 26th of an apparent lung ailment. During their short time together, father Nicholas made son John his primary heir and the executor of his will. And, he expressed his remorse about how he and John's mother Mary had not shown John what he now, facing death, realized was appropriate support for his son's marriage and his having children with his "Mena" more than a decade previously in far away Burma. Nicholas, who could barely breathe, squeezed John's hand and said, "I love you and I'm proud of you and ALL of your life so far. And I now consider it a privilege that I will be meeting your Mena soon. Tell your mother I said that."

At father Nicholas's funeral in Hoddesdon was John's uncle, James Stead (1767-1848) of the Islington suburb in London, a founding partner in the Oriental Import firm of Davison & Stead, who had, his fortune assured, just allowed his partner Robert Davison to buy him out so that he, then 70, could retire. With him was his youngest daughter, Mary Ann, a "maiden spinster" of 25, who had once, at age 9 when John had first declared to them his intention to enroll in Croyden's Addiscombe Military Seminary to become an officer in the Honourable East India Company, promised him that she would "pray for him" as a soldier of the British Empire and that she was confident that "God will take care of you."

Unexpectedly NOT with the Steads at Nicholas Croft's funeral was Nicholas's twin sister Mary Croft Stead, James Stead's wife and Mary Ann Stead's mother. She was, James said, "too ill to leave their home, having trouble breathing." When John told his uncle James and cousin Mary Ann that it had been a breathing trouble that had resulted in his father Nicholas's death, Mary Ann broke into tears, asking her father, "Might twins die together, Dad? Will mother also be leaving now?" James answered dismissively of that possibility, assuring his dismayed daughter: "She's just got some kind of cold, that's all. She'll be all right."

But Mary Croft Stead, John's beloved aunt, passed away only a month after her twin brother Nicholas Croft at the same age of 69 years. Her daughter Mary Ann was distraught but was able, at her mother's funeral, to read from a poem she had written into her personal notebook the previous year:

"As a shock of corn fully ripened lies
So she to her grave is come,
While angels are wafting thro' the skys
And shouting her 'Welcome home'."

Before January 1st of 1838, John, taking a lesson from his uncle James Stead's retirement buy-out arrangement with partner Robert Davison, negotiated the sale of the Croft Cask, Keg, and Barrell Company to a group of its employees headed by Chief Foreman Jed Carruthers, arranging for a total price of £30,000 to be paid in monthly increments of £250 for ten years from the company profits into an account he set up in his name at C. Hoare & Co. private bank on Fleet Street in London…his intent being to distribute equal shares of the money (i.e. starting values of £50/month each) to himself, to his widowed mother Mary Mann Croft, to his older sister Surrey Martha Croft Metcalf (1803-1865), to his younger brother Nicholas Croft, and to his sister-in-law, deceased brother John James's widow Elisabeth Wallace Croft (1800-1854)…all his father and mother's direct surviving heirs. Since Surrey Martha and her husband Thomas Metcalf were taking active care of their mother in their home, John was able to sell the family home and deposit the money (£500) also into the C. Hoare & Co. account. He arranged for the Metcalfs' share to be augmented by both Mother Mary's share as well as half of his own share and half of his brother Nicholas's share too, since brother Nicholas, then 24 years old, had moved away to Moscow, Russia. After Mother Mary's death in December of 1840, her share was split among the others. John kept signatory control of the money deposited into his sister's accounts, his sister-in-law's account, and his brother Nicholas's account because of the difficulties of drawing on the funds from Moscow.

For over three years, from February 1838 to June 1841, John Croft was involved in a largely sexual affair with Catherine Shairp Marryat (1796-1883). She was the wife of Captain Frederick Marryat (1792-1848) who had commanded the ship *HMS Larne* when John, a just graduated infantry ensign of 16, was first transported to Madras, India, with the HEIC 102nd Foot in 1823-4. Captain Marryat's wife Catherine, whom he had married in 1819, was accompanying him on the *HMS Larne*. She was the daughter of Sir Stephen Shairp (1757-1826), Great Britain's Consul in St. Petersburg, Russia. She had been born there, and was named "Catherine" after Russia's Tsarina (Empress) at the time called "Catherine the Great." She spoke Russian fluently and was interested in learning the languages of their immediate destination, India. She was the only woman in the shipboard Hindustani class that young John Croft was attending. But it turned out that Catherine was pregnant and the ship's physician diagnosed her with measles. Volunteers were called for to accompany her in the ship's lifeboat (of a type that was actually designed by her husband) which would be towed behind the ship to isolate her from the navy crew of 145 and the ship's 60 army passengers. Since John had survived the measles as a child, he volunteered, and, from among several volunteers, Catherine chose him because he was the only man she knew from her Hindustani class.

The lifeboat measles quarantine in the Indian Ocean was a trial made dangerously severe because of the storms the *HMS Larne* had to pass through during that time. So John Croft and Catherine Marryat, eleven years older than he and pregnant, became close friends in their miserable confinement before her improvement signaled that they could be returned safely to the ship. But because of the pregnancy, Catherine was to be left in Madras in January of 1824 to give birth while her husband sailed on to the Andaman Islands to meet other ships of the British 120-ship naval convoy transporting soldiers to a place near the conflict in Burma. John Croft and the other soldiers of the 102nd Foot were also left temporarily in Madras at Fort St. George, where in a nearby village he and two of his army friends witnessed a cultural horror—the triple "Suttee" pyre incineration of a deceased prominent villager's wives.

When in mid-March of 1824 Catherine Marryat gave birth to a son, she had him baptized in Fort St. George's St. Mary's Anglican Church. She found John Croft and his friends at the army dining hall and asked him to be the baby's godfather and hold him for the anointment during the service. At the ceremony she had the baby boy named Frederick Jr. after her husband, and asked John to inform Captain Marryat of the event if he should happen to encounter him during the impending events of the First Anglo-Burmese War. As it happened, infantry officer John Croft did more than once encounter and interact with Captain Marryat at the river port of Rangoon during the conflict and did indeed first inform him of his wife's health and the baby's status as a boy given his father's name baptized with him, then already Lieutenant John Croft, as the godfather.

For several years, John Croft had been aware that Captain Frederick Marryat had resigned his commission in the British Navy in 1830 and taken to writing novels. John had sought out Frederick Marryat's book, *The King's Own,* and liked the former Captain's vivid portrayal of the lives of sailors at war. But in the first week of January 1838 he happened to see in a London bookstore a graphic display featuring Marryat's recent novels and he purchased one, *Mr. Midshipman Easy* (1836) to read. One of the bookstore clerks told John that he had heard that "Captain Marryat" had become wealthy enough as a popular author and "an associate of Charles Dickens" to buy a grand house called Gothic Lodge in a wealthy neighborhood of Wimbledon…and that he even knew the address, which he communicated to John.

John Croft went to visit the Gothic Lodge in Winbledon later that very week…indeed the house is STILL there… seeking an audience with Captain Frederick Marryat, telling the liveried household servant who answered the door that he was "Captain John Croft of Her Majesty's 102nd Foot, Retired." The servant, a Mr. Lawrence, replied that "Captain Marryat is not here. He is presently in the United States or Canada and will not be returning soon. Would you like to speak with the Lady of the house?"

Fatefully, John quickly answered "Yes, I would very much like to do so, thank you."

When Catherine Marryat entered the Gothic Lodge's parlor to greet "a military colleague of the Captain's," she was surprised when she saw her one-time lifeboat mate John Croft rising from his sofa seat and saying to her "How nice to see you. Do you remember me?"

She came right up to him and embraced him warmly, saying "Of course I remember you, John. And it is indeed nice to see you too. I have often wondered if I would ever see you again.

John told her, "I found you through a bookstore clerk who knows about your husband, the Captain. He's become quite famous now."

Catherine's face darkened noticeably and she said, "Yes, but we are separated. He is away, but he doesn't really live here with me anymore. He's leased a house in the city for himself and only comes by now and then to visit the children."

"Well, I'm sorry to hear that," muttered John, "But tell me about the children. Is my godson Frederick, Jr. all right? Can I see him?'"

Catherine answered with a smile, "No, Freddie's already followed his father into the Navy and is at sea. He's only 14 years old and is already in the Navy at sea."

"Have you had other children?" asked John.

"John, you may be surprised to learn that I've had ELEVEN children," she said. "Four boys including Freddie, and seven daughters."

John exclaimed, "What? Eleven?! Now, I really AM surprised. That's a wonder."

"Well, we lost three of the eleven as infants or babies…and are left with eight," she explained. "I've hired a Russian Nanny named Tanya to help me in the training and raising of them. Frederick has essentially abandoned all responsible parenthood. He only sends money."

And that was the start of their affair, in the course of which both Catherine and John found understanding and sympathetic confidants. Together they discussed the controversial issues of the day…slavery, revolution, colonial management, the nobles, business and trade…and found that they generally agreed with each other on everything. Only did they disagree on Frederick Marryat. Catherine praised his manifest genius in several spheres of achievement, but very often complained about him too…his needless expenditures, his constant travel, the frequent rumors about his liaisons with other women. John was not personally acquainted with any of Frederick's negative aspects. He could only praise his courage in combat, his able leadership, his able artwork and literary endeavors. But together Catherine and John contrived, with Nanny Tanya's cooperation with the children, to meet regularly at John's London apartment for light meals, long conversations, and, during Catherine's first post-menstruation week so as not to risk conception, truly enjoyable sex. They almost never appeared in public together. John did become acquainted with Catherine's children, notably young daughters Flo, Augusta, and little Emmy, during some visited outings or during intermittent visits to the Gothic Lodge for contrived reasons.

In June of 1841, however, 33-year-old John Croft and 44-year-old Catherine Marryat mutually decided that their affair should end for a number of completely sensible reasons…his lack of marital possibilities, her children. So those who had become so very close in life stepped apart and stayed apart for each other's sake.

John decided it was time for him to find a new wife. Catherine had often told him that "Mena would not be displeased, but would want him to find another wife while still in his reproductive years." So John confided in his friend George Davison, the 35-year-old son of John's uncle James Stead's former business partner Robert Davison, and the husband of James Stead's older daughter Jane, spinster Mary Ann's sister. George proposed that he and Jane find some desirable lady candidates and invite them to family dinners where John would be. It would be John's responsibility to choose to get to know better those he preferred… or not.

For the next year and a half, John had met several of Robert and Jane Stead Davisons' marital candidates and did make efforts to get to know three of them better with dates to London public events and even visits to their parents' homes and to their churches. But, he told Robert in the fall of 1842, "None of them are right for me…I just don't feel that 'spark,' you know?"

John was invited to dinner at his uncle James Stead's home in the London borough of Islington's Brixton section for Christmas 1842. The Davisons …father Robert, son George and daughter-in-law (and daughter of James) Jane…were there. Also there, from Ovingdean near Brighton in Sussex, were James's son, now the newly ordained Rev. Alfred and his wife, Emma Robson Stead.

When John arrived at the Steads' home, he noticed that his cousin Mary Ann was dressed up in all her best finery and with her dark brown hair dangling in curls below her ears. She was posing for a portrait, being painted by their mutual cousin-in-law, the renowned ivory turner and miniaturist Nathaniel Brown Engleheart (1790-1869). Nathaniel had married Margaret Croft Curteis, niece of John's father's older sister Margaret. Nathaniel was coaching Mary Ann in her posing position and facial expression as he worked in front of his easel, instructing "Just turn your face a bit to the right…don't grin so…just smile sweetly. That's it."

The meal was a memorable success, with patriarch James Stead at the head of the table giving the prayer of grace, after which fourteen family members seated around the table all engaged in conversation as they ate. And, after the meal, Mary Ann was able to show everyone her completed miniature portrait, holding it up alongside her face to demonstrate, "cousin Nathaniel's great skill in portraiture."

When John was contemplating Mary Ann's freshly painted portrait, he was remembering how she had once, in that very house as a nine-year-old girl, promised to pray for him when he was a soldier, saying that because of her prayers, "God will take care of you." And indeed he thought, "God did take care of me in Burma and since." Now, seeing her as an adult and her portrait, he thought to himself, "She really is a beautiful thing."

A black-and-white photograph of Nathaniel Brown Engleheart's December 25, 1842 miniature oil painting of Mary Ann Stead, age 30. From Croft Family Archives (henceforth "CFA")

John asked her, "Mary Ann, you are 30 years old now. Why have you not married?"

This was apparently a sensitive question to her and she snapped back, "And you are 35. Why have YOU not married?"

John was taken aback. He did not mean to cause her offense. And he was starkly reminded that she and the rest of her family members there did not know that he HAD married in Burma when he was a soldier just 17 years old... and that he had lost his wife and children there by the age of 20. He looked significantly at George and Jane and said, "I'm looking now, but just haven't met the right woman."

To his surprise, Mary Ann then asked, "Might we marry each other, being first cousins?"

John said, "Many people have married cousins. But perhaps not so many where the groom's father and the bride's mother were TWINS."

"You are a solicitor," Mary Ann said, "Is there any law against it?"

"Not that I'm aware of," answered John.

"Then I think you should ask my father for permission to court me," she said. Her sister Jane, who was standing close by, gasped involuntarily when she heard this. But she smiled when John answered, " I've known you all my life. And I truly think you would make me an ideal wife and mother. I'll do it right now."

So James Stead, when asked, made sure that Mary Ann did indeed want to be courted…with the serious intention of soon impending marriage…by her cousin John Croft. He warned John that he did not believe in dowries, about which John averred that he "didn't care." So James then said to him, "Then I give you my permission to court, and, hopefully, to marry, my daughter Mary Ann. May God have mercy on your soul." The guests, hearing this surprising announcement, were pleased and amused by their host's response.

On New Year's Day, 1843, John came to get Mary Ann in a carriage and drove her to the central London offices of Day, Son, and Hewitson where he worked. The offices were closed for the holiday but senior partner Arthur Day was there to collect some documents. When John introduced Mary to him as his "fiancée," causing Mary to blush, Arthur Day, a large corpulent man of 60, assured her, "My dear, I'm very happy for you. Here we think that John Croft is a man of real promise."

From his workplace John then drove Mary to the building of his London apartment…at 7 Northhampton Place, assuring her that he was "a gentleman, swearing that he had no present designs on her virtue in his bachelor's abode. He wanted her to see that he lived personally without pretense. "And I have some things to tell you about myself that you don't know. And that, after you've heard them, you may change your mind about wanting to marry me."

In the next hour, John candidly told Mary Ann about his time as a soldier in Burma, including that he married there and had children there…and then lost them, coming home a widower, and a very wealthy one. Only did he not mention his more recent affair with Catherine Marryat.

After only a few minutes of thought, Mary Ann answered, "Well, this is a lot to digest. You've killed many people in a war as have many exemplary biblical characters. All right, it was kill or be killed for the sake of our country…God will forgive you if you ask him to. You've married and had children. And God took them all from you. But it's also God's will that you can remarry and have more children. You've chosen another Christian faith…that of the American Baptists. But you can surely tolerate my remaining committed to the Anglican one you were born into. And perhaps I can convince you to be rebaptized into it. To God, as you say your Mena told you, all Christian faiths are one. And your fortune taken by chance there in Burma you have only done good things with, supporting a Christian mission and paying for your own education with which you mean to help others. All in all, I may dun you with endless questions and clarifications of your very sad past, but I will marry you in confidence that you are, deep inside, a very good man. I can say with pride that 'I love you and still want to marry you'."

In early March of 1843, Senior Partner Arthur Day became seriously concerned about the recent financial performance of Day, Son, and Hewitson's Sydney, Australia, office. John Croft's documentary study of the situation revealed that since a Mr. Ian Farley had taken control of that office as its Director, that office's revenues had drastically dwindled. So Arthur Day made John Croft an exciting proposition. "John," he said, "We think you should take a trip to Sydney to get to the bottom of this matter and hopefully turn things around. We will pay for your journey and for your residence there. And, if in fact, you can restore the Sydney office to its former level of profitability by this time in the next 1844 year, we will double your salary thereafter."

"My goodness, " exclaimed John, "I'll have to think about this. I admit that it's an attractive offer indeed and I thank you for your confidence in me to accomplish such a result."

"Well, don't think on it too long," advised Arthur Day. "We'll want to know by the middle of this coming week…Wednesday the Ides of March. The ship *Euphrates,* in which our company has a financial interest, will be departing Portsmouth on a five-month journey around the Cape of Good Hope to Sydney on Thursday, March 23rd."

When John reported the news of this offer to James and Mary Ann Stead in Islington the next day, Mary Ann exclaimed, "You're not going there without ME, are you?"

John quickly retorted, "No, you could come with me as my wife if you will have me as your husband. So this is my proposal. Will you marry me, and very soon?"

James Stead smiled as his daughter Mary Ann answered, "Yes, I will marry you and be your wife."

John told Arthur Day that he would indeed travel to Sydney and turn around the Company's profit deficiency. But the Company would have to pay for the journey and the stay for two instead of one. He invited Arthur to the wedding in Islington's Parish Church on the morning of Tuesday, March 21st. Arthur asked him, "Is it that young lady I met in the office on New Year's Day? She seemed lovely to me."

"Yes," said John, "That's her…Mary Ann Stead."

When John and Mary Ann Stead Croft boarded the grand ship *Euphrates* on March 23rd, 1843, they had with them their wedding certificate evidencing that the wedding of "John Croft, of full age, a bachelor solicitor and merchant of address 7 Northhampton Place, London, of father Nicholas Croft, deceased cooper, did, in the Parish Church of Islington in the County of Middlesex, marry Mary Stead, a spinster of address Acre Lane in Brixton, of father James Stead, a gentleman, as officiated by Alfred Burder, Curate, and witnessed on March 21, 1843, by James Stead, Jane Stead Davison, a Mrs. Berd, and a Rofser Woodward."

John and Mary Ann Croft were greeted specially by the *Euphrates* Captain Charles Campbell when they came aboard. They were shown to the ship's largest stateroom, the one adjoining the Captain's own cabin in the ship's stern. Captain Campbell's wife Caroline, a tall lean woman of 50 years, was accompanying her husband on this voyage. She told Mary Ann that they were two of only three women aboard. An English banker named Carl Worthington had his wife Sarah with him, as well as their two sons, ten-year-old Billy and seven-year-old Sam. They were among 46 passengers, served by 40 members of the crew.

During the long journey, seasickness was blessedly mild. Mary Ann told John that God was sparing them that experience so as not to interfere with their "wonderful intimate relations."

John and Mary Ann soon became good friends with three young Englishmen who were traveling to Australia to join older members of their families who were already well established and prominent members of Sydney society. Twenty-two-year-old Robert Tooth and twenty-one-year-old Edwin Tooth, born in Kent, were planning to join their forty-year-old uncle John Tooth, who had come to Sydney on the *Bencoolen* in 1828 and was now sole owner of the Kent Brewery on Sydney's Paramatta Road. Robert and Edwin said that their Uncle John wanted to lease the brewery to them for £4000 per year and that they planned to pay him from its profits while operating under the name R. and E. Tooth & Co., Ltd.

Also on board was twenty-three-year-old James Sutcliffe Mort, called "Jemmy," who was sailing to join his twenty-five-year-old brother Henry Mort, who had left England for Australia in 1840, and his twenty-seven-year-old brother Thomas Sutcliffe Mort, who had an adventurous journey to Australia on the *Superb*, arriving in February 1838. This brother Thomas Sutcliffe Mort had taken a Theresa Shepheard Laidley to wife in October 1841, and was establishing himself as a leading Sydney auctioneer and wool merchant.

The Tooth brothers, Robert and Edwin, and James Mort soon came to look up to fellow passenger John Croft as they gradually learned more about him. John was the bearer of a castled family's name who was ten years older than they. He was a retired Captain of the Honourable East India Company army who had been decorated for valor in combat in the Anglo-Burmese War and he had spent part of his army experience in India also, about which he regaled them with colorful stories. He had impressive legal credentials as a solicitor. And he shared the largest passenger stateroom on the ship with a quite attractive and erudite wife who, these others said, was a "daily joy to encounter." They later related that John Croft had a fine sense of humour, and that he spoke eloquently, but "without condescension" to everyone on the ship…Captain, sailors, and passengers alike. He was, they said, "a born leader."

Upon their arrival in Sydney on August 5th of 1843, John and Mary Ann were struck by the nearly naked Maori oarsmen of the harbor's pilot boat. When they went ashore and got their baggage amassed on the Circular Quay landing, here was a long line of horse-drawn carriages with drivers contending to transport them and their belongings to "wherever you want, my good man." One of them told John that he had a wealthy cousin who had a nice two-storey house for lease in an area called "Wooloomooloo." "I've never heard of such a place as 'Wooloomooloo.' Is that a good place for me and my wife to live? We are pretty sure that she is expecting a baby, you see. And is it near George Street? I'll be working on George Street."

For the next 14 years John and Mary Ann Croft do VERY well in Sydney, Australia, financially and socially. In short order after their arrival, John confronted Day, Son, and Hewitson Company's George Street office Director Ian Farley with evidence of his personal skimming of corporate accounts (to the tune of £5000), his losses of it all by gambling, and his cruel employee abuse…knocking him out cold when Farley attacked him physically and then having him arrested, tried, and sentenced to seven years in Sydney's Darlinghurst Gaol for embezzlement. The Company's Sydney branch office was quickly returned to profitability, exceeding previous records for revenue. But John hired James "Jemmy" Mort to manage the firm in his place so that he would be freed to involve himself in a host of enterprises with just about everyone prominent at the time in Sydney society. The list of these people is long, including a "who's who" of Sydney's movers and shakers of the 1840s and 1850s. From their already impressive rented estate in Wooloomooloo, they moved to the apex of Sydney's residential housing pyramid...with John buying and renovating an estate he called "Mount Adelaide" on the highest point of fabulous and exclusive Darling Point.

John's early chosen enterprises included a £1000 minority partnership in labor brokering (called scornfully "blackbirding" at the time) with the very colorful and controversial financier Benjamin Boyd (1801-1851) whose methods, opposed by John's religious wife Mary Ann, led John to drop his partnership with Boyd, who was later eaten by cannibals on Guadalcanal while "recruiting" native workers in Polynesia. But by that time, John, upon the advice of his recent acquaintance, storied and widely invested financier and New South Wales legislator Thomas Ware Smart (1810-1881), had already invested £500 or more into the Boydtown Whaling Company, the Sydney Railway Company, and the Australian Joint Stock Bank. He was well on his way indeed.

At the beginning of *John Croft, Aussie Tycoon*'s Chapter 14 are the following paragraphs:

"After January 1, 1853, John Croft took stock of his financial holdings. In all of the bank accounts under his control, both in England and in Australia, he had the grand sum of £216,000. The current worth of his May 1845 investments into: 1) Australian Gas Light Company; 2) Mort and Company Wool Auctioneers Company; 3) Thomas Whistler Smith Warehousiing Company; 4) Robert and Edwin Tooth's R & E Tooth Brewers; 5) Edye Manning's Australian Fire and Life Insurance Company; and 6) Edye Manning's Sydney-Paramatta Steamship Line, was £5000. His remaining January 1846 investments: 1) Sydney Railway Company; and 2) Australian Joint Stock Bank, were worth £2000. His August 1848 investment into the Sydney Exchange was worth £2500. His December 1848 investment into the Bathhurst Copper Mining Company was worth £1200. His 1849 investments into: 1) Kiama Steam Navigation Company; 2) The Bank of New South Wales; and 3) Thomas Sutcliffe Mort's Australian Mutual Provident Society (essentially an insurance Company) were worth £2000. His March 1851 investment into the merger of his Hunter River Steam Navigation Company stock into the Australasian Steam Navigation Company was worth £6000. His August 1851 investment into the Great Nugget Vein Gold Mining Company was worth £11,000. And his December 1852 investment into the Twofold Bay Pastoral Association (taking a government "squatters lease" on 448,000 acres of south New South Wales land in partnership with Robert and Edwin Tooth, Edye, William, and James Alexander Manning, and Thomas Sutcliffe Mort) was worth his initial stake in it of £32,000. The sum of the worth of these 16 investments into various companies' and banks' stock or into land speculation was £59,200.

In addition to the appreciating value of his stock, John had been paid yearly dividends by 8 of his 15 stock holdings totaling £660 across all the years of his holding. And he was drawing salaries from his board positions in the Bathhurst Copper Mining Company (as Chairman of the Board, £100/year), in the Australasian Steam Navigation Company (as Chairman of the Board, £250/year), and in the Great Nugget Vein Mining Company (as a board member, £100/year). But these had been deposited into his bank accounts and are therefore counted above.

So, in January of 1853, having lived in Sydney for less than ten years since they arrived on August 5th of 1843, John and Mary Ann Croft were worth £216,000 in liquid bank holdings, £59,200 in stock and land speculation investment, and he had dividend and board salary income of over £500 per year. Their estate of Mount Adelaide was free of debt and its conservatively estimated worth was £4500. And, John served varying terms on numerous unpaid social, religious, scientific, judicial, charitable, and educational boards, and to the institutions represented by these board memberships, he was a prominent donor. "Our net worth" he told Mary Ann as he handed her a concise report on it, is close to £300,000 (relative buying power in US dollars in 2023 is $54,312,060 per officialdata.org….LBC). Some of our Darling Point neighbors and partners may be richer yet, but we are clearly doing very well. And our future prospects are impressive as well."

John and Mary Ann were among the Sydney social elite invited to the New South Wales' Governor Sir Charles Fitzroy's "Queen Victoria's Birthday Celebration" in Sydney's Government House on Wednesday, May 24, 1854. It was a grand affair and John wore his British redcoat officer's uniform with gold epaulets and his medal for valor from the First Anglo-Burmese War pinned onto his chest. The next day several of their neighbors told them that an artist's illustration of the celebration had been published in the *Illustrated Sydney News* and that THEY were featured in the illustration. When they had obtained a copy of the newspaper and examined it closely, Mary Ann agreed that they were clearly depicted as the dancing couple just to the left of Governor Fitzroy and his partner Margaret Gordon in the middle of the drawing. John was not so sure, but Mary Ann insisted, "Look at your dark hair and sideburns, your impressive height and posture…look at my back, my hair…the way you are holding me. It's US, I tell you. The artist captured us perfectly. Anyone would recognize us. Our neighbors already have."

This is the illustration of the Queen's (Victoria) Birthday Ball at Government House, Sydney, 24 May, 1854, from: Illustrated Sydney News as reprinted in Jill Buckland's Mort's Cottage, Kangaroo Press, 1988, p. 102. The artist is uncredited but speculated to have been Conrad Martens.

When John again told Mary Ann that they "were indeed doing well," she commented, "Yes, John, Australia has really been a land of opportunity for us and we should be grateful for this to God Almighty and to our wonderful dear friends here. But our greatest treasure sits with us at breakfast every day…our children May (Mary Anne…then

9) and Teddy (Edmund John…then 5). God grant us more children just like them. We'll be welcoming another in March and we can only hope it's a hardy child, capable of surviving more than a year. No amount of wealth can assure that…we can only pray." On January 15th of 1856, she gave birth to son Henry. He seemed to be a robust baby.

But not all is positive for John and Mary Ann in Sydney. Of the seven children Mary gives birth to in the twelve years between 1844 and 1856, four die in infancy from fever due to the heat, the water, and perhaps the mercury-based medications for the fever which they could afford. In late February of 1857, Mary takes ill with rheumatic fever, and, despite the efforts of their homeopathic physician Dr. Bellamy, dies on March 7th. John is wracked with despair…actually sick with grief. He has her interred in what is now called the Camperdown Cemetery of Australia's Pioneers, adjacent to St. Stephens Church in the borough of Newton…as he was on the cemetery's board of directors. The inscription on the 4'X8'X4" sandstone slab monument reads:

SACRED
TO THE MEMORY OF
JOHN
SON OF JOHN AND MARY CROFT
DIED 27TH MARCH 1846
AGED 7 MONTHS AND 13 DAYS
ALSO

JAMES NICHOLAS
SON OF THE ABOVE
DIED 12TH OCTOBER 1850
AGED 9 MONTHS AND 7 DAYS
OF SUCH IS THE KINGDOM OF HEAVEN
ALICE JANE
DAUGHTER OF THE ABOVE
DIED 29TH JULY 1852
AGED 10 MONTHS AND 7 DAYS
ALFRED
SON OF THE ABOVE
DIED 4TH JANUARY 1854
AGED 9 MONTHS AND 9 DAYS
ALSO
MARY
THE BELOVED WIFE OF JOHN CROFT
DIED 7TH MARCH 1857
AGED 45 YEARS

Before John and Mary had even sailed to Australia, during their short courtship, Mary had told John that she had written a poem relevant to the sad infant death of John's first-born son, with deceased wife Mena in Burma, in 1827. She asked John if he would like her to read it to him, and he, knowing of her poetry and her reading of it from memory, as she also sang many hymns beautifully from memory, told her "Please read it, Dear, I'm always in need of consolation." So Mary had recited:

"Pure as the early snow-cap to the view,
In spring's fair morning, and as transient too,
Didst thou, sweet pilgrim, in life's early day,
Thy opening beauties show, then fade away.
Too soon disease arose to blight thy frame,
And sink it into the dust from whence it came.
Planted in Heaven, the flower now seems to say:
'Remember, there's a resurrection day'."

The famous Australian architect, Edmund Thomas Blacket (1817-1883), a close friend of John's and Mary's who was actually present in the Crofts' Mount Adelaide estate when Mary died, was involved in the design and construction of Sydney's St. Andrew's Cathedral on George Street. He proposed that John donate money to have a stained glass window in a lateral wall of the Cathedral dedicated to Mary as a lasting public memorial. This stained glass window was to be made by stained glass master John Hardman Powell (1827-1895), a recognized world leader in such art. The window, of religious as well as artistic significance, was to illustrate four parables of Christ that were dear to Mary. So John gladly donated £180 for the window to be placed. It took several years for that to be done, and this wonderful artistic memorial is there to this day where five generations of Mary Croft's descendents have come to see it and marvel at its beauty. The plaque below the high arching window, corrected in 2018 from the previous sign saying just "John Croft

Donor," thanks to my cousin, Dr. Robert Craig of Brisbane, Australia, now reads as it was intended: "Donated by **John Croft**, of Mount Adelaide, in memory of his wife, **Mary Stead Croft**, who died in 1857, following the death in infancy of four of their seven children."

This is a photo by Dr. Susie Crawford in 2019 of the Mary Stead Croft Memorial Window in Sydney's St. Andrew's Cathedral.

In 1858, John decides, in consultation with neighbor Thomas Sutcliffe Mort, (who was also planning similarly), to leave Australia and return to England to raise his three children there. He sends a letter to his deceased wife Mary Ann's brother, the Rev. Alfred Stead in Ovingdean, Sussex, that he and his three children wanted to accept the Reverend and his wife Emma's invitation to come back and stay with them to help their resettlement there in England. He sells "Mount Adelaide" to Henry Mort and sells all his furniture and his art, asking Henry to retain for at least a year all his estate's staff at their current pay, taking from Henry less than the appraised price of Mount Adelaide to compensate him for this (i.e. he accepts £4500 when the appraisal was £6000). He liquefies all his investments, changing them into gold (he was a gold transfer agent in partnership with Thomas Whistler Smith), diamonds, cash, or transferrable monetary instruments. And he resigns all his board memberships and civil positions. All this took him almost a year.

When John first told the three children, "May" (Mary Anne, b. Feb. 2, 1844), "Teddy" (Edmund John, b. May 31, 1848), and baby "Harry" (Henry, b. Jan. 15, 1856), that they would have to say farewell to their friends and sail away to England, the older two were not well disposed to the idea. Especially daughter May resisted the notion, arguing that she couldn't imagine living in a new place without all her friends. But John promised them that they would be happy to make the acquaintance of their Croft, Stead, Davison, Metcalf, and Atkinson cousins in England, and that they would easily make new friends as well. And he told them what a "grand adventure" the trip itself would be. "We'll be sailing around half the world," he said. "Living as a family on board a ship for five months will no doubt be tough and tiresome for us at times. We will likely suffer some from seasickness. And I'll need you, May, to take some adult responsibility for little Harry. He's just becoming potty trained now, and he'll need all kinds of help from his big sister who is no longer a girl but a young woman. We've got to watch him every second lest he fall overboard while running as he now does around the deck. We'll keep a safety tether on him. A trip like this with a child of this age is bound to be challenging, and I will need your help, and, Teddy, I'll need your help as well.

On Tuesday January 4th, 1859, John, May, Teddy, and baby Harry boarded the 1750 ton *HMS La Hogue*, a former warship of 74 guns commissioned to Royal Navy command in 1812 that had been converted to a three masted sail-rigged screw-propeller type wooden steamship in July 1849. It was renovated and assigned to colonial passenger service after March of 1858. The Captain was Sir John Moore, C.B., who had been knighted in July of 1855 for his able command of other warships during the Crimean War. He and his crew of 135 were transporting 236 passengers. John Croft and his children were given two adjacent staterooms on the second deck, from where they could order food to be served to them in the children's stateroom twice a day and have their clothing laundered and returned weekly. Toilets and shower stalls were at the aft end of their staterooms' hallway.

The 13,000 mile sail to England was indeed a challenge for John and his children. John and the boys had to cope with seasickness early on, but May was blessedly spared this for no perceptible reason. Captain Moore had a small piano in his stateroom and allowed a crewman called "Mr. Bellini" to teach piano lessons to several passengers who could pay for it…and this included both May and Teddy. John and May and Teddy played a lot of checkers and chess and took turns feeding baby Harry.

Six weeks out of Sydney in the Indian Ocean one of the ship's crew was attacked by smallpox, making John grateful that he had had all the children vaccinated at St. Mark's Church on Darling Point…as part of a program he had financially supported for the whole congregation. The sick sailor was ordered into a lifeboat to be towed a hundred yards behind the ship accompanied by a cabin boy whose face indicated that he had previously survived the smallpox. John told the children about his experience accompanying a measles-in fected woman, the Captain's pregnant wife Catherine Marryat, in a lifeboat towed behind the *HMS Larne*, also in the middle of the Indian Ocean, back in December of 1823. He told them how a storm had made that experience quite a scary adventure. But, in the case of the *La Hogue* sailor, the weather was kind to him and his cabin boy companion and, after eight days, he had recovered and he and the cabin boy were returned to the ship and noone further was infected.

At the island of St. Helena in the Atlantic, the ship took on lime juice and watercress plants to address a problem with scurvy affecting several of the crew. John and the children were happy to drink the lime juice and eat the watercress rations themselves, although they did not feel at all ill. John told the children that St. Helena was where the French Emperor Napolean Bonaparte had died in May of 1821. He told them that his former sea-captain Frederick Marryat of the *HMS Larne* had then been assigned, due to his coincident stationing on St. Helena when the French Emperor's death took place, to write a verifying report for the British Admiralty…and that he had drawn a famous sketch of the former Emperor on his deathbed there as a result…his last direct likeness.

On the 10th of May, 1859…21 days short of Teddy's eleventh birthday…the *La Hogue* arrived at the English port of Gravesend. They spent the next day and night in a local hotel. But the day after that, John arranged for their travel from there by coach westward along the south coast of England to Brighton, from where they also traveled the short distance back east to Ovingdean where they arrived at the Rev. Alfred and Emma Robson Stead's rector's house steps from St. Wulfran's Church.

CHAPTER TWO: Residence "Back in England" with the Steads of Ovingdean. John visits the Garretts and meets the Flicks.

The Steads welcomed John and the children very warmly. Emma Stead told them that she had been praying for their safe passage from Sydney since the first of the year, and that she had only three days before had a dream that they had safely arrived. "The Lord be praised," she said as she embraced John and the children and hugged them. "I know Mary is watching from above," she said. "And she's happy to see us all together."

Emma Robson Stead (22 June, 1810—8 April, 1888). Photo taken in 1885. From CFA.

In the next month in Ovingdean, John and the Steads came to an agreement about the financial aspects of the Crofts' stay. John insisted, despite both the Steads' objections, that he pay the Steads a "reasonable rent" for the time there while he sought to purchase a more permanent place for them elsewhere. John knew that Rev. Alfred had long been well engaged with a series of expensive renovations to the rectory's main house, which they had occupied since 1844…modern plumbing, floor leveling, fine paneling and banistering the inside…and the process of "flinting" the brick exterior. He was adding a garden in the rear yard with a cement-lined pond adjacent to St. Wulfran's Church's cemetery. And there were a stable building and a carriage house and a kind of shop building with room for storage that all needed substantial renovation as well. Trees were being planted to line the home's hundred-yard curving carriage driveway.

Rev. and Rector Alfred Stead (20 June, 1810-5 September, 1889). CFA Photo taken in 1885.

After considerable discussion, Rev. Alfred told John, “The £200 per month of rent you insist on paying is just far too much. My salary here is less than that per YEAR. I will deduct £50 of that per month to go to Rev. Arthur Thomas, the primary curate of St. Wulfran’s Church, as your family tithe. He and the Church’s elders will then not begrudge at all your becoming active members of our Church family.

St. Wulfran’s Rectory “Cottage,” first built in 1804, as it appeared in 2008…now a private residence owned by the Kilburn family which is again renovating it and the home’s grounds. Photo by JG Davies from mybrightonandhove.org

The Steads’ children were: Emma Barbara, a young woman of 20 years, born July 18, 1838; Catherine, 16 years, born in 1843; Alfred James, born in late 1845 so that at 14 he was part of a year behind May Croft, who had turned 15 in February, and Robert St. John, born in 1847, and, at 12, a year older than Teddy Croft, who celebrated his 11th birthday at the Steads' Rectory Cottage on May 31st of that 1859 year.

The Steads had lost their second child, 1840-born daughter Margaret Jane Stead, three years before in 1856. She had been buried in the St. Wulfran's Cemetery, where the Stead family had a plot in which grandfather James Stead had been interred as its first occupant in 1848. When the Crofts visited this grave close behind the Church together with Rev. Alfred and wife Emma, John noticed the inscription "M.J.S., 21st June, 1856" had been inscribed on the side of James Stead's gravestone. John thought this strange...that teenaged daughter Margaret Jane did not have a separate grave of her own and that only her initials, and not her full name, were inscribed on her grandfather's gravestone. Rev. Alfred and Emma gave no explanation of this, and so John did not ask them about it. Some time later, inquiring about it in private with St. Wulfran's primary curate, Rev. Arthur Thomas, he was told that Margaret Jane had "died in disgrace" and that her parents had opposed her burial in the family's "sacred ground" in the cemetery. Rev. Thomas himself had overruled Rev. Alfred to have her buried in the St. Wulfran's cemetery at all, but "without a named stone." John chose not to mention this to his own children, May and Teddy and Harry. Years later, John heard the rumour that unmarried pregnant Margaret Jane and her baby had died in childbirth while estranged from her family, and that her parents were unable to forgive her and give her a named grave in their family plot.

The elder daughter, Emma Barbara Stead. was a very smart and energetic person, who, at 21, had become a kind of "second mother" to her younger

Emma Barbara Stead (18 Jul., 1838-21 Dec., 1916) taken ca. 1900. From CFA

siblings…always suggesting ways they might "improve themselves in the Lord's eyes." Whenever she would say this to the boys, Alfred, Jr. and Robert, they would roll their eyes and say, "Yes, mum!"

In the summer of 1859, while living at the Steads' rector's "cottage" of St. Wulfran's Church in Ovingdean, Sussex, John Croft was able to travel alone by train and coach to Leiston in Suffolk to see his former client Richard Garrett of Richard Garrett & Sons Manufacturing Company, one-time employer of his younger brother Nicholas, who died with two of his baby daughters in a St. Petersburg, Russia, cholera epidemic in 1845. Richard Garrett welcomed him warmly at the Garrett's shop and invited him to come to visit the next day, which was a Saturday, at the Garretts' grand Carlton Hall near Aldeburgh, which made a strong impression on John. He told Richard Garrett's wife, Elizabeth Dunnell Garrett, that this was just the kind of home he was looking to purchase for himself and his children.

"What do you do for a living, Mr. Croft?" asked Elizabeth Garrett. "A named estate house like this costs a great deal of money."

John answered tersely, "I've got enough money, and I'm looking to invest it."

The Garretts' Carlton Hall near Aldeburgh, Suffolk. From CFA.

There at the time also were the Garretts' twenty-one-year-old daughter Sarah Louisa, their fourteen-year-old son Frank, and the Garrett's nineteen-year-old daughter Jane Emma and one of her suitors, a Mr. Hyla Elkington.

John immediately asked Hyla Elkington, "Are you related to George Richards Elkington of the gilding company in Birmingham? One of my first jobs as a solicitor was to advise him on assuring his patents would apply internationally…this back in the late thirties…1836 or 1837, as I recall."

"I'm his sixth and youngest son," replied Hyla. "But we have a yet younger sister Emma too."

Richard Garrett commented, "Hyla's father George is a long-time friend of ours…we've done business with him."

John asked, "How is he?"

"Well, I think Hyla would agree that he's had some troubles coping with the death of his wife and Hyla's mother Mary last year. He's been sort of withdrawing from his business affairs…trying to have four of Hyla's older brothers gradually take over the business."

Richard Garrett III (1 Feb., 1807-26 Jun., 1866). From CFA.

"That's too bad," said John. "How old is he?

Hyla answered, "He's getting close to 59."

"That's not that old," said John. "He may still recover his vigor and stay involved in things."

Daughter Sarah replied to this curiously, saying, "If I may presume to ask, good Sir, how old are you?"

"That's no presumption at all, Miss," answered John. "I'm still 51 in this year…born in July 1807."

"That's my birth year also," said father Richard. "But my birthday for this year was in February. So I'm now already 52."

Son Frank smiled and asked John, "How old do you think I am?"

John smiled back at young Frank and answered, "I would guess you to be sixteen…adult robust but not yet shaving."

Frank's smile turned to a grin, and he exclaimed, "What a good guess! But people say I look older than my age. I'm still fourteen."

Mother Elizabeth asked John, "You mentioned children, John? How many and how old ?"

"I have three children, all born in Sydney, Australia," answered John. "Daughter May is fifteen. Son Teddy is eleven, and son Harry is just three."

"That's wonderful," Elizabeth gushed, "We'll just be so happy to meet them…hopefully soon."

There was then a sumptuous mid-day meal with a competently busy household staff serving two dozen people…the Garretts, Richard and Elizabeth, with ten children in attendance and several guests, not all of whose names John could later remember. After the meal he and Richard separated themselves and went into a separate parlor to have a private conversation of some length.

When John explained to Richard that it was his intention to find his brother's widow and give her the money that he felt his brother had been entitled to, Richard was able to help him with some information that he did not know: "The widow's birth name was Caroline Fink," he related, "And she was born in 1807…your and my own birth year. Her birth place is unclear, but she had grown up in a German community east of Hamburg in a Duchy called Mecklenburg-Strelitz. The Ducal family there has close heriditary connections to the royal houses of both England and Russia. One of the previous Dukes, Duke Carl, even became the King of Greece in the 1830s with the help of his brother-in-law King Friedrich Wilhelm III of Prussia and his cousin, our former King George IV of Great Britain. The Current Duke George negotiated the marriage of his son George to Grand Duchess Ekaterina Mikhailovna of Russia, the sister-in-law of the Tsar. The official Duke's palace is on an island in the Zieker See close to a town called Neustrelitz. Your brother's wife, then Caroline Fink, grew up in that town.

Schloss Neustrelitz ca. 1920, from wikipedia.org

In that town lived a family named Marsow, who professed being descended from a long-ago Baron Heinrich Marsow, who had owned a section of the local land and lived in fine castle there in the beginning of the last century. But in this century the land and castle were gone and the Marsow family lived in relative poverty in an ordinary house in Neustrelitz. Yet Caroline married a 'Baron' Marsow in 1825 at the age of 18. This Marsow…I don't know his first name…was in his fifties or more, and he was somehow associated with a German banker named Ludwig Seyler and the famous Berenberg Bank, which was then opening foreign branches in other countries. In 1833 or 1834 Caroline somehow moved with her husband to Moscow, Russia, where they took up residence in what is still called there the 'German Quarter.' Her husband's plan was to open a Berenberg Bank branch there, but, sometime in 1835, he unexpectedly died, leaving Caroline only very little. She had to move in with German Quarter friends. She was in a quite unfortunate situation. Her only asset was her ability in the Russian Language, which she apparently had a talent for learning.

As Caroline was running out of hope she met your brother Nicholas, who arrived there in 1836. She was introduced to him as a person he could pay to teach him Russian…and she did that wonderfully according to his notes to me attached to his machine orders. Unfortunately, I just threw those notes away after I read them…being personal as opposed to business, you understand. I couldn't have known what would happen to him over there in Russia."

John commiserated, saying "I understand. I rarely save personal letters any more."

Richard continued, "So Englishman Nicholas and German Caroline fell in love and got married in Moscow in the English Church there in the fall of 1837. By that time, Nicholas's sales for us, especially of the farm implements, were rising with his Russian fluency, and he informed us that, right after the marriage, he would be moving to the Russian capital in St. Petersburg…which was our primary shipping point to Russian customers anyway. Because of his able sales work, they were able to rent from some Russian nobleman with an '-ov' name a grand flat off St. Petersburg's main street, called Nevsky Prospect…I have the address of it somewhere, but, of course, they aren't there any more. And their marriage was fruitful also, blessed by children, as Caroline's previous marriage was not. She got pregnant and had a daughter there named Mary after his and your mother. This was in 1840…fall as I remember. And then they had another daughter, named Martha, perhaps after Caroline's mother, I'm not sure, in 1843. Things were going well. But then came the cholera in early 1845. They were all severely stricken, among the first victims of a great Russian epidemic of it. The two daughters went first, then, on March 7th, 1845, Nicholas himself, but Caroline survived. Perhaps the fact that she was pregnant helped her somehow. The British consulate in St. Petersburg contacted us here with the report that Nicholas and the girls had been buried in St. Petersburg's Foreigners' Cemetery and that they had a single monument naming them all. But they wanted our Company to send funds to help Caroline get back to Germany…which we promptly sent. "Neustrelitz" was the listed destination, and when she got there she nicely sent us a letter reporting that fact. The letter's return address said only "Caroline Croft, Neustrelitz," in English and "Deutschland" in German. Then, in January of 1846, we got another letter from her reporting the birth on September 22nd of 1845 of a healthy daughter, named Catherine Rose Croft. I did keep that letter, but without its envelope with the same unhelpful address…it's here at home and I can find it and give it to you."

"I'd greatly appreciate it, Richard," said John. "Thank you so much. I'll now be figuring out just how I'm going to travel to this "Neustrelitz" and find her."

Richard responded, "I think I can help you with that, John. To travel to Neustrelitz in Mecklenberg-Strelitz you will most conveniently travel first to the major German seaport of Hamburg. Neustrelitz is 150 miles east of there by coach. And my brother Newson Garrett, who lives near us here, in Alde House, has a malting business with most of its customers in Hamburg. He delivers the malted barley for the German brewers directly by sea and the River Elbe by sail-rigged barges. These barges sail from his River Ald Landings at the village of Snape to Hamburg via the River Elbe in 6 to 10 days unless the weather turns bad. All you would have to do is sign on one of the barges…either as a passenger or even as a paid barge seaman.

"That's so very helpful, Richard," replied John, "Might you write me a note of introduction and I will go to your brother Newson's place and meet him right away from here if that's possible? Is his place far?"

"Not at all, John," said Richard, "It's only twenty minutes away by carriage. And certainly I'll write you an introduction and a request that Newson give you all possible help in finding your brother's widow in Germany."

As John was leaving the Garretts' Carlton Hall with Richard's letter to his brother and with widow Caroline's hand-written missive as well, mother Elizabeth asked John also to give a personal note she had written and sealed to her sister Louisa, who was Newson's wife.

"You two sisters are married to brothers?"

Elizabeth proudly said, “Yes, we sisters of the Dunnell family are both married to two of the Garrett brothers, my Richard and Louisa’s Newson. I’ve had fourteen children with Richard, losing four in infancy. And Louisa has had eleven with Newson, losing only one, meaning that we’re both busy raising twenty Garrett children, ten each. And I daresay that all twenty are doing very well.”

John was touched by Elizabeth’s revelation. Smiling through swelling tears he shared with her that, “My wife Mary Ann and I lost four of our children in infancy in Australia. I know what such losses feel like, Elizabeth. We’ll carry the pain with us for the rest of our lives. But I lost my wife Mary Ann also. She was only 45 years old. And now I’m trying to raise our three back here in England by myself.”

“I’m so sorry to hear that, John,” Elizabeth said, almost whispering. “That’s a hard, hard fate. But you should remarry while your children are still young. Every child needs a mother. No matter how much you try, you can’t be a mother to them, and they’ll suffer for it.”

Elizabeth Dunnell Garrett (1806-1884), from long-shopmuseum.co.uk

"The best I could do now is to find a woman to marry who would willingly become their step-mother," answered John. "But I thank you for your kind advice."

In the late afternoon, John arrived at the estate of Newson Garrett on some uplands outside the town of Aldeburgh. Newson was five years younger than his brother Richard, but John thought he looked older because of his longer gray beard. His wife Louisa, who was very pleased to receive the sealed letter from her older sister Elizabeth Garrett, might have been considered by many Elizabeth's twin, so similar to each other did they appear.

Newson Garrett (1812-1893) ca. 1865. From CFA.

John soon met several of Newson and Louisa's children—the two oldest, then in their twenties, were daughters Louisa (b. 1835), named after her mother, and Elizabeth (b. 1836), named after her Aunt. Both had been born while the family lived in London and Newson worked as a silversmith and pawnbroker. Then two sons, Dunnell Newson and Newson Dunnell, were born two years apart, in 1837 and 1839 respectively, but the first of these, Dunnell Newson, died at 6 months of age in May

1838. Son Edmund was born in 1840, after which Newson and Louisa left London and moved to a house across from the church in Aldeburgh, Suffolk.

It was in March of 1841 that Newson bought a barley and coal business near the Snape Bridge only a few miles from his home and began shipping the barley into Europe on Thames barges from the Snape Landing on the Ald River. This business was soon buying up local barley crops and transporting over 200 tons of them per year into Hamburg and on further into Europe.

Newson and Louisa continued to have children...Alice in 1842, Agnes in 1845, Millicent in 1847, Samuel in 1850, Josephine in 1853, and George in 1854. By that time Newson decided to master the malting of the barley crops himself and sell the already malted barley to the Hamburg breweries in their production of beer and ale. This move decreased his transportation costs and dramatically improved his profits. He had a large malting facility built at Snape and hired its workers from all over Suffolk.

After son Samuel was born in 1850, Newson and Louisa were able to afford to have a grand estate home constructed on a hill near their former house site. They called their new mansion "Alde House."

Newson Garrett's Snape Maltings, from en.wikipedia.org

Newson Garrett and John Croft got on famously, conversing during the family dinner and afterwards until it was dark. Newson instructed his servants to prepare a bedroom for John's occupancy, since, he said, "It's too late to travel anywhere now."

John retired to the well furnished bedroom thinking to himself how he had achieved his intended goal. Newson had offered him free passage to Hamburg, declaring "You can go any time you want. You are a friend of this family now, John."

And, when John had mentioned that he was seeking to buy an estate of his own in England,

Newson seemed excited by the prospect that he might buy or build an estate near them in Suffolk.

"I am close friends with the county's leading real estate broker, Samuel Flick. Believe me, he knows more about British real estate than anyone else you can find. He is now of such an age that he has apprenticed his son Robert into the profession of brokering and auctioning real estate, and they make a fine pair indeed. I would gladly introduce you to both of them tomorrow after breakfast. They are at Theberton only seven miles from here."

John assented to this plan, wondering to himself, "What must have Newson's brother Richard written about me in that letter of introduction? He just can't seem to do enough for me."

At breakfast of ham, eggs, and fresh baked rolls, John sat at the long family table next to their second daughter, then twenty three years old, Elizabeth. He asked her, "What are you doing these days, Miss?"

"I'm studying," she answered.

And just what are you studying? Aren't you finished with your schooling?" he inquired.

"I'm studying human anatomy and curative medicines. I plan to become a medical doctor," she said proudly.

John was surprised by this and did not respond right away. So Elizabeth continued: "My teachers have always said that I'm a very smart person. Whenever I have taken an exam I've always gotten

A portrait of Elizabeth Garrett (Anderson) (1836-1917) in the 1860s from Wikipedia.

the highest grade in the class on it. So, I've considered my choice of a life's career to be more than marriage and motherhood, which my older sister

Louisa is already away and involved in. I want that too, but I want a profession first. I want to help people who are ill in the most impactful way…as a physician."

John then answered, "Well, I can only applaud and support a young woman's having lofty goals to help others. I knew such women when I was a young soldier in Burma. They were missionaries there for the American Baptist Church."

The mention of America caused Elizabeth to speak further. "The United States has beaten us to certifying a woman medical doctor to practice. Elizabeth Blackwell was certified there in 1849… ten years ago. And I met her earlier this year in London when she presented a paper titled "An Appeal in Behalf of the Medical Education of Women." After that talk she managed to have her name entered into the British General Medical Register…the first woman's name so entered."

John asked, "Did you just hear her presentation of that paper or did you meet her personally?"

"I am a member of our British Society for Promoting the Employment of Women," Elizabeth told him, "And that Society was the sponsor of Elizabeth Blackwell's appearance here. So, through the Society's officers, I requested a personal interview and, to my pleasant surprise, got one. It took place in Dr. Blackwell's hotel room. I got to ask her all kinds of questions and her answers were inspirational to me."

"What kinds of things did you find out, Elizabeth?"

"I found out that the male students of her medical school, Geneva College of Medicine in Hobart, New York, were asked to vote to approve her admittance to the College. If even ONE of them had voted no, she would not have been admitted, but they approved her for admittance by unanimous vote. She had no social life there at all, she told me…just isolation and study. But, two years later she received the highest grade on the final medical qualification exam. She told me that she had originally desired to become a surgeon, but that an accident with an eyewash solution caused an infection in her left eye so severe they had to remove the eye. It looks a bit disfigured now. So she had to embark upon a general practice as a physician. Surgeons definitely need both eyes. Just her telling me this story caused her adopted companion, eleven-year-old Kitty Barry, to start weeping, so that both of us Elizabeths had to console her."

John just nodded his head from side to side, then said to her, "Dear Elizabeth, I will henceforth be praying for you to succeed in your efforts to become a medical doctor and a licensed physician. I have only two pieces of advice for you. One is to 'LEARN EVERYTHING.' Never ask 'why do I have to learn this? You never know in life WHAT you might have to know. Knowledge truly IS power...so LEARN EVERYTHING.' and two is simple— 'NEVER GIVE UP, never quit, just keep pressing onward this way or that way until you are where you want to be'."

Elizabeth looked into John's eyes intently and replied, "I will take that advice and accomplish it all just as you say, Mr. Croft. Thank you."

John looked significantly around the breakfast table at all the younger boys Edmund, Newson, Jr., Samuel and George, and the girls Alice, Agnes, Millicent, and Josephine...all bright young faces. He leaned closer to Elizabeth and said in a quieter voice, "Please remember to repeat that advice to your sisters here as well. Women should command more of this world than they now do."

After breakfast, the Garretts' stable boss had hooked up John's borrowed horse and carriage and brought them to the ready in front of the Alde House's entry portico. The entire family was gathered there to see John off with father Newson sitting alongside him on the bench seat. Newson told John as they drove away, "It's our family custom to wave friends and family away as a group. They'll keep waving until we are out of sight."

Less than an hour later, Newson was able to introduce John to Samuel and Charlotte Flick and their son Robert Flick at the house in Theberton that Robert and his wife Anna Maria Stanford Flick had recently acquired. John could tell that the Flicks were delighted to see their old friend Newson Garrett.

Newson immediately qualified John Croft as a "qualified client" of the Flick's real estate business, telling them that, "John here is an investor who is returned here to England from 16 years in Australia and is seeking a named estate somewhere convenient to London."

Samuel Flick turned to John and asked, "Do you prefer to buy an estate as is…meaning with furniture in situ and with the estate's horses and carriages…and will you take on the former staff? Many of our agency's properties of this nature are sold in that way because the original owners have passed away and their beneficiaries can't afford to live in such places. Sometimes the owners have defaulted on loans and the banks have taken over the properties…meaning you would be paying them…and this ordinarily includes the estate's horses, carriages, and staff."

John thought a bit and answered, "I would prefer to purchase a property with all those things included…horses, carriages, and current staff retained."

Robert Flick then asked, "Will you be seeking a loan or paying outright?"

John answered, "I will pay outright, drawing on my accounts at C. Hoare & Co. bank in London."

Robert smiled and asked further, "And how much are you willing to spend, my good man?"

"In my mind I am alloting 20 thousand pounds to purchase an estate I can be proud of…but of course I'd like to pay less if possible," answered John. "And perhaps some of the estates I would consider would have some sources of income as well…rental homes, loggable forests, or farmland or coal mines or something. Is that a possibility?"

"Indeed it is," said Robert. "And how much time are you alotting in your mind to make a significant purchase of this nature?"

"We're now in the last half of 1859," answered John. "And I'd like to be moved into a new residence by the end of the next 1860 year. Is that a possibility?"

"It definitely is," Robert assured him. "And you'll have many exciting choices. We'll prepare you a list of 20 or more candidate properties with descriptions of the buildings and the terms."

"And what do you charge to help me in acquiring the chosen property?"

"We will charge you 3 percent of the agreed -upon purchase price," quickly answered Robert. "Does that seem all right with you? If it does, we ask that you sign a witnessed document of contract with us and give us your address and that of your designated solicitor. You would then be looking at prospects within two weeks."

"I am myself a London licensed solicitor," said John. "So you'll just need one address. I'm living temporarily in the Rectory cottage at St. Wulfran's Church in Ovingdean, near Brighton in Sussex with my late wife's brother and family. I'll give you that address right away."

"So do you agree to sign a contract with us?" asked Robert, looking at his father Samuel as he spoke.

"Yes, I'll sign," declared John. "Right now if you like.. I assume you will accept my friend Newson Garrett here as a witness." Then he turned to Newson and asked, “Will you be a witness for me?”

Newson replied, “Surely.” And then he thought to ask John, “Will you be shipping out to Germany right away, before you buy a place, or will you be waiting until you are settled into a place?”

John thought about it and answered, “I have to put my family’s needs first and wait to go to Germany until I’ve purchased a permanent place for us to stay. So the trip to Germany on your barges might be next year or even later. Is that all right?”

Newson nodded his head, assuring John that, “Yes, that’s fine. The time doesn’t matter to me. As long as I’m in charge of the barges, you can use them to get to Germany whenever you want.”

So the deal with the real estate agents was made, and the document of contract signed and witnessed. And after a pleasant noon meal, John was able to drive away with his horse and carriage on his journey to Leiston where he would catch the first train south to London and then back to Brighton in Sussex, where he would hire a carriage to take him back to the Ovingdean rectory. Robert Flick would use his own horse and carriage to return Newson Garrett north to his home near Aldeburgh.

CHAPTER THREE: John Croft's Estate Matters, a Historic Excavation, and His Travel to Germany.

When John returned to the Steads' St. Wulfran's Church rectory in Ovingdean, he came to more financial agreements with Rev. Alfred. Alfred told John that he regarded the work needed to restore the rectory itself to be nearly complete. "I had most of the major work done back in 1849-1850, and now we've gotten all seven sleeping chambers plastered and carpeted and finely furnished with beds and bedding," he said. "But now I want to take charge of renovating the St. Wulfran's Church building itself. It needs a complete new slate roof. The congregation is embarrassed by the leaks in the present roof. Sometimes the people don't even come to church if it's raining, and the leakage is getting worse. And I want the outside of the building flinted to match the rectory. Also, the nave needs all new pews with kneeling stanchions. And, I want to have the ceiling painted by a young local artist who was once a sunday school pupil here with our daughter Emma Barbara. He's one of us, so to speak.

John asked, "Who is that?"

"He's the son of our late Ovingdean church-stalwart Nathaniel Kemp...Charles...the one who has decided to spell his name with an 'e' on the end of it as 'Kempe'." Barbara tells me that he was always a bit strange, but she has a real affection for him anyway, and she raves about his artistic abilities. He has a noticeable stammer when he talks and he's quite shy in demeanor. But he has established himself as a church artist of the first rank… especially in the design and composition of stained glass."

Charles Eamer Kempe (29 Jun., 1837-29 Apr., 1907) in 1860, from Wikipedia.

"Stained glass?" said John, "You know I had Australia's leading architect, Edmund Blacket, have a stained glass window put into Sydney's St. Andrew's Cathedral as a memorial to our dear Mary Ann. The stained glass artist was John Hardman Powell, and I was told by people who know that he's the world's leading stained glass artist. His office is in Birmingham. Have you considered him?"

"John, we aren't adding any stained glass. We just want the ceiling painted in a complementary way. And there's the always sensitive matter of cost. Young Kempe says he'll do the painting for us personally for only the £30 cost of the paint."

"I would happily pay for that, if you would allow," suggested John. "And I'll endow a special church account for you to draw on to get the other things done too. When would you like to get started?"

"It's hard to get church matters like that decided with any dispatch, unfortunately. I have a good relationship with our Curate, Rev. Thomas…but we both have to deal with a committee or two which could delay things for a year or more. But if the money's already in the church's accounts that might accelerate things for us."

John said, "Alfred, I'll deposit £500 into an account you can be a signatory of this very week."

John related to the Steads that he had made a plan with Newson Garrett to travel to Germany to find his deceased brother Nicholas's widow Caroline, but that, before he did that, he wanted to purchase with the help of Samuel and Robert Flick's real estate agency a prominent estate to which he and his children could move. "But," he asked Alfred and Emma and also Emma Barbara, "I will still need someone close to take care of my three children for me while I am gone. Might I ask you all for that considerable favor?"

All three of the Steads nodded affirmatively, with Emma saying definitively, "Of course we will do it. You and yours are like our own to us now."

In January 1860, John got to thinking about the art and science of photography one day. He thought about how his beloved Mary Ann was an early devotee of photography and how she had engaged a Sydney photographer named M. Brown to take photographs of their family guests at the Mount Adelaide housewarming celebration on Darling Point in November of 1849. He could still recite the photographer, Mr. Brown's, clever poetic advertisement that "Of those for whom we fond emotions cherish,/ Secure the shadow ere the substance perish." So he transported his three children to the studio of a Brighton photographer and had a photograph made of all three of them together—Mary Anne (May) at age 15, Edmund John (Teddy) at age 11, and Henry (Harry) at age 3.

May, Teddy, and Harry Croft in early 1860. From CFA.

When John showed this photograph to Rev. Alfred, he asked John why little Harry had been posed in a girl's dress. "That's just the way photographers and artists depict children of that age in posed settings. I think it has to do with the fact that all children are baptized as infants in a baptismal gown, which is a kind of dress. And that later toilet training may keep children of that age in dresses until they can reliably pull boys' pants on and off by themselves…I don't know. It's just how it's done."

"Have you seen other examples of this…boy toddlers in girls' dresses?" asked Alfred.

I have another example with me," replied John, taking a fancy notebook out of his vest pocket and handing it to Alfred, "Look at the painting of Harry on the cover of my personal calendar notebook."

“Is that Harry?” asked Alfred. “I can’t tell for sure.”

“It’s Harry,” answered John. “Parents can easily recognize their children in paintings by this artist. It was done by the one-armed genius Richard Noble, whose studio at 246 George Street in Sydney was close by my Gold Agency Partnership with Thomas Whistler Smith. Our Royal Assurance Company was there too, at number 390.”

Alfred shook his head and turned the notebook over and back in his hands. “Is this framing made of real gold? I’d swear it’s actual gold.”

“You are right. It is real gold, assayed and smelted from a huge nugget of gold ore from my own Australian Great Nugget Vein Gold Mining Company. I was a founder and the board chairman of it from 1851 to 1858.”

“My goodness, John,” said Alfred, “You really have become wealthy in this world. What else do you have made of gold?”

John smiled and said, “My signet ring is also made of the same gold, dug out and refined from my own mines.”

“How many mines did you have?”

“Three copper mines owned by my Bathhurst Copper Mining Company and two gold mines owned by my Great Nugget Vein Company.”

With that John went upstairs in the rectory to his sleeping chamber, in which was a writing desk, and withdrew his signature stamp and a sheet of paper from the desk drawer. When he came back downstairs he handed it to Alfred:

John Croft's personal gold-and-cut-glass signature stamp. From CFA.

“My cursive initials ‘J.C.’ for ‘John Croft’ are cut into the glass…not an easy process to be sure…so that, when I press the signet ring’s face into the melted wax sealing my ready-to-send envelopes, the letters ‘J.C’ appear indelibly in the wax seal.”

With that explanation, John handed Alfred the sheet of paper he had removed from his upstairs desk. “See the initials in the seal,” he said.

John Croft’s cursive initials “J.C.” stamped into blue sealing wax across an envelope’s opening. From CFA.

In July of 1860 John Croft, accompanied by Robert Flick, went on a tour of two properties—one called Belmont House in Hoddesdon in Hertforshire where he had grown up, and the other called Dalton House in Saddington in Leicestershire. Both were very grand late 18th and early 19th-century brick and stone primary house buildings whose former owners had modernized them with running water and indoor plumbing. The three-level Belmont House was within the Hoddesdon city limits and had its water piped in from the city's own water sources, whereas the larger Dalton House had its own pure-water well coming up into its large ground floor kitchen from where it was piped to toilet rooms with baths and shower stalls on each floor. The property adjoined a sizeable and scenic reservoir as well.

Belmont House was on a six-acre city lot with attractive trees and gardens surrounded by a low stone wall, with a turreted gateway onto the passing roadway. The Dalton House property was more rural and included a "Fleckney Farm" of 496 acres, which contained 32 separately named pastures from 1 to 43 acres in size totaling 354 fenced acres under already arranged leases for animal grazing, plus four larger pieces with both forest and arable sections for logging and farming. Both Belmont House and especially Dalton House had numerous outbuildings for various purposes, including small houses for members of the respective household's staffs of servants.

Belmont House had nine bedrooms with a staff of eight comprising the members of two families already happily in place in two separate houses and hoping to stay on. The four-level Dalton House (including an entire basement), with 16 bedrooms on the upper two levels of its grand main house, had a resident staff of twelve. Both houses included impressive furnishings, and came with stables of horses and carriages of different types.

"So the owners of both these properties and their families are already out of them, John," explained Robert Flick. The last of the Belmont owners has recently passed away, and the Dalton family has moved out and occupied a deceased Duke's mansion in London. They decided that a rural lifestyle did not suit them anymore."

Robert and John spent days together in the Flicks' home in Theberton in Suffolk going over the financial terms, with John trying to see the "bigger picture" of what acquiring either this or that of the two candidate properties would cost him in pounds and how his life and the lives of his children would be impacted by his acquisition. During his time with the Flicks, John also got some time to spend with both the Richard and the Newson Garretts. To his surprise, both Richard and

Newson advocated that he choose the Belmont House "city property" in Hoddesdon, advising him not to take on the Dalton House and Fleckney Farm's management of animal pastures and croplands which would be "more trouble than its worth in income."

At Richard and Elizabeth Garretts' Carlton Hall, John spent considerable time talking with their daughters Sarah Louisa, who was then 22 years old and Jane Emma, who was then 20. And at Newson and Louisa's Alde House he asked for information about the Boarding School for Ladies in Blackheath, London, where they had sent their daughter Elizabeth who had so impressed him with her stated commitment to become a medical doctor and a licensed physician. He was thinking of it a place where his own daughter Mary Anne might go.

It was Sarah Louisa Garrett at Carlton Hall who asked John directly, "How much will these estates you are considering cost you?"

John was impressed by Sarah's straightforwardness and could not immediately think of why he should demur to answer the question. So, even though her grandmother, her parents and sister Jane were also listening in curiosity, he forthrightly answered, "They want £8000 for the Belmont House in Hoddesdon, and £18,000 for the Dalton House and Fleckney Farm in Saddington."

"Whew!" Sarah said. "That's a lot of money."

John commented, "Just the lesser amount is almost twice what I sold our 'Mount Adelaide' estate on Darling Point in Sydney for two years ago."

Richard Garrett inquired, "Was your Sydney estate the equal of the two places you're looking at here?"

"In my judgement it was," said John. "The 14 acres of it comprised the highest residential lot on the most exclusive place to live in Sydney…Darling Point.

"Well that shows how house and land values are escalating throughout the empire. No doubt Robert Flick has informed you of this."

"In fact he has. And as I have been considering that cost escalation, I think that buying a house now is sure to be a better appreciating investment than keeping my money in a bank account. That's why I'm thinking that I should buy BOTH the Belmont House estate in Hoddesdon and the Dalton House and Fleckney Farm estate at Saddington. The children and I can live in one and I can lease out the other profitably as well."

"Not a bad idea, at all, my good man," said Richard. "Likely the Flicks could provide the leasing management for some low percentage fee as well. But finding someone to take over the running of the Saddington estate will be quite the more difficult, I think."

So John Croft did purchase both estates, withdrawing £27,000 from his C. Hoare and Co. primary bank account to cover the Flicks' commissions and also his projected moving and resettlement expenses. The sales were finalized by contract before Christmas of 1860.

A 2022 photo of the Belmont View Care Home on the previous Belmont House site in Hoddesdon, Hertfordshire. It is now a two-storey brick building of expanded size, featuring 85 en suite bedrooms with bath/showers for its senior-living tenants...gardens with a duck pond. cf. quantumcare.-co.uk

A 2022 photo of the expanded twentieth-century reconstruction of John Croft's Dalton House in Leicestershire, which is now The Grange Nursing & Residential Home with 46 single rooms, 16 with ensuite WCs. Notice on the right side the tower with a clock in its face…this was the Dalton House Carriage House. The website is thegrangecare-home.co.uk

John and his children left the Steads' rector's residence at St. Wulfran's Church in Ovingdean in Sussex in January of 1861. The Rev. Alfred and his wife Emma and all of his children, including the *de facto* nanny Emma Barbara, were sad to see them move to the closer of the new residences, the Belmont House in Hoddesdon. But Rev. Alfred himself physically helped in the moving and accompanied them on their first family trip to Hoddesdon. "I thank you, John," he said, "For leaving my access to your 'support account' with me…I won't overdraw it, you may be sure. But the church will miss your munificent tithes."

At Belmont House the Crofts settled in comfortably and they found the staff in place there very kindly accommodating too. Only did John have to engage the services of a nanny, who would be taking care of young Harry who then had just turned five years old. He managed to hire away an experienced Hoddesdon school teacher, Mrs Edna Jones Gould, to be their family nanny. Her husband Norman Gould could dependably transport her in his delivery cart to and from the Belmont House from their nearby cottage five days per week. Harry soon got used to "Mrs. Gould" and didn't like to see her leave every day before dinner.

John did all he had to do in order to arrange to get son Teddy accepted for admission to Eton, England's and the world's most prestigious boarding school for boys aged 13 to 18. He was to enroll in the fall of that 1861 year. Daughter Mary Anne went away in May to enroll and reside at the Blackheath Boarding School for Ladies in London. She and her father John, who took her there for her registration, were both in tears as they said "Good bye and God bless!"

John had not forgotten about his intention to travel to Germany on one of Newson Garrett's malted barley barges, and he stayed in touch with both the Garrett families as best he could. Richard and Elizabeth Garrett's daughter Sarah Louisa asked John if he and she might begin an "epistolary correspondence" so that the families could remain in closer touch while now farther apart. She said she would take delight in opening letters that John would write to her and use his gold signet to seal. John told Sarah that he would seek her father Richard's approval to participate in such a correspondence, and, during that very visit, he did just that."

Richard's response to the proposed correspondence was a positive one. "Indeed I favor such a correspondence, John," he said. "I just don't have enough time on my hands these days to do much personal writing myself."

Then he asked, "John, did you purchase these large residential estates because you eventually plan to remarry and have more children to be raised in them?"

John answered, "I bought them based on my lifelong fancy that I would someday be wealthy enough to live in some grand mansion. And my plans included marriage and having a family with as many children or more than you and Newson have. Now it turns out that my dreams of wealth have become reality, but my dreams of a large family have been thwarted by fate so far. Even though I lost my dear wife Mary Ann four years ago now, I don't yet feel ready to seek another wife."

"Well, when you are ready to remarry, you couldn't do better than to consider our daughter Sarah Louisa," Richard replied. "She's our smartest and most practical child. And she's somehow not had any fit suitors. Now she is thinking that her younger sister Jane and her beau Hyla Elkington will be announcing their wedding any day, whereas she, the older sister, seems doomed to spinsterhood."

"My goodness, Richard," said John. "You and I are the same age. Does not that age difference between Sarah and me bother you?"

"Not at all. And it apparently doesn't bother her. Also, I would tell you that the merging of our two fine families appeals to me greatly," was Richard's answer.

In May of 1862, John received an invitation in the mail to accept being appointed an usher during the wedding of Jane Emma Garrett and Hyla Elkington, which was to take place on the 10th of July. He wondered to himself about how his "epistolary correspondent," Sarah Louisa Garrett, would regard her younger sister Jane's going before her into marriage. but he soon received a letter from Sarah expressing only her sincere happiness for Jane and her high regard for the groom-to-be, Hyla.

In June of 1862, John decided that he should move his family from Hoddesdon's Belmont House to Saddington's Dalton House and Fleckney Farm. They accomplished this move in less than a month. The only trouble was that the Flicks had been unable in several months of trying to find anyone of financial substance who would lease the Belmont House for any sensible amount of money. So John made Norman and nanny Edna Gould an offer. He would continue to pay his current Belmont House staff as he had been (except for the horse staff which would be invited to move with the Belmont House horses to Saddington), including Edna's nanny's salary even though she would have nobody to nanny… son Harry, of course, would need another nanny in Saddington. And John would pay her husband Norman a caretaker's salary of £30 per month if they would move into the Belmont House and take care of it, so that John and his family could come back and stay in it at any time they wanted.

After some consideration involving Norman having to find a renter for the Gould's cottage in Hoddesdon, John's offer was accepted. He and his family could move to Saddington without worrying about the status of their Belmont House property, which, with Norman and Edna Gould's management, would continue its financial appreciation.

When John and family were comfortable with their Dalton House abode and another nanny, a Mrs. Smythe, for Harry had been engaged, John decided that he wanted to have a photograph of himself made in his new house. So he hired a local photographer to come take the picture. This one which he himself titled "John Croft—Master of Dalton House, Saddington" is shown below.

According to a later physical description of his father by son Edmund ("Teddy"), John Croft was 6

feet 2 inches in his shoes, weighed just over 14 stone (200 lbs.), and had hair, sideburns, and beard of very dark, almost black, brown hair.

The July 10, 1862 wedding of Jane Emma Garrett and Hyla Elkington took place at the small Saint Peter's Church within sight of Carlton Hall in Suffolk near Aldeburgh. John took Eton freshman Teddy and nanny-taught Harry with him, because they were home at the time. May was at Blackheath Ladies School in London.

Saint Peter's Church at Carlton, Suffolk, from Wikipedia.

Jane's sisters, Betsy Maria Garrett Grimwood, Sarah Louisa, and Clara Garrett Peck, were her attendants, with closest in age Ellen Garrett Johnson her maid of honour. Hyla's groomsmen were four of his brothers, Frederick, James, and Alfred, with closest in age Howard his best man. Almost all of the Newson and Louisa Garrett children were there, except for the oldest sisters Louisa and future physician Elizabeth.

The beautiful bride, Jane Emma Garrett Elkington (1840-1909), from CFA.

The handsome groom, Hyla Elkington (1839-1901), from the CFA.

The groom's father, George Richard Elkington (1801-1865), portrait by Samuel West, from Wikipedia.

John was especially pleased to be reacquainted with Hyla's father, George Richard Elkington, whom he had last seen in the course of his solicitor's career in the mid 1830s. He was impressed that George recognized him and was even more impressed when, at the reception in Carlton Hall after the marriage service, George introduced him to his "new wife" Margaret Morgan Jones Elkington and to John Hardman Powell of Birmingham… that very world famous stained glass artist who had created John's memorial to his late wife Mary Ann Stead Croft in Sydney's St. Andrew's Cathedral.

George Elkington, not knowing about the connection John felt with this man, introduced him as "The artist who made the stained glass memorial for my wife Mary, who died in 1858, in the Selly Oak's St. Mary's Church that I funded the establishment of and that we all attend and support."

John, who had only heard of the man from his architect friend Edmund Blacket in Sydney, embraced and hugged him, to Powell's surprise, and told him, "You've also created a stained glass window masterpiece for me in memory of my wife Mary Ann, who died in Sydney, Australia, in 1857."

John Powell was elated by this felicitous coincidence, exclaiming, "My God, I remember that work well…done for the 'Sydney Wren'," Edmund

Blacket. How I'd like to meet him. I sent him the window as a construction kit. Four of the parables of Christ, wasn't it?"

"Indeed it was…indeed it was," gushed John. "Just imagine, both George here and I having wives named Mary memorialized by your stained glass work as far apart in the world as places get. Indeed what hath God wrought?"

George and John and John Powell all three clasped hands and looked into each other's tearing eyes. George was the first to separate, saying to his wife Margaret, "We really are blessed."

Stained glass master John Hardman Powell (1827-1895), from thepuginsociety.co.uk

The Carlton Hall reception hosted by Richard and Elizabeth Dunnell Garrett was a veritable showcase of family conviviality. When John and Teddy and little Harry left for home in Saddington they all felt that they, already Crofts and Steads, had become members of yet another family…and a prominent one, the Garretts of Suffolk.

In early August of 1862, John received a letter from Newson Garrett informing him that the barges would be ready to sail for Hamburg, Germany, "before the end of the month." So John, whose daughter May and also son Teddy were away at their boarding schools—Blackheath Ladies School and Eton, took son Harry with him by train and coach from Saddington in Leicestershire to Ovingdean in Sussex (160 miles) asking the Rev. Alfred Stead family there to care for Harry until he came back from Germany. Thanks to Emma Barbara's immediate kind attention to Harry, John was able to leave him without much trouble. He then traveled back north by train and coach the 130 miles to Newson Garrett's Alde House in Aldeburgh, Suffolk.

At Newson and Louisa Garrett's home, John was told that he would have to wait until the "right barge," called the *Unicorn,* returned from Hamburg for reloading to make his passage on it back to Hamburg. It could be two days of waiting, or, it could be two weeks, he was told. Meanwhile,

Newson said, "You could stay here, but I'd rather you visit a friend of mine at Snape and wait at his place. He has a project going on that may interest you. He lives close to the landing and he will get you on the *Unicorn* when it's ready. The *Unicorn's* Captain Ole Hodgson is a relative of his wife's. His name is Septimus Davidson.

Newson drove John to the house of Septimus Davidson and his family, just east of the Snape Church. It was a fine house of medium size with a tiled roof and a grand carved wooden front door. Newson knocked on this door firmly and the Davidsons' young son Hugh answered the door and excitedly shouted to his parents within, "It's Mr. Garrett and he's got someone else with him!"

So Newson Garrett left John Croft as a household guest of the Septimus Davidson family in Snape. The rest of that day and evening, Septimus, a tall solicitor of 45 years of age with a close-cropped reddish beard, regaled John with his project, which was the excavation of a large tumulus...a smooth elevated hump...of soil on his property to see what it contained. "I've long figured it to be some kind of early cemetery," he told John. "And indeed we've dug up quite a few fired-clay funeral urns filled with ashes and bone fragments. But there's something much larger buried down deeper and we're trying to figure out what it is. Tomorrow at church I'll introduce you to my lead excavators and afterwards you can see the project for yourself."

After the morning service at the Snape Church, which was within easy walking distance of both the Davidsons' house and the project, John was introduced to a Mr. Francis Francis and a Dr. Nicholas Hele who were supervising about a dozen volunteer neighbors and friends in the digging activity on the Davidsons' tumulus. Together the four of them walked to the project site.

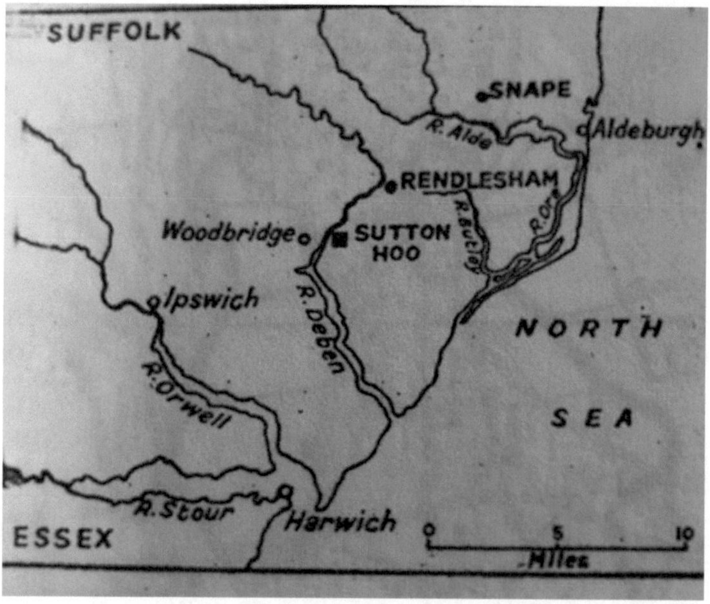

A map of the Snape environs from the work of R.L.S. Bruce-Mitford of the Suffolk Institute of Archeology.

When John first saw the project he was impressed with the scale of it. What had been a plot described by Septimus Davidson as humped up ground over 70 feet in circular diameter and sloping upward to a height of almost 5 feet in the middle of its top was now changed. It now had an east-west ditch of 50 feet in length partially bisecting it to a middle depth of 4 feet below the mean ground level. This meant that 9 feet of the soil had been taken out carefully, sifted through, removing the funeral urns in random positions, and then piled up at some distance away, revealing the contours of what appeared to be a boat that was close to 50 feet in length with tapering sides almost 10 feet in width in its middle and having its east aft end stubbed off square and its prow quite well pointed to the west so that its implied course followed the sun.

Dr. Hele explained, “We had an experienced boatwright give us his opinion that we have unearthed an Anglo-Saxon or a Viking sailboat that is hundreds of years old. We found no sign of any sails, nor the masts. The wooden substance of the vessel has been almost completely eaten away by the earth and its worms and such until most of the wooden parts can’t be seen at all anymore. But it was built in the Viking or Anglo-Saxon ‘clinker’ fashion using iron ‘rivets and roves’ to hold the strakes onto its frame and keel…and those rivets

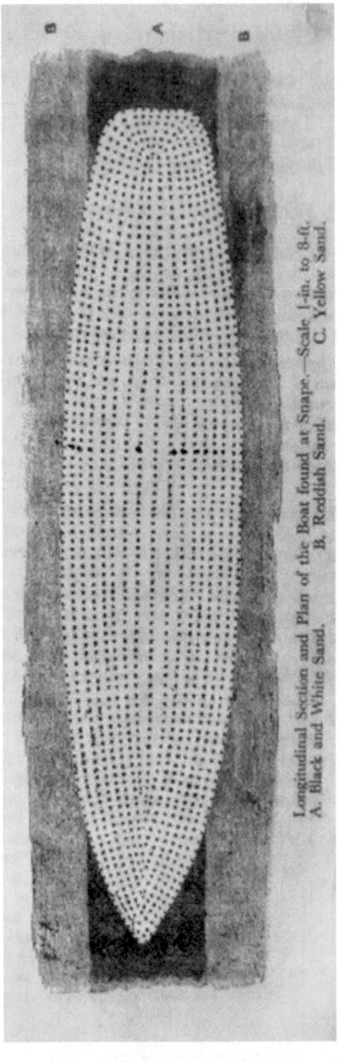

The Snape Boat Excavation—rivets and roves, from: Rupert L.S. Bruce-Mitford's "The Snape Boat Grave," Publication of the Suffolk Institute of Archeology.

and roves, now fused together in rust, are still in the exact places they were in when the boat was buried here. In our excavation we have made every effort not to disturb them. The yellow sandy soil at their depth around the rivets was removed not with shovels or trowels, but with soft brushes, so that we have precisely 17 rows of them running from stern to bow…8 rows on each side of the row that held the keel's top joist. Only have they fallen from the slopes of the riveted gunwales to a flat excavation floor."

"I can only marvel at the team effort to get this done," commented John. "How long did that take you?"

Francis Francis answered, "Pretty much the entire summer…always with about ten people working at it as we directed them."

"And are all these people doing this without pay?" John asked.

"Nobody is being paid, John," said Septimus Davidson. "Most of them started out on it thinking we were going to find and share with them some fabulous treasure…gold and silver objects of Viking plunder, perhaps. But gradually, as no such treasure was found as the shape of the ship was emptied, most of them kept at it because of their historical curiosity."

"So how did a ship of that size come to be buried here so long ago? That's an important question to be answered, eh?"

Francis replied, "It certainly took a lot of labour to get that done. The sea is a half mile away."

"And why was it buried here? Was it some historical figure's sarcophagus? Was some particular Anglo-Saxon or Viking King or Prince or Commander buried in it?"

Dr. Hele opined, "We do think that was the case…that the ship was used as a grandiose coffin, and likely that of a historical figure who lived in this area at the time. But we have no real evidence of this theory. We haven't unearthed any human tissue at all or inurned ashes within the ship's dimensions…some gobs of hair maybe, but that could be animal in origin too."

John asked, "Where is there any record of the Anglo-Saxon Kings going back, I would guess, several if not many centuries?"

Dr. Hele said, "There is the work of the Venerable Bede, a Northumbrian monk who started writing his '*Ecclestiastical History of the English People'* in 731 AD. He focused most of his attention in his five books on the Anglo-Saxons who inhabited this area…and he tells stories of their Kings, descendents of the legendary King Wuffa…going clear back to Roman times. I've been reading Bede's work closely since I became involved in Mr. Davidson's excavation project…and I can only imagine that one of those Kings of Bede's descriptions was buried in this ship here by his succeeding King as a kind of memorial. His descriptions all precede 731 AD in time, and we have no way…at least no way yet…to determine what the time frame of this burial was."

John's curiosity was further piqued by Dr. Hele's apparent scholarship. He asked further, "Is there any opinion about what type of craft this was? Was it a warship, a fishing ship, or a King's personal yacht?"

Dr. Hele continued, "We've found no cannon, and no helmets nor armour. We found two metal spear points, not within the excavated inside of the ship, but outside it in the mound. Those could have belonged to someone other than a crewman on the ship. So far, I'd guess that we haven't found a warship…or at least not a warship that had cannon. But, all in all, it's just too early to tell what kind of ship it was."

John Croft decided that, while he was waiting as the house guest of the Davidsons to join the crew of the Thames barge *Unicorn,* he would spend his days helping with the excavation. He wore what he considered his work clothes and shoes.

Three days passed, and John found himself digging at the excavation site supervised by excavation leader Francis Francis. Neither Septimus Davidson nor Dr. Hele were there that morning… only Francis Francis, John, and five other volunteer diggers and sifters. Francis Francis came to think that the diggers, including John, should dig from one side of the mound itself a deeper ditch which would wind up making a kind of tunnel close under the shape of the ship clear into its center. By noon the end of the mound ditch's tunnel extension, which would only allow room for one digger at time, was just a foot under the middle of the ship.

"I think we've gotten to where we've been wanting to go, lads." Said Francis. "Let's take a lunch break."

The men all shared ham and cheese sandwiches which had been prepared by Mrs. Elizabeth Davidson with young son Hugh's help. There was also a keg of German beer…made with Newson Garrett's malted barley, they were told. The other men, who all knew each other well, were curious about newcomer John. When Francis had introduced him to the others that morning, he called John "Mr C." apparently remembering only John's last name initial. John made no protest to this, and so he thereafter became "Mr. C." to them all. He took a few minutes to tell the men about his being a friend of the Garretts and his intention to travel on the *Unicorn* to Hamburg and further into Germany to find the widow of his late brother and give her this brother's money.

One of the men joked, asking "Hey, Mr. C., why don't you just give us the money?"

John said, "I might just do that if I don't find his widow and daughter to give it to."

All the men chuckled at this.

Francis then handed John a trowel and a pail and said, "Lunch is over, Mr. C. You take first turn under the center. Scrape away carefully there. Put whatever you find other than dirt in the pail. Good luck."

John crawled into the tunnel and began scraping the top of the end of it up toward the ship. He wondered what would happen to him if the narrow sandy-soil tunnel collapsed on him. The tunnel did not admit enough light for him to see clearly what his scrapings were. So he just sifted them through his fingers, sensing nothing of such substance as to be deposited in his pail. But then he suddenly noticed a few sizeable and sharp shards of glass. He took a few moments to examine them. Apparently he had dislodged the already broken pieces of a decorative vase or similar small ceramic vessel. And there was something spilled from it of spherical shape with a piece of tanned thin leather covering it, maybe two inches in diameter. He put the glass shards and the skin covered ball into the pail and crawled carefully back out of the tunnel into the ditch and beyond to where Francis and the other men were waiting for their turns. Francis asked, "Find anything, Mr. C.?"

John poured the pail's contents on the ground at their feet, "I've got some pieces of glass and something else."

He reached down and picked up the unknown object from among the sandy soil and glass pieces. With his fingers he peeled off its leather covering and put it into his pocket. He then dropped the object and gasped loudly. On the ground at his feet was a GOLD RING. He pounced back to the ground to pick it up in his hand, and held it high for the others to see.

"It's a gold ring…and a fancy one at that," said Francis Francis. Others similarly exclaimed, "It's got a stone in it," "Worth a king's ransom, I'd say," and "Try it on, Mr. C."

John put his right forefinger into the ring and discovered that the ring was too large to fit tightly there. "It's definitely a big man's ring…a large kingly kind of ring," he said.

"Well, I know what Dr. Hele will say when he sees it," said Francis Francis. "He'll say that such a ring is evidence enough that we've unearthed a King's ship. He'll be overjoyed."

John said, "Mr. Francis, would you mind if I take a break and go to show it to Mr. Davidson?"

Francis Francis answered, "I imagine that Septimus might be there by now. Let's ALL go."

When Septimus Davidson saw the ring in John's hand, he broke into tears, saying, "I knew it. I knew it. I knew it. I told everyone the mound held a king's sarcophagus. So the sarcophagus was the king's ship. I knew there would be some treasure found. And now treasure has been found. I knew it. I knew it. I knew it." John ceremoniously placed the gold ring into Septimus Davidson's hands. They both were grinning at each other.

When later Dr. Hele saw the ring, he echoed Francis Francis's prediction of what he would say, "Such a magnificent specimen of a ring is surely a king's possession and surely evidences that King's burial here in his ship. We've all made a world class historic find. We can be proud of ourselves now."

Ring from 7c Anglo Saxon Ship burial found in Snape

These photos of the Snape Boat-Grave ring is from Snapevillage. info site and the East Anglian Archeology Publication #95 from 2001. Notice the intaglio...an upright human figure cut into the back of the oval gem. See a full description of the stone and its discovery and its loss for 88 years (1862-1950) in Rupert L. S. Bruce-Mitford's "The Snape Boat-Grave" 1952 Publication of the Suffolk Institute of Archeology Vol. XXVI (Part 1) accessed at https:// suffolkinstitute.pdfsrv. co. uk which dates the burial with more modern technologies to the 7th century (635-650 AD) with the ring, now in the British Museum, being less than a century older. Reading diverse sources, including the writings of the Venerable Bede, I personally (LBC) opine that the buried Anglo-Saxon King was King Anna (d. 654 AD, successor Aethlehere), son of the Wuffagas-line King Eni, all of the noted vintage.

Sail-rigged barges at the Alde River landing near Newson Garrett's Snape Malting Center, from longshopmuseum. co. uk.

Three days later, when John Croft was already aboard the *Unicorn* sailing in the North Sea for Hamburg, he happened to reach into the pocket of his work pants and notice the thin and waxy piece of leather that had been the covering of the Snape boat-grave's gold ring that he had discovered and turned over to Septimus Davidson. The leather was still partly flexible, no doubt due to its having been contained in the sealed glass vase or vessel that he had dislodged with the scraping of his trowel.

When John closely examined the side of the leather piece that had been in contact with the ring, he noticed a number of symbols scratched into its under-surface, and recognized them to be runes, the ancient alphabet letters of the Germanic peoples, including the Anglo-Saxons and the Vikings. He tore a sheet of paper out of his gold-framed notebook and copied the runes as best he could onto the white paper page. This is a copy of what he wrote thereon:

The inscribed runes on the leather wrapper of the Snape Boat-Grave's gold ring.

John showed his copy of the runes to Captain Ole Hodgson, a man proud of his Norwegian Viking heritage. "Can you read what these runes say?" John asked him.

"I did indeed get some study of the ancient runes when I was in school," answered Ole. "But I can't easily make out just what this is. I think it's a list of numbers, perhaps dates…though I'm pretty sure the first and the last numbers are the same… both are 'FIVE'. Where did you get these runes?"

"They are on the underside of a leather wrapper that enclosed the gold ring I found for your cousin-in-law Septimus Davidson. I put the wrapper into my pocket and forgot about doing so. Now it appears the wrapper may have a value of its own as a relic. I'll have to get it back to Septimus and see if he can get it properly deciphered. Maybe the runes tell the date of the burial…or the birth and death dates of the person there buried. It could be important historically."

"Well, I'll be getting back to Snape before you do, John," suggested Ole. "You just go on from Hamburg to Neustrelitz and take whatever time you need to find and help your brother's widow, and I'll take the leather wrapper with the runes on it back directly to Septimus in Snape as soon as we unload our barley and return there. By the time you come back through Snape, the meaning of the runes will likely have been made clear. You know that Septimus will be most appreciative of this."

"I will gladly entrust this task to you, Ole. Thank you very much."

John had prepared himself for the trip to Germany by going to the Bank of England in London the previous month and exchanging 100 British pounds (£100) that he previously had transferred there from his primary C. Hoare & Co. account in order to obtain a Bank of England signed monetary account statement in the amount of 1326 German Hamburg Marks Banco (GHMB). In Hamburg he could use this statement to open an account in the Hamburger Bank that he could then draw upon using bills of exchange. He would initially draw out about a tenth of that in german 32-schilling coins (2 GHMB for each one) for day-to-day travel needs. At this time in Hamburg a German worker was used to working 14-hour days 6 days per week, and earning 168 schillings (meaning 10 GHMB at 2 schillings/hour) therefrom. So John's Hamburger Bank account containing 1326 GHMB would be enough to pay the average German worker for more than two-and-a-half years of work.

The voyage on the *Unicorn* across the North Sea and up the Elbe River to Hamburg took only five pleasant days as the weather was good and the wind both brisk and steady. John had also enjoyed his contact with Captain Ole Hodgson and his crew. They advised him that the best place for him to find someone competent in both German and English that he could hire to accompany him on his trip to Neustrelitz was at the Anglican Church of St. Thomas-à-Becket in the center of the city. That Church of his own faith had been established in Hamburg in the 17th century and had an English Chaplain who was offering the Church's services in the English language.

So it was that John Croft, then on his own in Hamburg and positively impressed with the city, went first to the new "Hotel Hafen," then to the Hamburger Bank, and then to the Church.

This, with the grand city hall in the background, is Hamburg's Anglican Church of St. Thomas-à-Becket at 22 Zeughausmarket. From Wikipedia.

When John entered the Church, he was immediately greeted with an English "Hello, and welcome to our Church" spoken by an elderly deacon. John asked him, "Excuse me, sir, but how do you know that I understand English?"

The deacon answered, "I didn't know…but I always address individual visitors in the same way. So what can I do for you today?"

"I need help in finding an English-competent German guide to accompany me to the town of Neustrelitz 150 miles east of here. I'm trying to find my own deceased brother Nicholas's widow, with whom I have lost contact. She was last known to be living there. My intent is to give her money to help her and my brother's daughter who should now be 17 years old."

"I see," said the deacon. "So, let me introduce you to our Chaplain. His name is Charles Frederick Weidemann and he's served our congregation well since 1853. He's the author of our hymnal, *Psalms and Hymns for Use in the English Episcopal Church*, and he is sure to know just who would be the ideal one to help you. Would you be willing to come to our service tomorrow at ten in the morning and contribute a one-time tithe? And are you intending to pay the person that Chaplain Weidemann recommends? If he is suitable to you, of course?"

"Yes, of course, I'm willing to pay what's reasonable to the right person. And I'll gladly come to the service tomorrow and contribute."

So the deacon asked John to wait in the nave while he went to get the Chaplain. After John had walked a circle around the pews and read several memorial plaques, he saw the deacon bringing with him a balding man of medium height with a close-cropped beard and moustache in his clerical robe of purple and white.

Chaplain Weidemann came up to John and said, “May I ask your name, my good sir?”

John answered, “I am John Croft, an English solicitor and a gentleman. I am hoping you will recommend an English-speaking German guide to help me find my deceased brother’s widow and daughter in Neustrelitz.”

Chaplain Weidemann shook John’s hand and formally introduced him to the deacon, whose name was Karl Schmidt. Then he said, “I am acquainted with some of the Knight family who purchased the Croft Castle near the Wales border in Herefordshire in the last century. Are you related to those castle Crofts?”

“I assume that I am, but I don’t know exactly how,” answered John. “I can trace my family line back through a John Croft who was the brother of the composer William Croft who created the ‘St. Anne’ melody to the hymn ‘Oh God Our Help in Ages Past.’ That was in the early 1700s, and I think the line goes further back through the Crofts of Claughton Hall in Lancaster and eventually to the castle Crofts. I’ve never been to either place in my life but I plan to visit them both in the near future. Perhaps I can find records in the churches in those locations which will establish my connection.”

The Chaplain then told John that: "the hymn 'Oh God Our Help in Ages Past' is included in my own hymnal here. I think we should sing it in tomorrow's service while you, the composer's relative, are with us. Would you favor that?"

"Indeed I would," replied John.

Deacon Schmidt asked, "My good man, are there any other hymns that you favor…that have been spiritually important to you?"

John thought a moment, then answered, "My late wife Mary Ann was an oft-praised singer in church choirs and when I am caused to remember her singing William Cowper's baptismal hymn 'There Is A Fountain Filled With Blood' tears well up in my eyes."

Deacon Schmidt said, "I know it well," and took up singing that hymn.

There is a fountain filled with blood,
Drawn from Emmanuel's veins.
And sinners plunged beneath that flood,
Lose all their guilty stains,
Lose all their guilty stains,
Lose all their guilty stains,
And sinners plunged beneath that flood
Lose all their guilty stains."

Chaplain Weidemann smiled to hear Deacon Schmidt's rendition, but interrupted him after the first verse to tell John, "We can see that you are indeed one of us, good sir. So, I will introduce you to a well-qualified young man tomorrow after the service. I think you will like him. If he can't promptly find your dear ones for you in Neustrelitz, they simply aren't there."

John spent the night of Saturday, September 6th, 1862, at the Hotel Hafen, which was within walking distance of St. Thomas-à-Becket Church, and attended the next morning's service, singing "Oh God Our Help in Ages Past" with the congregation and putting an envelope with three 32-schilling coins in it into the offertory pan passed to him. As the congregation filed out of the church after the Chaplain's benediction, he noticed that Deacon Schmidt was waiting for him in the company of a young man who looked to be about twenty years old.

"This is Herr…I mean 'Mr'…Daniel Wolk," Deacon Schmidt said, putting his arm around Daniel's back. "He's serving his apprenticeship with us, intending to become a vicar. He's a native German, but attended an English school in London when his father was employed there as an official of the Berenberg Bank. We recommend him heartily to you in your search for relatives in Neustrelitz. He has an uncle who lives there with his family."

John heartily shook young Daniel's hand, being positively impressed with his firm grip, saying, "That sounds very good to me, young fellow. Will you accept 3 marks per day to accompany me to Neustrelitz…to search there for my relatives…and return?"

Daniel grinned broadly and glanced at Deacon Schmidt, who nodded positively to him. Then he reached out to shake John's hand again, saying, "That's most generous, Mr. Croft. I accept your offer and I will do my best to find your relatives."

John again shook Daniel's hand and said, "Please call me John. Can we begin tomorrow?"

"We could well begin today. There will be an east-bound coach leaving our central station at 2 pm."

It took John and Daniel a week to get to Neustrelitz on the Zierker See in the Mecklenburg Lake District. While riding together in the coach for that time and sharing the same rooms and meals at inns along the way they became well acquainted with each other. Daniel heard all the known details about John's brother Nicholas and his family tragedy in Russia.

Daniel Wolk found Caroline Fink Marsow Croft's mother Martha Fink on their first day in Neustrelitz. He and John had waited outside the Neustrelitz Stadtkirche after the Sunday morning service…this because Daniel didn't know his Uncle Wilhelm's home address in the town, but he knew that Wilhelm was a devout Lutheran and had a number of pews there permanently reserved for his family. He was a retired soldier, having served years in the Prussian army under Generalfeldmarshall Friederich von Wrangel as an aide-de-camp with the rank of General, and was last active in the Prussian army's reconquest of Berlin after the 1848 revolution there against King Frederick William IV.

Neustrelitz's Stadtkirche, from de.wikipedia.

"We won't have any trouble picking him out of the crowd coming out of the church, John," said Daniel. "My mother once told me that he always wears his general's uniform and his medals to church."

And it was a touching reunion. General Wilhelm Wolk embraced Daniel vigorously when he was confronted by the young man who called him "Uncle Wilhelm" and identified himself. "You are the very image of your father at your age, Daniel. It's such a pleasure to meet you while I am still in this life. You know your father, my younger brother Henry, died while I was commanding troops during the 1848 revolution, so I could not attend his funeral in Hamburg. Even then I had not seen him for several years."

Daniel answered, "He passed away from some fever at only 50 years of age. I was only six. My mother Maria is doing well there though…she's now 63. She raised me, her only child, as a single mother, only helped by her own parents, Edward and Ethel Schiltz."

"That's a hard loss, my boy…a hard loss." said Wilhelm. "I only met your mother once. It was at their wedding in 1840."

Wilhelm's wife Anna and two of his sons, Henry and Karl, were with him…and Henry's wife Henrietta and their twin daughters Ingrid and Irma… and Karl's wife Helen and their son "Willie" who was named after Wilhelm. They invited Daniel and John to their grand home near the Schloss Neustrelitz (cf. p. 56). Wilhelm said, "They've just finished the construction next to the schloss of a grand new Schlosskirche. It's an example of what is called 'new Gothic' architecture. But even though it's much closer to us than the Stadtkirche, we're set in our ways and will continue our membership where it now is."

In the Wolks' comfortable parlor was hanging a gold-framed portrait of his long-time Prussian army commander-in-chief, Generalfeldmarshall Friederich von Wrangel.

Generalfeldmarshall Friederich Graf von Wrangel (1784-1877), from Wikipedia.

Daniel was interpreting from the German into English when Wilhelm pointed to the striking portrait and said, "Can you believe it? He entered the army as a 12-year-old dragoon in 1796 and is still commanding troops in it after 66 years at age 78. The King won't let him quit. We all called him 'Papa'. This portrait is actually a copy of the original by Franz Kruger. He painted it five years ago."

At the early afternoon Sunday meal, John had the chance to tell the Wolks, through Daniel's able interpretation, the reason for his trip to Neustrelitz…that he was trying to find his deceased brother's widow and her daughter so that he could give them his brother's inheritance money. When Daniel relayed his mention that the widow's maiden name had been Caroline Fink, Wilhelm's oldest son Henry immediately announced in German, "I know her. She was four years ahead of me in school here. She was a very pretty girl and very popular in school. To me she was a goddess. I lost track of her after I joined the army at fifteen and I didn't see her again until I was discharged for injury in 1846 and came back here to marry. She had returned here from Russia by then and moved in with her mother Martha, where she gave birth to the child. Henrietta will recall that I once introduced her to Caroline with her mother and the baby in the very church we attended this morning. That's the last time I saw her, in fact. But I know where her mother's house is and I can take you there today."

When John and Daniel were being driven in Henry Wolk's carriage to find the house of Martha Fink in a poorer section of the town, it began to rain. Henry said, "So now it rains, eh? Good thing I've got this covered carriage. We're coming to the house now. It's that small one on the right side of the road, just there…"

John could see the small house Henry indicated. It had two windows in the front looking out, and had whitewashed stucco walls that were mottled and gray, and a roof of slate tiles with a brick chimney rising out of it on the west side. There were only flat stones constituting the walkway across the now muddying bare dirt yard to the brighter, white-painted wooden door. All three of the men got out of the carriage to go to the door. Henry lashed the horse's yoke to a scrub bush sticking up along the roadside.

At their knock, a very old woman wearing a gray dress and a knitted shawl opened the door and asked in German, "Are you men sure that you are in the right place? Why would you come knocking at my door?"

Daniel told John what she had asked and John answered for him to relay to her, "If you are

Martha Fink, the mother of Caroline and the grandmother of Catherine, I am here to give you all some money. I am John Croft, Caroline's deceased-in-Russia husband Nicholas Croft's brother. Caroline is entitled to Nicholas's inheritance money and I'm here to see that you all get it. Do Caroline and Catherine live here with you?"

"No, they have been in England for some time…more than ten years now…looking for her husband Nicholas Croft's relatives," the old woman answered, "But I am Caroline's mother, Martha Fink…long a widow myself and now alone here in the world at age 82. Might I ask you men to come in and help me put some buckets around to catch the rainwater dripping through my leaky roof?"

John turned aghast to Daniel and said, "So they are in England looking for me? And they've been there looking more than a decade? What hath God wrought?"

"Well for much of that time you were in Australia, John," said Daniel in English. "All the Croft-named males in your immediate family have died…you are the only one left. Your surviving sister does not bear the Croft name."

"And if she inquired of the Garretts, who employed her husband, they likely told her that I was in Australia and they had no address for me there," John reasoned. "If she found Croft Cask, Keg, and Barrel in Hoddesdon she might have been told that her case for support depended on me and that I was in Australia. Still, it just seems bizarre that in all that time we weren't able to connect to each other in any way. Did she remarry soon on and stop looking?"

Martha Fink, listening to this interpreted-for-Henry conversation outside her door, interjected in German, which Daniel interpreted, "No, she has not remarried to my knowledge. And Catherine is now 17 years old. I will give you their address. They live in a place called Middlesex in London. Now, please, you men, come on in and help me with the buckets. You are getting drenched."

In the next three days, John gave Martha Fink 10 32-schilling coins, prepaid for a carpenter's crew to come retar the tile underlayment of her roof to stop the leaks, and made a generous financial arrangement with Henry Wolk to continue to support the very elderly Martha Fink in whatever ways were needed for the remainder of her life in her Neustrelitz house, something that Henry was clearly happy to do. He and Daniel then left Neustrelitz to return to Hamburg. Martha had given John the address of Caroline Croft in London. She and daughter Catherine lived in a flat above The Swan Inn at number 1 Swan Street in Isleworth, Middlesex, London. John told Daniel, "I should easily be able to find them with this information, thank you very much."

On the way back by coach to Hamburg, John became even more positively impressed with the character and life goals of young Daniel Wolk. Daniel was the sole support of his own mother Maria after the recent death of her father Edward Schiltz…and Maria had taken her 80-year-old mother Ethel into her home where she and Daniel lived. Ethel was getting more and more difficult to take care of.

"So how did your grandfather Edward die, Daniel," John asked.

Daniel answered, "The doctor said it was rheumatic fever. He started having strange dreams near the end, even when he was awake. I think that's what got my father too when I was six."

John was easily sympathetic to this, saying, "I've lost two beloved wives to fever, Daniel. And six children too. We can only pray that medical science will come up with some effective remedies against the infections that cause these damned fevers. Tomorrow wouldn't be soon enough for me."

When they got back to Hamburg and were sitting in the Hotel Hafen's lobby together, John asked the desk clerk for a piece of paper and a pen and told Daniel as he jotted down the figures: "When I got here to Hamburg I deposited £100 into my new Hamburger Bank account. That was worth 1326 GHMB. I immediately withdrew 100 GHMB in Schillings…50 32-Schilling coins to spend while I've been here. In addition to the coach fare and meals for the both of us both ways, which took 50 GHBM or 25 coins, I gave 3 coins to the Anglican St. Thomas-à-Becket Church here and 3 coins to the Stadtkirche in Neustrelitz and another 10 coins in Neustrelitz to Martha Fink. I paid 8 coins to the carpenters for the roofing job on her house That totals 49 coins, and indeed I have only 1 left from the 50 here in my bag. The problem is that I figure that I owe you 3 GHMB for each of 18 days of your fine work and companionship. That's 54 GHMB or 27 coins I should pay you. But here I only have 1 coin. Do you understand me so far?"

Daniel replied, "I do."

John continued, "I'm going to have to pay this hotel for two or three or more nights' stay…until I can catch another free barley barge back to the Snape landing in England. This will require 12 coins or more. The point is that I do not have enough coins to pay both you and my own way back home. I do have some British pounds on me as well, but you'd have some bother to get them changed into GHMB."

Daniel said, "Well, it looks like we should take a walk together to the Hamburger Bank where you can draw more of your German money out of your original account. By my math, you still have 1226 GHMB there, don't you?"

"Not really," replied John. "I've signed a bank withdrawal authorization in the amount of 500 GHMB to your cousin Henry Wolk to use to help him support my brother's mother-in-law Martha Fink for the rest of her life in Neustrelitz. So actually I can only withdraw 726 GHMB from my bank account here. But I do agree that we should just now take a walk to the bank. Let's walk!"

As they walked to the Hamburger Bank, John informed Daniel that it was his intent to keep the remaining 32-schilling coin in his pocket, and that he planned to withdraw another 20 from his account for his own use in addition. But that he intended to sign the remaining 706 GHMB in his account over to Daniel.

Daniel was astonished to hear this and sputtered, "But, but…that's ….far more than enough to pay me..that's a year's pay for a senior vicar."

John was firm. "That's what I want to pay you. I trust you will use it to the benefit of your mother and grandmother as well. I know you will."

After their session together in the bank, John and Daniel parted ways. John said, "I hope that I will see you again some day, Daniel. If you are ever in England, be sure to find me by using the addresses I've given you. I would love to introduce you to my family. In this life, you never know what future awaits you. You might one day find me in distress and come to my aid… You never know."

"God bless you, John Croft…and good-bye until we meet again," said Daniel as he walked away.

John was fortunate enough to catch the barge *Unicorn* under Captain Ole Hodgson in the port of Hamburg in order to sail back to the Garretts' Snape landing near Aldeburgh in Suffolk. Captain Hodgson told John that while he was away on his visit to Neustrelitz the *Unicorn* had made another complete trip back and forth to Snape. He also told John that Septimus and Dr. Nicholas Hele had an explanation for him about the runes on the gold ring's leather wrapping material.

When John returned to the house of Septimus and Elizabeth Davidson they were celebrating their 16th wedding anniversary, having been married in 1846. "Sixteen happy years married," exclaimed

Septimus, putting his arm around Elizabeth's shoulder and kissing her cheek, "With 8 of the country's most wonderful children…SO FAR."

Everyone laughed at this comment. Newson and Louisa Garrett were there, as was Dr. Nicholas Hele and a dozen other guests. They had all warmly welcomed John back into their company, and seemed very pleased that he now had an address for his late brother's widow…especially when they learned that she had apparently moved to England more than ten years ago. "I imagine that you'll be finding her in person soon now, John," said Newson. "I wonder if she's become a citizen of our Queen Victoria's Britannic empire yet. I hope she has."

In the evening after the other guests had left, Septimus and Dr. Hele took some time to explain to John what they had decided the runes on the gold ring's wrapper meant. They had even prepared three hand-scribed diagrams to show him.

"It's a NUMBER PRAYER, John," Dr. Hele said. "The runes in it (see p. 114) are in a three-by-three array of the spelled names of the numbers in the prayer. The old Anglo-Saxon words are: 'fife, twenii twa, and æhtatyne in the top row; twenii eahte, fiftyne, and twa in the middle row; and tuaelf, eahte, and twenii fife in the bottom row. The first drawing here translates these number names into our English:"

Five	Twenty-two	Eighteen
Twenty-Eight	Fifteen	Two
Twelve	Eight	Twenty-five

John studied this drawing and said, "So what makes you think this bunch of numbers is a prayer?"

Septimus Davidson answered, "Part of the reason is the number names being arranged in THREE tiers of THREE. This represents the triune nature of our Christian God as the Father, the Son, and the Holy Ghost. But we found there's more to it as we gave it more and more and yet more thought. These are not just any numbers put into threes. If you look at the next drawing you can see the names rewritten numerically…and, if you add the numbers up in all the ways they can be added THREE at a time…every row, every column, and the two corner-to-corner diagonals…you get the SAME SUM, which is 45."

5	22	18
28	15	2
12	8	25

John added the rows, columns, and the three-element diagonals together and, sure enough, agreed that all the sums were indeed 45.

"What kind of person could have created such an array of numbers?" John asked.

"It had to have been a very smart person. Likely a king's magus, sage, or high priest," said Dr. Hele. "But still that isn't all of this particular array's powers. We have discovered yet more."

Septimus Davidson corrected Dr. Hele here, saying "It was not 'we,' but YOU, Nicholas Hele, who discovered what is more."

Dr. Hele bowed deeply in Septimus Davidson's direction, and said, "If we count the numbers of the runes themselves used to express the names of the numbers, we get another array…the one shown in this next diagram:

4	9	8
11	7	3
6	5	10

John asked for clarification here, saying, "So this array is made up of the number of runes used to form the NAMES of the previous array's numbers. As there are four runes used to spell the name of the number 'five,' nine runes used to spell the name of the number 'twenty two," eight runes used to spell the name of the number 'eighteen' and so on and on to the ten runes used to spell the name of the last number 'twenty five'. Is that it?"

"That's it, precisely, John," replied Dr. Hele. "And you will notice that all the ways you can add these numbers of the number-spelling runes

THREE at a time on any row, column, or diagonal comes to the common sum of 21."

John could see that Dr. Hele was right…all the sums were 21. He said, "That is indeed a miraculous marvel. It's awesome just to be in the presence of such a wonder. This had to have been wrought by God's inspiration."

Septimus said, "That's well put, John. That's why we call it a 'Number Prayer.' We figure that our buried King's court sage gave him this array to put into contact with his gold ring…to polish it and contain it…so that the ring would then transfer the array's power into the King himself as he wore it. We conjecture that this may have happened at the King's investiture and that the array's power was created by his sage to enable the King to live to be 66 years old…the sum of the arrays' common sums of 45 and 21. Or, perhaps, the age of the King at his investiture was 45, and the age of the sage was 21, or… Well, we just don't know."

"Well, I know this…" John responded. "The value of the discovered ring far exceeds its weight in gold. It and its runed wrapper are national historic treasures indeed. I feel so blessed to have been a part of these discoveries. Thank you both for your astonishing revelations here today."

John had nice visits in Suffolk with both of the Garrett families after he departed from the Davidson's home in Snape. At Richard and Elizabeth's Carlton Hall near Aldeburgh he was able to speak at length about his trip to Germany with their daughter Sarah Louisa, his "epistolary correspondent." At first she had expressed her disappointment that he had not found Nicholas Croft's widow, but only her mother. But John said, "Well, my trip was not a success in quite the way I imagined it would be, but it turned out even better in some ways. I was able to give some much needed aid to Caroline Croft's elderly mother, and I met some very fine people who were most willing to help me. I found out that Caroline and her daughter Catherine moved here to England to look for me more than ten years ago when I was in Australia. I now have their address in London, and I will be able to find them living close enough to us to be present members of our family instead of being far away in Germany."

Sarah said, "I like it that you always try to see the positive aspects of every situation, John. I think I should try more often to do the same." Then, with her characteristic directness, she asked, "When you find Caroline in London, how much money will you be giving her?"

John smiled patiently, and answered, "It all concerns the price I negotiated for my father

Nicholas's cooperage firm, Croft Cask, Keg, and Barrel, in late 1837, the year he died and named me the sole executor of his estate. Five heirs were to get £50 per month for 10 years…totaling £30,000. The payments commenced in January of 1838 to me, my mother Mary, my sister Surrey Martha, my brother Nicholas, and my sister-in-law Elisabeth Wallace Croft, the wife of my late older brother John James Croft. After Mom's death almost three years later in December of 1840, the remaining four of us heirs each got a fourth of a monthly share more per month…that is, £62 and 50s. This means that brother Nicholas was owed 36 months times £50 until Mother's death, then 39 months times £62 and 50s until his own death in March of 1845…then by my reckoning his widow should get the remaining 33 months of the payment term at £62 and 50s per month that was bequeathed to him. That all together totals £6300, but I must also add the C. Hoare's bank account interest at 3% compounded per annum without any additional deposits for 10 years. That makes it £8466. Moreover, your father Richard, an eminently fair man, has informed me that he has arranged to pay the Richard Garrett & Co. employee Nicholas Croft a £1000 death-in-service benefit as of his date of death and compounded at the same rate since to be awarded to his widow. That will add from YOUR family enterprise another £1085. So, Caroline Croft will be getting, from two sources, a total of £9551."

"Whew!," exclaimed Sarah, "That's a lot of money. I should think that her life should be substantially easier thereafter."

John spent Christmas of 1862 at Dalton House in Saddington with all three of his children there enjoying the family festivities. It was a happy time for all…John, May, Teddy, and Harry, who had tolerated well his stay with the Rev. Alfred Stead's family in the Ovingdean rectory for the four months that his father had been away on his trip to Suffolk and Germany.

After May and Teddy had returned to their schools away, Blackheath Ladies School and Eton, John traveled to London and visited with his sister Surrey Martha and her husband, candle-maker Thomas Metcalf, who was ill at the time and not working. Their son Thomas, then 36 years old, was living away from them in Hastings-St. Leonard in East Sussex on the south coast.

"Surrey, I'd like you to accompany me to find and meet our brother Nicholas's widow Caroline and her daughter Catherine at the Swan Inn in Isleworth," he said. "It turns out that they've been here in London looking for us, their deceased husband's and father's family, for more than ten years. They live in a flat above the inn. Will you come there with me?"

Surrey immediately assured him, “Of course I will.”

On Thursday, January 8, 1863, John parked his one-horse rented carriage in front of the Swan Inn at 1 Swan Street in Isleworth, Middlesex, London. It was a nice looking place, established in 1845 according to its sign.

The Swan Inn in Isleworth, shown in 2010, from pubwiki co uk.

John and Surrey entered the building and spoke to the man at the registration booth who had a name tag pinned to his vest reading “Mr. Chapman.”

John said to him, “I’d like to ask you about a woman and her daughter who, her mother in Germany has informed me, live in a flat above us here.

Their names are Caroline and Catherine Croft. We are members of their Croft family who have never met them. Are they living here? Are they here to-day?"

"They do live here and they are both here now, but all we who also live…and work…here would not like it at all to see them bothered in any way," Mr. Chapman answered with a seriously protective look in his eyes.

John spoke back quickly, "Mr. Chapman, I assure you they will be most pleased to speak with us. Caroline's husband Nicholas Croft, who died tragically with two of their children in a cholera epidemic in St. Petersburg, Russia, in 1845, and is Catherine's late father, was our younger brother. We want to make their acquaintance. We are told that they have been looking for us futilely for more than ten years, but now here we are. Please be so kind as to have someone go upstairs and inform them that we, John Croft and my sister Surrey Martha Croft Metcalf…their closest Croft relatives…are here to see them."

Mr. Chapman said, "I'll go up myself and ask them to accompany me back downstairs You two go sit at a table in the tavern over there and I'll bring them to you if they want to come."

In a few tense waiting minutes, Mr. Chapman, alone, came into the tavern's restaurant and quite politely asked them, "Can you please wait here for them for a few minutes? They are very excited about your presence here and they want to change their dress and fix their hair to meet you 'more properly'."

John smiled at this and said, "We will gladly wait, thank you very much." And Mr. Chapman left them to get back to his registration booth in the Inn's guest lobby entrance.

They waited more than fifteen minutes, until John asked Surrey, "Do you think they're really coming? Maybe we should just order a meal or drinks or something."

But then two ladies entered the tavern from the lobby and Surrey, who saw them first, whispered strongly to John, "Here they come…and a beautiful pair they are."

John did not say anything back to Surrey, but his eyes agreed with her assessment. The women were very clearly mother and daughter, resembling each other closely at different stages of life…the mother at 55, John's same age, and the daughter just radiant at 17, only a year younger than his daughter Mary Anne…both slender and lithe, both light blondes with their hair fixed similarly to cover their ears to their necks…both with straight white teeth fixed in smiles. They had on similar one-piece dresses, the mother's green to match her eyes and the daughter's an also eye-matching azure blue.

It was clear that Mr. Chapman had told Caroline and Catherine Croft just who it was that was awaiting them. They walked rapidly toward John and Surrey's table, and John and Surrey rose and stepped forward, opening their arms to invite warm embraces.

Caroline, who was hugging John, said in his ear, "My God, we've found each other at last. I had given up on finding you." And Catherine, who was hugging Surrey, asked, "So are you my Aunt? Do I have any cousins I don't yet know?"

There was simply too much time, too many life events, to catch up on. They talked and talked and talked for two hours, stopping only to have Caroline, who worked the evening hours in the tavern as a bar maid, order them all a nice beef and potatoes meal made in the Swan Inn's fine kitchen.

At one point John was relating as briefly as he could that he had married and moved to Sydney, Australia in 1843, and, in sixteen years there, became wealthy enough to return to England with his three children after his wife's death to purchase two named English estates. But his sister Surrey, noticing that Caroline and Catherine were not wearing any jewelry at all, interrupted John's relation to ask them, "Do you have no wedding or engagement rings?"

Caroline answered tersely, "I had to sell both my previous wedding rings so that we didn't starve."

Surrey was jarred a bit by this, and said to her, "I can't imagine that a woman as beautiful as you are…and who can speak not only English, but German, and Russian…has not had many suitors over the past seventeen years. Are you still single by choice?"

Caroline said with some pique, "Of course I'm single by choice. And good choice too. Every suitor had flaws of some kind I couldn't abide. None could match Nicholas in my mind as a life's partner. Only now might I have found my 'Mr. Right'. But he spells his name with a 'W'."

Catherine reacted to this with a "Mo-om?"

Caroline explained, "I am now officially being courted by the prominent home-builder Robert Wright, the father of Catherine's own persistent suitor David Wright, who is an aspiring foreign service officer, now at Oxford. We may soon announce our engagements…a mother and daughter Croft to marry a father and son Wright."

"That's wonderful…wunderbar…chudesno!" said John in three languages to which he had previously been exposed. "And you will now be able to afford any size dowry a groom might require."

"Robert Wright will not be demanding any dowry, I can assure you," Caroline replied. "He's proud of me for working all these years to support myself and my daughter…and he won't be asking me to quit unless I want to. But what do you mean to say about my being able to afford a dowry?"

"What I mean is that I am the executor of my father Nicholas Croft's estate, recorded and proven in 1837 while you and brother Nicholas were in Russia. I am ready to sign over to you all the funds from that estate and from my brother Nicholas's employer, Richard Garrett & Co., to which he was well entitled…a sum very close to £10,000. That money is, I am happy to say, already YOURS and I will help you gain bank access to it all within the next week or so."

Caroline was stunned. "£10,000!?" she gasped, then repeated, "**£10,000**!?"

John added, "Well…almost…actually £9551, but if you want, I will personally add the extra

£449 to total £10,000. However, there are going to be some important legal matters we will have to discuss concerning any impending marriage."

"What legal matters are those?" Caroline asked.

John Croft explained to her: "As a licensed solicitor, I think you may not be aware of the legal concept of 'coverture' whereby a married woman and all her possessions are considered the property of her husband…he controls all of their common estate, no matter who owned it before the marriage."

"I do not know of this." Caroline said. "Does that mean that if I become Mrs. Robert Wright, all the money you say I have coming from Nicholas's inheritance will be his?"

"That is correct. His assets and your assets will be his property after the marriage and only he can sign to withdraw it from the common bank account to spend it on anything at all," answered John.

"Do you think my Robert knows this?"

"I am quite sure he knows it. All men know it…and think it their right," said John. "But you say that he wants to marry you and that he will not demand a dowry. That likely means he thinks that you have no appreciable financial estate and he wants to marry you anyway. That is a good thing. It likely means he really loves you for yourself and doesn't care that you don't come to him with any financial assets."

"But what if I want to keep control of the money once I get it into a bank account in my name... even after I marry Robert?"

"You can stay single in the eyes of the law," explained John. "You can find a Church to get married in that will honour your request not to report the marriage to the civil registry. You'll then be married in God's eyes, but not the Queen's. You would then keep all your personal identification as Caroline Croft in your legal and banking affairs, but you would be Mrs. Robert Wright to God, Robert, and everyone else. Socially, you might prefer the now acceptable retention of your first name as Mrs. Caroline Wright. And, importantly also, you would ask Robert to make a will naming you, as Caroline Croft, the primary beneficiary of HIS estate in case of his death. You wouldn't legally be his wife to be the probated heir without the will's specification."

"Well, I will have to discuss this with Robert," said Caroline. "But please go ahead with getting me the money as soon as possible."

So within two weeks John got Caroline Croft a bank account in her name at C. Hoare & Co Bank in London and deposited into it £10,000. She told him that Robert Wright, having consulted his own solicitors, would agree to marry her without the church's report to the civil registry…and he would tolerate her remaining legally Caroline Croft in order to maintain control of her £10,000. And he agreed that he would, immediately after their marriage, write a will naming Caroline Croft as a beneficiary equal to his THREE sons. In the course of this, John was able to meet Robert Wright at the Swan Inn one day at Caroline's insistence.

John agreed to meet Robert for lunch at noon, and he arrived fifteen minutes early. But Robert was already seated at one of the tavern's restaurant tables, and got up to greet John as he walked in. John quickly saw that Robert used a cane to walk, having a noticeable limp.

Robert was about John's height and weight, but he was clean shaven and had thicker hair on his head that was more completely gray than John's. As the men drew close, Robert said, "You must be John Croft. Caroline described you to me."

John smiled and held out his hand to shake Robert's hand firmly, saying, "Yes, I'm John Croft and I'm happy to meet you. I've only recently met Caroline, but my position as executor of my late brother Nicholas's estate has cast me in the role of her financial advisor. And, I am a licensed solicitor also."

Robert also smiled and replied, "She tells me that you were in Australia for 16 years and that that's why she had trouble finding you. She says you did well in business there, and that you know a lot about the business world…and that you have recently purchased two named estates here. Also, she related that you traveled to Neustrelitz in Germany in an effort to find her, and that, while there obtaining her London address, you helped her mother Martha get a new roof and find some much-needed financial support. For that I can only thank you and see you as a valuable future family member."

"So you are indeed committed to marrying Caroline, even despite her desire to retain control of the money her inheritance has now given her?"

"Yes, I am," answered Robert. "I don't need any of her money and I love her…rich or poor."

John replied, "Now THAT is the answer I most wanted to hear…the right answer in the most important matter of essence. But may I ask you some further questions about yourself? If you don't want to tell me anything, just say so."

"Ask me whatever you want. I see that you are taking a protective role in Caroline's life here…a paternal role, even…and I admire you for that. If I were you, I'd do the same."

"Where and when were you born? How do you describe your family life? How did you become a home-builder? And, how do you now earn a livelihood?"

John and Robert took seats at the table. A male waiter came to take their lunch orders…sandwiches and beers. And Robert related: "I was born here in London in 1805 and baptized into the Anglican Church. I am the oldest of six Wright family children, all still alive, three brothers and two sisters… all now married and with a lot of children, all of whom I could name. All are doing well in life…no criminals or problem debtors…only patriotic citizens, devoted to the Queen Victoria."

John felt he had to comment, "That's extraordinary in a family that large. You are two years older than I am. Are either of your parents still living?"

"No, they are both gone, God bless their souls."

"Tell me about your marriage."

"When I got back from Burma I…"

"What?!,' interrupted John, "You were in Burma? Tell me about that."

"I was there for the first stage of the war. I trained at the Royal Military Academy at Woolwich, became an ensign of artillery, and was transported to Rangoon with the 41st Regiment of Foot under Colonel Sir Edward Stopford. I got there via the Andaman Islands on the *HMS Slaney* under Captain Charles Mitchell."

"Did you know Henry, called 'Larry,' Lawrence? He was my roomie at Addiscombe and was an artillery ensign in the 41st Foot, like you."

"Yes, of course I knew him," said Robert. We were in combat together at the Kemmendine Stockade with its elephants. I took a musket round in the leg there, breaking my right shin badly, and it got infected. I spent three months in The Rangoon military hospital fighting for my life. I was there until October of '24, then invalided back to England and then out of the service by summer '25. The leg eventually sort of healed up but has never been the same. That's why I use this damned cane."

John took a deep breath, and said, "I was at Kemmendine too and saw Colonel 'Fighting Bob' Sale of the 13th Foot end the conflict by killing the

Burmese commander who tried to flee the fortress on his elephant. ”

Robert frowned and said, “I heard about that later. In fact, it was Larry Lawrence who told me about it when he visited me in the Rangoon hospital. He was later in there too, after I left, with a fever he barely survived.”

“I was there myself after being wounded at Donubyu in April ’25. Have you remained in touch with Larry?” asked John. “I heard he became a General and was even knighted.”

Brigidier General Sir Henry Montgomery Lawrence, KCB (28 Jun., 1806-4 Jul., 1857), engraving ca. 1850 after an unknown photographer, from Wikipedia.

"Larry never forgot a friend," said Robert. "But he spent his whole career in India, Afghanistan, and Nepal. So I never saw him after Burma. He died a hero at the Siege of Lucknow during the Indian Rebellion of 1857. He is buried there in Lucknow with his tombstone saying "Here lies Henry Lawrence who tried to do his duty." He founded 4 Military Asylums in India for the education of the children of British soldiers. For that his eldest son Alexander was elevated by Queen Victoria to be the 1st Baronet Lawrence in consideration of his father's military services to the crown. A few years ago a statue of Larry by John Lough was placed in St. Paul's Cathedral and I was there for its dedication."

Statue of Gen. Henry M. Lawrence in London's St. Paul's Cathedral, from Wikipedia.

"I'll definitely be visiting St. Paul's just to see that," said John. "I had no idea he'd been so honored."

Both men were silent, contemplating the surprising coincidence of their similar military service and their mutual acquaintance in it. In a minute or two, Robert said, "I finished my military service as a Lieutenant in 1825. You?"

John answered tersely, "Captain. 1828."

Robert decided to continue his answering John's inquiries. He went on, "In 1826 I married Mary Burgoyne of 'the' Burgoynes and…"

But John interrupted him again, asking, "Is she possibly related to another of my Burma soldier comrades…Matthew Burgoyne? He and I came back from Burma to England on the same ship, the *HMS Boadicea* in 1827-8."

"Well, I don't know a Matthew Burgoyne, I'm afraid, even though I know many Burgoynes," replied Robert. "They are a large family, though, as you may be aware. So likely he is related, but belongs to another branch of the family."

John did not answer this. So Robert continued: "And Mary and I had three sons. The older two,

Phillip and Thomas, are married now and have two children each. My youngest son, twenty-one-year-old David, is at Oxford studying foreign languages and hoping to gain a foreign service appointment. You know that he is madly in love with Caroline's daughter Catherine and wants to marry her in a common service with Caroline and me. My dear wife Mary died of a heart ailment in 1855, so my sons and I have been without her for almost eight years now, and it's still difficult sometimes."

"I lost my own dear Mary in 1857, and so I understand," said John. "I have three children, a daughter May and sons Teddy and Harry, that I'm trying to raise on my own…and it is a challenge. But how did you become a home-builder?"

"In the 1830s I was among the first to study architecture at King's College here in London. After I received my certificate I found employment as a draftsman with the Cubitt brothers, Thomas and William and Lewis, who were then building large blocks of luxury private residences in Belgravia, Pimlico, and Bloomsbury. I also helped with the homes at Kemp Town in Brighton."

John refrained from mentioning that he had been in King's College's first law classes and instead asked, "Wasn't William Cubitt the Lord Mayor of our city of London?"

"He was until just this last year when he lost election to the clothmaker, Sir William Rose," answered Robert. "But he was our Mayor for the two previous years."

Then Robert continued: "So, the Cubitt brothers all sort of went in different directions professionally. And I had to choose one to follow. So I followed Lewis, the youngest of them, because I got on so well with him. His particular specialty was

Portrait of Lewis Cubitt (29 Sept., 1799-9 Jun., 1883) by William Boxall, 1845, from Wikipedia.

home design and that appealed to me. I thought of a kind of business slogan for him. It was 'building homes that look good from the outside and are comfortable on the inside,' and he appreciated my efforts to advertise and sell the homes he designed.

But five years ago I decided to create my own business…using a set of already proven designs to build larger numbers of homes in blocks or tracts of real estate here in London and perhaps, in the future, in other cities. I have now succeeded in registering my home building business, called High Quality Homes Ltd., as a common stock offering on the London Stock Exchange. The trading symbol is HQH and the price yesterday for a single share was £2. The offering began with 50,000 shares outstanding, but we now have stock holders owning almost 30,000 of them. I am the Chairman of the HQH Board of Directors."

John was impressed with this information to be sure. "How many HQH homes have you built and sold and where are they?"

Robert seemed a bit disconcerted to answer this, but confided, "We've built ten homes in Wimbledon in the past two years and sold eight of them. But we are looking for less expensive land to build more such homes on."

John persisted, "Have you paid any dividends to the stockholders?"

Robert answered, "Not yet. Our books still show that we are in debt. The land we had to buy cost more than we received for the eight houses we sold. But, of course, we will become profitable soon as we continue our operations. It can't fail. People want to buy our homes. Might you, John Croft, become one of our stockholders?"

"How exactly would I do that?"

"Well you could give me a bank draft to pay for the number of shares you want and I'd get you a certificate for that number of shares from our company accountant. But I'd prefer to take you personally to the Stock Exchange to buy stock in our company through a licensed broker. That way the price will be fixed at the time of the recorded transaction instead of having to respond with addition or rebate according to the rapidly changing price on the market. AND, the stock exchange is an exciting place to see. You might enjoy it."

John explained, "In Sydney I was not only an investor in several companies on the stock exchange, but I was an investor in the new Stock Exchange itself. I owned Stock in the Stock Exchange. And I frequently was there to see it in operation. My partner and close friend, Thomas Whistler Smith, was the President of it. This is how I know that what you are saying is true."

After Robert Wright left John's company at the Swan Inn's restaurant, John went upstairs and knocked on the door of the apartment of Caroline and Catherine Croft. Caroline answered and, seeing John standing in the hallway, asked in a voice lowered in volume but elevated in importance, "How did it go?"

John chuckled and answered, "Well, Mr. Wright is indeed 'Mr. Right'. The weddings, both of them, should proceed without further delay."

When he said this, he was quite surprised that Catherine, who had turned her ear to the conversation at the door from the main table in the tidy apartment, jumped up and kept on hopping up and down in excitement, saying "That's GREAT! Yay! Hooray! I can't wait to tell David!"

The next day at the London Stock Exchange, Robert helped John purchase 100 shares of stock in High Quality Homes, Ltd.

The London Stock Exchange in 1810, engraved by Thomas Rowlandson, et. al. from Wikipedia.

CHAPTER FOUR: Beginnings and Endings... Weddings and Funerals.

By the time of the dual wedding on April 4, 1863, Caroline and daughter Catherine had become beloved members of the Croft family...and they met and got along well with the Steads and the Garretts as well. Robert and David Wright had become acquainted with John's sister, Surrey Martha and her husband Thomas Metcalf, because they were London residents who lived near them.

The wedding took place in St. George's German Lutheran Church at 33 Little Alie Street near Goodman Fields in an east-end area that had been home to German emigrants who worked in the sugar refining and processing industry. This church offered Sunday services in German at 9:00 a.m. and English at 10:30 a.m. Pastor Louis Cappel told Caroline and Robert that he could also perform their ceremony in Latin if they so desired, and he was amenable to marrying two couples in one ceremony and to not reporting the senior couples' marriage to the civil registry. Only did he suggest a church subsidy of £60 which groom Robert Wright gladly paid.

Caroline told John that St. George's German Lutheran Church had celebrated its 100th year in London just the year before, in 1862. She said she was impressed by the church's addition in 1859 of a two-storey brick annex behind it that was an "Infant School" for children under three to be taken care of while their parents were in the church nave, with its old-style box pews. The money to build the Infant School was donated by Johann Goethe's publisher, W. G. Göshen. Above the altar and the pulpit in the church itself was a large wooden plaque engraved with the coat of arms of English King George III (1738-ruled 1760-d. 1820) of the German Hanover dynasty.

The altar and pulpit seen from the nave aisle in St. George's German Lutheran Church in London, from: spitalfieldslife.com.

St. George's German Lutheran Church's Infant School, from spitalfieldslife.com.

The wedding ceremony itself was quite unorthodox. The guests in the box pews on the grooms' side of the aisle included the families of both Phillip and Thomas Wright, Robert's older sons and fellow groom David Wright's brothers. Also there was Lewis Cubitt, Robert's former boss and HQH, Ltd. investor, and his wife Sophia. On the brides' side were John Croft, with daughter May and seven-year-old Harry, and Surrey Martha Croft Metcalf and her husband Thomas, and also Mr. Chapman and two of Caroline's fellow bar maids from the Swan Inn. There were no bridesmaids or groomsmen…no maid of honor…no best man. Only did the guests hear Pastor Cappel's reading from *Ephesians* 5: 22-24, exhorting "Wives, submit to your husbands as to the Lord. For the husband is the head of the wife as Christ is the head of the church, his body, of which he is the savior. Now, as the church submits to Christ, so also should wives submit to their husbands in everything." And from the longer exhortation in *Ephesians* 5: 25-33 to the "Husbands, love your wives, just as Christ loved the church and gave himself up for her to make her holy, cleansing her by the washing with water through the word, and present her to himself as a radiant church, without stain or wrinkle or other blemish, but holy and blameless. In this way husbands ought to love their wives as their own bodies. He who loves his wife loves himself. After all, no one ever hated his own body, but he feeds and cares for it, just as Christ does the church—for we are members of his body. For this reason a man will leave his father and mother and be united to his wife, and the two will become one flesh. This is a profound mystery—but I am talking about Christ and the church. However, each one of you also must love his wife as he loves himself, and the wife must respect her husband."

After this, Pastor Cappel said, "Now I tell you all what this church and its members believe…that marriage is a covenant of fidelity. Thus I advise you simply '**PLAY NOT, STRAY NOT**'…lest you lose your marriage, which is an important blessing from God, and your immortal soul."

Then he asked the marriage couples…first Robert and Caroline, then David and Catherine to repeat this vow after him to each other: "I______ take thee_________ to be my loving (wife/husband) from this day forward, in joy and in sorrow, in plenty and in want, in sickness and in health, to love and to cherish, as long as we both shall live. This is my solemn vow."

When the vows were completed, Pastor Cappel announced that by the powers vested in him by the Holy Church and its ministry he there and then pronounced the two couples to be husbands and wives, and told the "Gentlemen, you may now kiss your brides." The guests all applauded politely when this was done. The couples then walked together down the aisle to the church's foyer where cakes and tea were served in lieu of a more formal reception. The wedding certificates were signed in triplicate there in the foyer by the couples and their designated witnesses, followed by Pastor Cappel's signatures. When he signed there was another round of applause. The weddings were over.

John first shook David's hand and hugged Catherine, and asked them, "Will you have a honeymoon?" David smiled and replied, "Dad has rented us our own furnished flat in Oxford…so we'll have our honeymoon there. Study must go on."

So John asked the same question when he was congratulating Robert and Caroline. Robert answered, "We're taking the train to Wales to stay two weeks at the St. George's Hotel in Llandudno in Conwy County…the Queen of the Welsh watering places abutting the Great Orme peninsula."

The St. George's Hotel, est. 1854, on the Llandudno Promenade in Wales, from stgeorgeswales co uk.

"Well, I've heard it's a great resort," said John. "I wish you a wonderful time there. And after that?"

Robert went on smiling and said, "After that she'll be coming home with me to Belgravia…and it'll be just she and I and the home staff there now that David and Catherine have a place of their own in Oxford. Caroline won't be working on her own anymore. She's quit the Swan Inn and is moving out. Also, Caroline wants us to travel to Neustrelitz in Germany soon so that she can introduce me to her mother Martha before she gets any older. "

John was pleased to see the close relationship that had formed between the seventeen-year-old bride Catherine and his now nineteen-year-old daughter May. After the wedding he could see it in the way they hugged each other and spoke closely into each other's ears for privacy and giggled. Even though Catherine had grown up the daughter of a working single mother and had matured through a life of hard work and frequent stress, she viewed Blackheath Ladies Boarding School graduate May as a kindred soul. She told her. "We're the first of our families' children. You're the oldest and I'm the only…no other child before either of us. We are both fated to rule our own roosts, and raise hordes of little cousins."

During the break in Eton's 1863 term schedule between the Lent and Summer "Halves," Teddy's fellow Eton student Robert "Bobby" Tooth, son of Edwin and Sarah Tooth of Sydney, Australia, came to Dalton House in Saddington in Leicestershire, at his parents' mailed insistence, to spend the break with the Croft Family. Bobby's father Edwin, then at age 21, had been on the ship *Euphrates* together with his older brother Robert and John and Mary Ann Croft when they were all sailing to Australia in 1843, twenty eventful years before.

Bobby was four years older than Teddy and had actually been a six-year-old classmate of May's when they started school together at Sydney's Christ Church St. Laurence School. His father Edwin was one of John Croft's oldest and closest friends and partners, sharing in a number of business ventures together.

When Teddy and Bobby got out of the carriage in front of Dalton House, John was there to meet them with both May and Harry. Bobby was clearly now a good-looking young man and he was dressed in a suit and tie, with highly polished black shoes. John strode to him first, shook his hand vigorously and said, "My word, Bobby, you've grown up well. I'll now have to start calling you Robert, I'd guess, eh? I remember teaching you to fish on May's boat *Adelaide* on Double Bay in Sydney. Do you recall?"

"Yes, I do, Mr. Croft. And I've been going by 'Bob' now for some time." He looked and smiled at May who had put on her prettiest yellow dress to come out and meet him, and added, "May, you've obviously grown up well also. Are you still in that boarding school? You were always the brightest of us."

May picked up her skirt and stepped quickly over to give Bob a warm hug, and answered, "No, I'm done with school now. I can't decide if I'm now a 'proper lady' or not, but I've finished school."

Bob said, "I've got one more 'halve" to go at Eton…we have THREE 'halves" per year, you know. I'm going back to Sydney then to help in the family businesses. There was some talk of Oxford or Cambridge, but that's not for me. I'm going home."

Almost fifteen-year-old Teddy was watching his family welcome his senior fellow Bob. He ran to John and May and hugged them, saying, "I've got more Eton to go. But I'm far enough along to avoid the fagging now…no more having elders and oppidans beating me and making me serve them."

Bob charitably commented to May, "Ted has been earning high marks. He's a class leader and you should be proud of him. I'm sure he'll be accepted to university study wherever he applies." Then he turned to seven-year-old Harry, and asked him, "Are you coming to Eton too?"

Harry proudly stated, “NO, I’m studying at home here with Mrs. Anna Smythe. She says that I am ‘precocious’ and that she’ll teach me Latin, Greek, Biology and Algebra…and that I should go instead to Rugby when I’m thirteen.”

“It sounds like you’ll be well prepared, Harry,” said Bob. “Do you play chess?”

“We have a nice chess set, and I know how the pieces move, but I haven’t really played anyone a serious game. Dad is too busy and Teddy and May have been away at school. Mrs. Smythe has played me some checkers on the chess board, though, and I’ve liked doing that.”

“Well, you and I will play some serious chess, Harry,” said Bob. “And some checkers too.”

John suggested, “And we have some good fishing possibilities around here as well…bream, carp, chub, garfish, pike, trout…you name it, we’ve got them…even eels. We can fish the River Soar and the Saddington Reservoir. And the cook will make us a fine meal of what we catch.”

Bob asked, “Do you have all the right tackle and gear?’

John pointed to a wooden shed on the property a short walk away and said, “The former owners were avid fishermen and left all their gear and tackle in there for us. I haven't closely gone through it, but it looks more than ample for any number of us. We may have to dig our own worms for bait, though."

Bridge over the River Soar at Navigation Barrow, from Wikipedia.

May was not an advocate of the fishing. She said, "You men can do all the fishing you want. I'll stay here. Fish are too slimy for me and the very thought of what has to happen to them after you catch them is…is…bbbrrrr! I'll stay here."

Teddy joked, “May, you haven’t had trouble eating them before, though, have you?”

May responded, “You dig the worms, catch the fish and gut, behead, and clean them, the cook filets them so there are no bones, then fries or bakes them with seasoned breading, and I’ll eat them. That’s how fishing works here at Dalton House.”

So on one of the days of the Eton break visit of Robert Tooth, the “men”—John, Robert, Teddy, and Harry all dug worms and went fishing for half the day. They returned with a wicker creel filled with ten already gutted, beheaded, and cleaned brown trout of about two pounds each. Dalton House cook Beatrice Stamper made a delicious meal of them, which even May cnjoyed. “Who caught the most fish?” she asked.

Teddy answered cryptically, “Three of us caught three each and one of us only caught one.” He was looking over his shoulder at John when he said this.

John said, “But that one was the biggest one caught.”

Bob, Teddy, and Harry all erupted in unison, “That’s not so! I caught a bigger one!”

Throughout the next two years, John Croft mostly stayed at Dalton House in Saddington. He and May resolved to travel somewhere else for a day or two to visit their relatives and friends once per month, lest they "stagnate" in constant residence in one place. Teddy was away much of that time at Eton. Only younger Harry continued his education with the able teaching of Mrs. Anna Smythe.

Mrs. Smythe knew that John had taken a subscription to the monthly *Gentleman's Magazine and Historical Review* that was published from St. John's Gate in Clerkenwell, Middlesex, London. This 200+ page small-print but worldwide circulation publication was essentially the world's first multi-topic "magazine." The first editor, Edward Cave (1691-1754), had coined the word "magazine," meaning then only a "storage place," to describe his literary product back when he began it in 1731. The succeeding editors into the next century, who all used the pseudonym "Sylvanus Urban," wrote that their magazine "provided access to so much information that it was the 'intelligencer' of the world's English-language culture." John spent at least an hour reading it every morning. So Anna Smythe asked him to take another hour every week day to simply have a session with son Harry to "read whatever you find interesting to him and discuss it with him afterwards." John did this and soon came to regard it as important for many family reasons. He asked May to join in these sessions from time to time as well.

The *Gentleman's Magazine* substantively advanced the genre of the obituary…not only informing the public about the demise of its citizens in long lists every month, but informing also of these citizens' contributions to public life…and also listing their grieving survivors and the cemeteries where they were interred.

John had long read these obituaries in the magazine whenever he encountered a copy of it. With a pen he would circle the name of that person who died that month at the oldest age. Or he would circle the name if, as sometimes happened, he had personally known the person who died. He would count the generations and number of the deceased person's survivors, if they were listed, keeping a record of those whose human "issue" extended to double and even triple great grandchildren in their lifetimes.

Once, in their Sydney *Mount Adelaide* house on Darling Point in 1856, John was reading an older issue he had found somewhere of the *Gentleman's Magazine* from August of 1852 and encountered an obituary on page 213 that read: " June 22: At Frankfurt-on-the-Maine, Germany, Jane, wife of Mr. George K. Davison and eldest daughter of James Stead, Esq., of Acre Lane, Brixton, Surrey, age 45." This was the shocking way he and Mary Ann found out about the tragic death of Mary Ann's older sister Jane Stead Davison, to whom she had been so close. Mary Ann immediately wrote and mailed a letter about it to her brother, the Rev. Alfred Stead in Ovingdean, asking him for more information about this jarring loss. But, by the time the answering letter from Alfred arrived at *Mount Adelaide* nine months later, Mary Ann, in March of 1857, had taken ill and died. She never learned the circumstances of her dear sister's death. Rev. Alfred's letter reported that she and George were on a Maine River cruiseboat vacationing in Germany when she slipped on the rainy deck, fell overboard and drowned.

Alfred had mistakenly assumed that Jane's husband George Davison would have sent Mary Ann and John a letter about this tragedy, but no such letter made it to them in Australia if he did.

George Kearsley Davison (1801-1880)
in 1863, from CFA.

In Ovingdean in 1859, when John and Alfred discussed this, Alfred related about how he and Emma had become upset with George due to his making a drunken proposal to marry another woman within a year of Jane's death. Since then, they had no subsequent contact with him at all and considered him also to be dead to their family. George and Jane's only child, daughter Jane Kearsley Davison, called "Janie," then twenty-five years old, had left her father's house to marry, on July 4th of 1857, London solicitor Richard Broadhurst Postans in St. Wulfran's Church in Ovingdean with her uncle, the Rev. Alfred Stead, presiding and her father not in attendance.

Alfred and Emma gave to John the address of Richard and Janie Postans in London so that he could establish contact with them and, through them, with her father on his own if he wanted, which he did. His own reunion with George at his Keppel Street house near Russell Square was charged with both sad and glad emotions. It was apparent, however, to John that George was having severe mental problems and that he was engaged in excessive self-destructive drinking and had begun to neglect his business responsibilities as well.

John and May and Harry had a deep discussion about the death of "Aunt Jane" whom they had never met but only heard of, and about how "Uncle Alfred and Aunt Emma" could be so upset with her husband "Uncle George" that they considered him "dead to the family." John couldn't help but think about what he had been told of how Alfred and Emma's sixteen-year-old daughter Mary Jane Stead had so displeased them with her falling in love with a young man they disapproved of that, when she died giving birth to that young man's baby unwed, they wouldn't allow her to be buried with her own gravestone in their St.Wulfran's Church cemetery plot. St. Wulfran's Curate Arthur Thomas had to overrule them to have her buried in her grandfather James Stead's grave with only her initials and death date, "M.J.S., 21st June, 1856" etched into the side of his gravestone. But John did NOT mention this thinking to May and Harry.

When Harry asked, "Is it because Uncle Alfred is a priest that he got so upset with Uncle George?"

John said, "I don't think his being a priest has much to do with it. Priests are usually the very teachers of the value of forgiveness...people looking beyond other people's sins and shortcomings. I have heard your Uncle Alfred refer people to the book of *Matthew* Chapter 18 where Peter asks Jesus, 'Lord, how many times should I forgive a brother's sins against me? As many as seven times?' and Jesus said to him 'I do not say seven times, but seventy seven times.' When the people were crucifying him, Jesus called out 'Father, forgive them for they know not what they do.' I know your mother would have taught you about the need for forgiveness in life. She certainly forgave me a lot to marry me and become your mother. And, as for George Davison, I can assure you that he will always be your "Uncle George" in this family as long as I am the head of it. And you can remember this too—There is NOTHING you can do in this life that I won't still love you…NOTHING!" Then he smiled and said in a lighter tone, "Only do I ask you to think before you act, that's all. Then you won't need to be forgiven."

After this discussion, which took place in February of 1865, John and May decided they should visit Janie and Richard Postans in London. John realized that he had not yet seen their little girl Margaret Ellen Postans who was born in 1858 and was therefore six or seven years old. So John sent them a note asking them to give him a date and time when it would be convenient for him and May to visit and a date was made for Thursday afternoon, March 9th. The Postans lived in St. Pancras.

When John and May came up to the door of Richard and Janie's house, they knocked and it was six-year-old Margaret who opened the door for them and led them into the parlor to see her parents. May right away commented to Margaret's parents about how well she had greeted them and brought them into the parlor. Margaret, with her dark hair pulled tightly back into a bun, beamed with pride, and said, "Mummy says meeting people well is important…so I am practicing." Then she addressed John, saying "Mr. Croft, may I call you 'Uncle John'?" And to May, she said, "Miss Croft, may I call you 'Cousin May'?" Both John and May, delighted, said, "That would be fine."

Janie told John and May that Richard would give them a tour of the house and a look at the backyard garden, and then they would all gather around the kitchen table for scones, tea, and conversation.

Richard Broadhurst Postans (1828-1901) in 1865. From CFA.

Janie Kearsley Davison Postans (b. 7 Aug., 1832) in 1865. From CFA.

The house was not large, composed of three bedrooms, a storage room for clothing, a combined kitchen and dining area, a parlor, and a "utility room" with a laundry washing station and a kind of shop…with a workbench on which a vise was mounted and a toolbox sat. Richard said, "I do some carpentry here, making birdhouses and a wooden rocking horse for Margaret and such. I do the laundry scrubbing in the tub for Janie and haul the water in and out." The house had a bath, shower, sink, and toilet room with running water also. John realized that this was a licensed solicitor's household without a paid staff…no maids, butlers, horses and carriage hands, no nanny…it was "just them" who were proud of their house and their lifestyle. He thought of how he would once have dreamed of having such a house when he lived as a youth with his parents and several siblings in a house with a dirt floor and an outdoor toilet house with no water, except what they hauled in pails on a shoulder yoke from a nearby well. And, he had not visited anyone's house in a long time that did not have a staff of servants and a staffed stable for horses and a carriage house. He realized just what a life of wealth and privilege he had come to think of as normal.

The conversation with tea and scones at the kitchen table was very pleasant while May and Janie talked about all the Croft relatives of their mutual acquaintance. But John and Richard started talking about the American Civil War. John had had no cause to read anything about it except for newspaper articles and for articles in the *Gentlemen's Magazine.* So he was impressed with the details that Richard could relate about the recent battles in the United States between the Union and Confederate armies and the successes or failures of the commanding generals involved."General Ulysses S. Grant has made a big difference in the conduct of the war," he maintained. "I'd have to say that the Confederacy's days are now numbered. Our Manchester clothing mills will be lacking even more cotton now."

John asked, “Do you not favor our neutrality in the conflict?”

Richard became more emotional, answering, “When I thought that it was a mere disagreement over the rights of the individual states to determine their own political fates, I figured we should just stay out of it. But President Lincoln has convinced me with his Emancipation Proclamation that the only real ‘states’ right’ the Confederacy is fighting for is the right to buy and own slaves. We banned all transportation of slaves on the high seas in 1810, and banned slavery in the entire United Kingdom in 1833. You’d think our Prime Minister, Lord Palmerston, would just declare our neutrality over and done and take the Union side, even if we all have to wear wool.”

“Huzzah to that, Richard,” said John. “Well said. The world would be a much better place without slavery, that’s for sure.”

Little Margaret was sitting on her mother’s lap. She squirmed a bit, causing Janie to put her back onto her feet by the table. Margaret asked them all, “Am I the youngest of all our relatives?”

May answered, “I can’t think of anyone younger than you, Margaret. You may well be the youngest. What do you think, Dad?”

John could only agree, telling Margaret, “I think you are indeed the youngest.”

Margaret continued, asking, “Are you the old-est, Uncle John?”

John chuckled and answered, “No, I’m not the oldest. My sister Surrey Martha and her husband Thomas Metcalf are both four years older than I am. AND, have you heard of our ‘Aunt Peggie Croft Curteis’?”

“No, I haven’t,” said Margaret. “How old is she?”

“She was born in Whittington, near Kirkby Lonsdale in Westmoreland in 1763…well before the American Revolution…and she’s still alive. So how old does that make her now in this 1865 year?”

Margaret looked stumped, so Richard coached her, “1763 to 1863 is 100 years…and to get to 1865 is two more. She is 102.”

“Did my mother know her?” asked Janie.

“She did, and she liked Aunt Peggie as does everyone else who knows her. She’s very nice and very wise.”

Margaret "Aunt Peggie" Croft Curteis (b. 1763) in September 1865 when she was "in her 103rd year." From CFA.

Janie asked, "Who are her children?"

John explained, "Aunt Peggie…whose real name is Margaret just as your daughter here, married her older sister Eleanor's husband, the Rev. Samuel Curteis, two years after Eleanor's death in 1830 at age 69…so this marriage for her at 69 in 1832 was too late in Samuel's and Margaret's lives to have children. So, Aunt Peggie has no children of her own…but remains a second mother to her sister's brood of seven with her husband Samuel Curteis, who then passed away in 1844. One of those children, Samuel and Eleanor's son Jeremiah, is a Church rector just as his father was and he and his wife take care of Aunt Peggie in his rectory in Shelton, Norfolk."

Rev. Jeremiah Curteis (1804-1881) of Shelton Rectory, Norfolk, in 1865. From CFA, script by Edmund J. "Ted" Croft.

In the remaining months of 1865 death took a hard toll on the Crofts' family and friends. John received a letter in April from Caroline Croft

Wright that included a printed funeral announcement for her mother Martha Fink in Neustrelitz in Germany. Caroline and Robert Wright were visiting her there when she took ill, stopped eating, and simply did not wake up the next morning.

Caroline's letter informed John that his one-time German interpreter, Daniel Wolk, had earlier traveled from Hamburg to Neustrelitz to visit his own family and told Martha that he and his mother Maria were living well, although his grandmother Ethel Schiltz had passed away. Henry Wolk insisted on paying for Martha's funeral expenses, including her place next to her husband in the Neustrelitz Stadtkirche's cemetery. He and wife Henrietta and twin daughters Ingrid and Irma, "surprisingly still unmarried," attended the funeral, as did his brother Karl. But Henry and Karl's father, the General Wilhelm Wolk, had also passed away and they were caring for their mother Anna.

Caroline's letter also said that her daughter Catherine Wright was now in Madras, India, with her husband David, who had been posted there as a foreign service officer assigned to the British Administration Office. This caused John to write in his answering letter to Caroline to inform Catherine in subsequent communication that he, her Uncle John Croft, had been in Madras at Fort St. George from January to April in 1824 on his way to fight in the Anglo-Burmese War, and that he and his friends Barnaby Crawford and Matthew Burgoyne had witnessed near there the burning alive of two willing "suttees"...the widows of a prominent Hindu magistrate whose name John could still remember as "Ghunnassam Mukherjee." His point was to encourage foreign service officer David Wright to do all he could to "stamp out the suttee practice entirely if it hasn't already been stamped out," such a horror was it.

On Thursday the 19th of May, John got a short letter from Thomas Metcalf saying that his older sister Surrey Martha was near death from a shortness of breath the doctors couldn't cure and that she wanted to see him before she died. John asked daughter May if she wanted to come with him, and she said she did.

When John and May arrived at the Metcalfs' house near Regents Square in London they had trouble finding a place nearby to leave their carriage. The stable where they finally left it was a long walk back to the Metcalfs' address at number 27 Gray's Road. May was thinking out loud as they walked, "Aunt Surrey is only 62 years old. She's got lots of life left to her. It's too soon for her to die."

John could only respond, "It's always too soon for a good person to die."

Thomas Metcalf, Jr. opened the door at their knock and directed John and May into the drawing room. His father Thomas had trouble getting himself up out of a padded chair there to shake John's hand and give May a welcoming hug. "She's in the bedroom," he said. "And it won't be long, I'm afraid. She's in and out of being awake. Dr. Stannard left here this morning saying there was nothing more he could do. Son Tom and I are sitting a death vigil here now."

"Can we see her?" asked John.

"Yes, just come with me into the bedroom," said Thomas. "There are some chairs alongside to sit on."

John and May followed Thomas into the bedroom and saw Surrey Martha in bed, covered up to her chest with a yellow blanket, her head resting on a white-cased pillow. Thomas then turned and left them alone with his wife. John thought that she looked calm and serene. Her face was unwrinkled. May whispered to her father that, "She looks better than Uncle Thomas to me. He's not doing so well."

To their surprise, Surrey opened her eyes and said in a low voice, answering May's comment, "Thomas is not in good health and my losing my breath has been hard on him."

John quickly moved close enough to the bed-side to take her hand in his. "Dear Surrey," he said, "It appears what claimed our father and his twin sister Ann is now claiming you. Is that the way you figure it?"

"Aye, Johnny," Surrey answered with a wheeze, using her childhood name for John. "God is taking my breath away minute by minute now. So I'd like to make my deathbed request of you before I can't say anything at all."

John squeezed her hand slightly and said, "What is it? Whatever it is, I'll do it if I can."

"I want you to take care of your nephew, our son and only child, Tom. He's 39 now, still single and childless, and has had some troubles with the law. We still support him as we are able, but that can't last much longer."

Surrey then paused to take a few labored breaths and continued, "I want you to help him while you are alive and leave him what you would leave your own sons in your will."

John said, "I don't have a will."

Surrey coughed twice and said, "But you know you will have one someday. Please promise me that you will do this."

John turned to look at May, who was standing just next to him. She raised her eyebrows and shrugged her shoulders as if to say, “Well, this is clearly what you have to do.”

John told Surrey, “I promise. I will give Tom what support I can and will include him in my will.”

The death vigil only lasted two more days. When Surrey passed away, on Monday the 22nd, her husband and son were at her bedside with her. John and May were in the drawing room with Dr. Stannard, who had brought a death certificate blank with him to sign.

Surrey Martha’s funeral was a particularly sad one for John. He told May, “I am now the last of my parents’ eight children…all the rest are gone.”

In late August of 1865, John and daughter May traveled by train to Norwich in Norfolk and then south by rented carriage to Shelton-Hartwick, where the funeral was held at St. Mary’s Church for Margaret “Aunt Peggie” Croft Curteis (cf. p.. 185) who had died “beyond her 102nd birthday and on to her 103rd.”

After the burial service in St. Mary’s Cemetery, the Rev. Jeremiah Curteis (cf. p. 186) hosted a reception at the Shelton Rectory. The Rectory building was a three-storey cube of brick with two chimneys on one side and brightly painted white windows looking in all directions.

The Shelton Rectory building today, from themovemarket com that touts a recent appraisal of £1.3m for the nine-bedroom private residence.

At the reception, John was able to introduce May to a famous artist of his long-ago acquaintance, Nathaniel Brown Engleheart. Engleheart had painted the miniature portrait (cf. p. 22) of May's mother, Mary Ann Stead, at Mary Ann's father James Stead's home in Islington's Brixton section on Acre Lane on Christmas day of 1842…the very day when John and Mary Ann decided to request her father James Stead's permission to begin their courtship. Nathaniel was married to Aunt Peggie's niece Mary Jane Curteis, who was the daughter of the Rev. Samuel Curteis and Aunt

Peggie's sister Eleanor Croft Curteis, and the sister of Rev. Jeremiah Curteis. Nathaniel and Mary Jane were the parents of 15 children…7 girls and 8 boys born in the 25 years between 1813 and 1838, all but two of whom were living and 7 of whom were attending Aunt Peggie's services.

Nathaniel Brown Engleheart (13 May, 1790-6 May, 1869) from francis-online co uk.

"So, May," Nathaniel joked when he had heard John's story about him, "My work may have been the cause of your birth. When your father saw how beautiful your mother was in my painting, he decided he just had to marry her."

"It is indeed a great painting, Mr. Engleheart," said May. "I've long admired it. It's the very image of how I still see my mother in my memory."

May also accompanied her father John Croft to the Saturday, September 30th, 1865, funeral of George Richard Elkington (cf. p. 97) at St. Mary's Church in the Selly Oak community of Birmingham, traveling there by both train and rented carriage. The Head of Birmingham's Elkington & Co. silver plating business that held the first patent on electroplating, George Elkington had been a founding endower of St. Mary's Church and a leading donor to many of its associated charitable causes, so that the church was filled to its capacity and more for the funeral service conducted by Incumbent Rev. Thomas Price.

The Crofts had gotten to the Church very early so that they could be seated close to the Elkington family members. They found seats near the front row of pews next to Richard and Elizabeth Garrett and their daughter Sarah Louisa who were sitting directly behind their daughter Jane and her husband Hyla Elkington in the front row. On the other side of the aisle sat John Hardman Powell and his wife Anne Pugin Powell. John Croft and John Powell acknowledged each other with nods.

Around one of the tables near the south end of the Pavilion stood Richard and Elizabeth Garrett,

Hyla and Jane Elkington, and John and May Croft. They were eating and drinking as they conversed. Sarah Louisa Garrett was still working her way through the buffet, but, as six people were all that could fit around their table, there was no obvious place for her to join them.

Selly Oak's St. Mary's Church with its South Transept's Stained Glass window illustrating Christ's parable of the Good Samaritan by John Hardman Powell dedicated in 1866 to George Richards Elkington, from stmarysellyoak.org.uk

After the service, a buffet of tea, small sandwiches, and sweet biscuits for the congregation was served in a very long and wide pavilion held up by a framework of steel poles. There were no chairs for the people to sit on. Instead there were standing-height round tables for as many as six people to place their teacups and food plates upon. There was a light rain drizzling down with a pitter-patter resounding on the canvas top.

About thirty hired workmen in gray woolen shirts and trousers were standing in the rain waiting for the people there to leave so that they could collect all the cups and plates and napkins and disassemble the pavilion.

Richard Garrett commented to John, “I think the clean-up crew should just wait out of the rain in the church itself now that we are out of it. They don’t need to be out here watching us all with our tea and biscuits.”

Hyla Elkington, having heard his father-in-law’s comment, said, “Excuse me, I’ll just have a word with Rev. Price about that.” And he left their table to look for Rev. Price.

Hyla’s wife Jane sidled closer to May, and said to her, “I know Sarah is going to want to stand next to your father so they can talk. They’ve been writing letters back and forth for some time now. When we see her coming, you and I should excuse ourselves to go back to the buffet for seconds.”

In only a minute they could clearly see Sarah carrying her teacup and plate toward them. So May politely followed Jane’s lead by excusing herself to "go back for seconds." But as they approached the start of the buffet line, she expressed her surprise to Jane by asking, "Sarah and my Dad?"

Jane smiled understandingly and answered, "Both Hyla and I think it's a match made in heaven. My parents agree as well. And Sarah is SUCH a catch. She's the smartest of us all."

"But she's closer to my age than to his, Jane. What about that?"

"She just turned 28 this month," said Jane. "So how old is your father?"

"He's 58. That's 30 years older."

Jane replied, "Men still sire children into their eighties. That's thirty years from now. That's plenty of time. They could have many children together. You could have a whole crop of stepbrothers and stepsisters…a houseful to be sure. Wouldn't that be nice?"

May didn't know what to think or say. But when she looked back to where her father was standing she could see he was definitely smiling as he and Sarah shared a conversation with her parents. Jane's husband Hyla had rejoined them also.

After they had returned home to Dalton House in Saddington after George Elkington's funeral, May deliberately engaged her father in a conversation about "the Garretts and the Elkingtons" thinking it desirable that he marry Sarah Louisa.

"Why do these friends of ours think you should get married at all, not to mention Sarah Louisa?" asked May.

John thought a bit, then related: "A few years ago now, I told Richard Garrett that he was correct in thinking that my underlying purpose in buying our grand homes back here in England was to remarry and raise more children in them. I told him at that time that I did not feel that I was ready to remarry. I was then only five years from the loss of your mother. But your mother and I shared the belief that the very purpose of life is to create more life…to have and raise children to continue our lives into the future through them."

"But you have already done that," observed May, "You have three children…Harry, and Teddy, and me. Isn't that enough?

"Once, when we found out your mother was expecting you, I asked her 'How many children should we have?' And her answer was that we should have 'as many as God sends'. It was never her intention to stop at three…she wanted us to keep on having children until we were both unable to do so. And I'm sure that from heaven she is happy now that I am still able to have more children. I feel that it is my family duty to do so. I am confident that if I had died in her place, as I then desired to do, she would now be telling you this also."

"So, do you believe that it is MY family duty to have as many children as God sends me?" May asked.

John answered, "Yes, I do. And your love for them will entail the further duty to raise them well so that they can someday do the same. That's how life works. Its most important purpose is procreation...bringing about its own optimum continuation."

May continued, "So, do you think that Sarah Louisa Garrett is the woman you would ideally have more children with?"

"Indeed I am coming to that conviction more and more now, and I hope when you have considered the matter thoroughly you will agree," said John. "Your opinion as my eldest child and only daughter is really the most important one I must consider in deciding when and whom to remarry."

For Christmas 1865, Teddy was home from Eton, and was facing only one more "half" term there before his graduation. He had received guidance there from an academic advisor who helped him send applications for admittance to both Oxford and Cambridge universities in the fall term in 1866. Three of the Eton faculty members who had taught him in different subject areas wrote letters of recommendation for him. He was anxious about his prospects for admission to these very exclusive and prestigious universities. "Oxford and Cambridge get hundreds of applications for admittance from the best students in the best schools in the land," he explained. "Only the top 15 percent are offered admission. I just can't be sure of getting into either place."

Both John and May tried to reassure "Ted," as he now wanted to be called, that his chances of admission were good. "You've gotten high grades in your studies at Eton, and you have strong recommendations from Eton's faculty members. You've traveled around the world from Australia to seek your higher education here in England. And your family is capable of donating large amounts of money to whatever university accepts you."

Ted was still not sure. But May continued the family's assurance, telling him "And I'll be praying for your admittance too."

The topic of John's consideration of his marrying Sarah Louisa Garrett now included his sons, Ted and Harry. When they were first struck by the possibility of their father's remarriage they reacted negatively. Harry said, "I don't like the idea of a new mother living with us. I'm happy just the way we are." And Ted added, "A new mother in the house likely means more children too. Our half-siblings, that will be. How are we to deal with them?"

Daughter May found herself admonishing her younger brothers, telling them, "You are only thinking of yourselves. You aren't thinking of Dad and how strongly he is committed to adding more Croft children to our family. You should know by now that he will never love any of us any less if we have another mother and more children added to our family. It's only that he will have HIS dreams of having all the children he can fulfilled."

In early 1866 John noticed how his epistolary correspondent, Sarah Louisa Garrett, was not only sending more letters, but had added considerable expressions of affection into her letters, adding the superlative "Dearest John" as a greeting instead of the conventional previous "Dear John," and signing them off with "Love always, Sarah," instead of just "Your Friend, Sarah" as before. He decided to respond in kind, but merely with "Dear Sarah" and either "Love, John," or, a bit more daring, "Yours, John."

In early March, John traveled to Ovingdean near Brighton in Sussex to visit the Steads at their rectory. He confided in Rev. Alfred and Emma and their eldest daughter Barbara that he was thinking of making a proposal of marriage to Sarah Louisa Garrett, daughter of Richard Garrett of the Leiston Works in Suffolk. They were unanimously in favor of this, with Emma proclaiming, "I'm sure Mary Ann would approve of this, John. She's been gone from you now for nine years." Rev. Alfred even suggested a "good date" for the wedding, "Friday April 5th, four days after this year 1866's early Easter."

John realized that Rev. Alfred was assuming that he would be married in St. Wulfran's in Ovingdean and that he, the Rector Rev. Alfred Stead, would preside. But John said, "I think the bride's family usually decides such wedding matters and I think the Garretts may favour St. Peter's small church in Carlton (cf. p. 95) near their family home, Carlton Hall (cf. p. 52). That's where I attended the wedding of Sarah's younger sister Jane in 1862, you might remember."

"Well, that's fine, John," Rev. Alfred responded, "but if you can somehow get them to choose my suggested date, we will be able to attend."

"I will try," said John. "Seeing your family support as it is, I've now decided to travel there from here to make my proposal. Wish me luck. Of course, I will let you know either way."

So John arrived at Carlton Hall near Saxmundham in Suffolk unexpected. But he was greeted very warmly by Richard and Elizabeth Garrett, who were thrilled to hear that his intent, if they granted him their permission, was to propose marriage to Sarah Louisa.

Richard looked to Elizabeth for her nod of approval and told John, "Of course we give you our permission. We think Sarah will assent and that you will become not only our friend but our son-in-law. It'll be a joining of the Garrett family with the family Croft…a union surely God will richly bless."

Sarah came home that evening after spending the day shopping in London, and was surprised to find John Croft sitting in the Carlton Hall parlor with her parents sipping tea. "John, what are you doing here?' she instinctively asked.

John stood up from his seat on a sofa, then dropped to one knee and, taking her right hand in both of his, said, "I've come to ask you to marry me. Your parents have already given me permission to make this proposal. And now, here together, we await your answer. What do you say?"

Sarah, bursting into tears of joy, answered, "I say YES! I will marry you and be a good wife to you and a second mother to your children."

In the next hour before retiring for the night, John and Sarah and Sarah's parents, Richard and Elizabeth, decided where and when the wedding would be. Richard and Elizabeth thought that St. Peter's at Carlton might be too small for the large wedding that they foresaw. Richard suggested that the event should be at St. Margaret Church in Leiston officiated by the Rev. J. C. Blathwayt with whom he had a positive history of donation and attendance. But Sarah spoke up against her parents' preference and insisted that they marry in St. Peter's Church closer to her home. Richard and Elizabeth gave in to Sarah's choice, and said that they would host the wedding party members at Carlton Hall for preparations and for the carriage transportation the two miles distance between Carlton Hall and St. Peter's. They would also arrange and host the reception for all the guests afterwards. The post-Easter date of Friday, April 5th was agreeable to all. John and Sarah said that they would together go shopping for the engagement and wedding rings. Sarah told John she thought that Hyla and Jane Elkington should be his best man and her maid of honour, respectively. May would be a bridesmaid, and Ted and Harry would be among the groomsmen.

When John reported to his children that he was indeed going to marry Sarah Louisa Garrett within a month's time, they were full of questions about how this would change their lives. "Will we have to move or will she live with us here?" "What kind of say will she have in our lives?" "Will she be able to tell us what to do?" Harry especially wanted to know, "Will we have to ask her if we can have pets, go swimming, boating, fishing, hunting…?" "Will she be able to punish us if we do something she thinks is wrong?"

John told them that "She will be living with us here. She will be a second mother to you, but you are old enough now to benefit daily from her wisdom and concern without any punishments being needed. I expect you to welcome her here and to give her your respect. I love her and I'm sure that in time you will love her also. She's a special person in all ways. That's an important reason why I'm marrying her…to give you THREE the benefit of her special character and life experience."

The Garretts had thirty overnight guests at Carlton Hall for April 4th and the April 5th, 1866, wedding and reception. They had hired additional staff helpers and stable hands to help with the meals and the transportation in twelve carriages to and from St. Peter's. Most of the Garrett family members had guest rooms with which they were familiar. But other guests stayed the two nights in a large drawing room one-floor upstairs which was emptied of its former furniture and furnished with single bunkbed sets with a floor-to-ceiling curtain dividing the male from the female guests. John Croft had a bedroom to himself, but May, Ted, and

John Croft in 1865, from CFA.

Harry were consigned to the bunk room. Rev. Alfred and Emma Stead (cf. p. 47 and 46) got a separate room, but daughter Emma Barbara Stead (cf. p. 50) was with May in the bunks.

On April 5th the preparations at Carlton Hall were chaotic. Wedding party participants were trying to get formally dressed into pre-ordered matching and properly sized tuxedos for the men and gowns for the women. This caused the main staircase to be crowded so that people brushed against each other in both their ascents and descents. One of these incidental contacts has become legendary in family lore…the contact on the staircase of twenty-year-old Frank Garrett and twenty-one-year-old Mary Anne (May) Croft.

Frank Garrett, Sr. at age 19, from CFA.

May happened to be descending the staircase in a partial state of undress…"wearing a slip" some say…so as to exchange a too-large gown she was carrying with another from the racks below. She thence brushed against the ascending Frank, who had somehow never seen May before. He was struck "as if by lightning" by the sudden sight of her, which he later described as "pretty of face and smile and hair…bodily lithe yet very shapely." He asked Hyla Elkington who she was, and Hyla answered, "That's May Croft…John the groom's daughter. What do you think of her?" And Frank reportedly answered, "That's the woman I'm going to marry."

The wedding ceremony in St. Peter's was remembered by all in attendance as a very pleasant event.

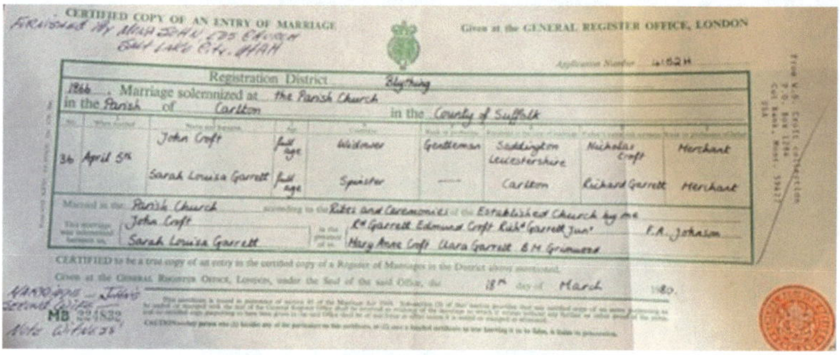
CERTIFIED COPY OF AN ENTRY OF MARRIAGE

Given at the GENERAL REGISTER OFFICE, LONDON

Application Number 4152H

Registration District Blything

1866. Marriage solemnized at the Parish Church in the Parish of Carlton in the County of Suffolk

No.	When married	Name and surname	Age	Condition	Rank or profession	Residence at the time of marriage	Father's name and surname	Rank or profession of father
36	April 5th	John Croft	full age	Widower	Gentleman	Saddington Leicestershire	Nicholas Croft	Merchant
		Sarah Louisa Garrett	full age	Spinster	—	Carlton	Richard Garrett	Merchant

Married in the Parish Church according to the Rites and Ceremonies of the Established Church by me F. A. Johnson

This marriage was solemnized between us, John Croft, Sarah Louisa Garrett, in the presence of us, Rd Garrett, Edmund Croft, Richd Garrett Junr, Mary Anne Croft, Clara Garrett, B M Grimwood

CERTIFIED to be a true copy of an entry in the certified copy of a Register of Marriages in the District above mentioned.

Given at the GENERAL REGISTER OFFICE, LONDON, under the Seal of the said Office, the 18th day of March 1980.

MB 224832

John and Sarah's Marriage Certificate. From CFA.

The Rev. F. A. Johnson, especially in Rev. Alfred Stead's experienced opinion, made his prayers, pronouncements, and his declarations with "admirable fervency." The attending guests showered the couple with rice and flower petals as they exited the Church at the end of the ceremony. When she was later asked what part of the ceremony she had most enjoyed, Sarah Louisa said, "When Reverend Johnson said to John, 'You may kiss the bride'."

Sarah Louisa Garrett Croft in 1868, age 30, CFA.

When John and Sarah had discussed their honeymoon, Sarah recalled from her letters in which John had described to her the honeymoon site chosen by Robert and Catherine Croft Wright, the St. George Hotel in Llandudno, Wales, the "Queen of the Welsh resorts"…and about what a wonderful place it was. John agreed, but advocated instead the Grand Brighton Hotel in Sussex.

John explained, "Since the children and I stayed in Ovingdean six years ago, the Stead family in the St. Wulfran's rectory have been extolling the construction of the now complete Grand Brighton as the "Palace by the Sea." It's in a grand seafront parade building which features the first lift outside of London to elevate us effortlessly to a high room with a balcony overlooking the just completed West Pier ending in a recreation pavilion. And, of course, it's only a short carriage ride from there along the coast to the Stead's rectory in Ovingdean where I could introduce you to their entire family."

Sarah readily assented to selecting the Grand Brighton Hotel as their honeymoon location. They should, she said, spend two weeks there, "getting to know each other more intimately."

A sketch of the Grand Hotel on King's Road in Brighton, from regencysociety.org

The West Pier and Parade across from the Grand Hotel in Brighton in 1912, from arthurlloyd co uk.

John and Sarah's room in the Grand Brighton Hotel fronted the sea on the fifth floor. They delighted in using the lift to get to it accompanied by two porters carting their baggage. The room had a "huge bed" in it with an *en suite* bathroom. The view from the balcony was most impressive…and tickets to the nearby Oxford Music Hall could be ordered from the hotel's concierge. "It really is a GRAND hotel," said Sarah. "We made the right choice."

Their initiation of sexual relations that first evening was "a GRAND success," according to John. He explained to Sarah that he had been "a bit worried about my own ability to perform well, because of the 'infirmity of age and disuse'." But, he assured her, "your patient 'ministrations' served well to 'raise me up in the effort'."

After the honeymoon, John and Sarah took up married life together with his children at Dalton House in Saddington, Leicestershire. Sarah had little difficulty settling in as the new "Lady" of the estate. She had arranged to bring with her 55-year-old widow Laura Killick to serve as her personal maid. She was given an upstairs bedroom. "Mrs. Killick" was a member of an extended family of staff at Carlton Hall and had been Sarah's maid since 1854, when her husband James Killick had been killed at the Battle of Balaclava during the Crimean War. Sarah also added her personal riding horse named "Princess" to the Dalton House stable, and a dark red brougham carriage whose driver and stable hand "Arthur" was housed in one of the outbuildings on the property. Sarah liked to ride, but she also liked to drive the brougham by herself…so that her horse Princess did double duty.

May and Harry were at Dalton House when John and Sarah returned from their wedding and honeymoon. Son Ted was at Eton in Windsor, studying through his last half term. Sarah soon came to appreciate the intellect and experience of Harry's nanny, Mrs. Anna Smythe, who was tutoring ten-year-old Harry for four hours in the house's billiards room every weekday. Sarah and Anna

Smythe shared a love of reading English literature…the poems of Samuel Taylor Coleridge (*Rime of the Ancient Mariner, Kubla Khan, and Xanadu),* Alfred Lord Tennyson (*Charge of the Light Brigade*), and Elizabeth Barrett Browning (*Sonnets from the Portuguese*, especially No. 33 ("Yes, call me by my pet-name.") and No. 43 ("How do I love Thee?")), and the novels of Jane Austen (*Sense and Sensibility, Pride and Prejudice, Mansfield Park, and Emma*) and Charles Dickens (*David Copperfield, A Tale of Two Cities,* and *Great Expectations*).

Once when John happened to be included into the women's literary discussions, he admitted to Sarah that he had, in his past, impressed people with recitations aloud of poetry he had memorized, and that he could recite the entire text of Coleridge's long *Rime of the Ancient Mariner* in a half hour, and of Tennyson's *Charge of the Light Brigade.* Sarah requested that he recite to her, May, nanny Anna Smythe, and maid Laura Killick Tennyson's *Charge of the Light Brigade.* But John demurred, saying a bit oddly that he preferred to recite the shorter, but euphonous, work of the American poet, Edgar Allan Poe…his poem called "Eldorado." And read it he did:

"Gaily bedight, a gallant knight,
In sunshine and in shadow,
Had journeyed long, singing a song,

In search of Eldorado

But he grew old—this knight so bold
And o'er his heart a shadow—
Fell as he found no spot of ground,
That looked like Eldorado.

And as his strength, failed him at length,
He met a pilgrim shadow—
"Shadow," said he, "where can it be—
This land of Eldorado?"

'Over the Mountains of the Moon,
Down the Valley of the Shadow,
Ride, boldly ride,' the shade replied—
'If you seek for Eldorado'!"

Later, Sarah and May asked John why he did not want to recite the "exciting *Charge of the Light Brigade*." John answered that he did not want to recite this work because he thought it might "bring sad thoughts to the maid Laura Killick whose husband had been killed in the Crimean War's Battle of Balaclava in which the 'Charge of the Light Brigade' had taken place."

John related to Sarah that he had been personally acquainted with the late famous novelist Frederick Marryat, who had once been the Captain of the ship *HMS Larne* that transported him to India during the Anglo-Burmese War forty-three years before…and that he had enjoyed reading Marryat's popular novels about military life, *The King's Own* and *Mr. Midshipman Easy*. He also told her about his "long-ago relationship of affection" with Marryat's wife Catherine Shairp Marryat.

John had read in the *Gentleman's Magazine* (*GM*) articles about how the author Charles Dickens had criticized the "British East India Company" for its harsh treatment of its "mutinous Sepoy soldiers" during the Indian Rebellion of 1857-8. John remarked to others that it was "faulty reasoning to expect the Sepoy soldiers to use their firearms against 'their own people'." "They served us well elsewhere, as in Burma, for example." he said, "But it's much better that we are now enforcing our colonial rule in India with our own English soldiers. It's only common sense."

John also read in *GM* about how Charles Dickens had only the year before become averse to riding on trains…this because he was a passenger on a train that partially fell into a construction-caused rail gap on a bridge near Staplehurst south of Maidstone in Kent on June 9th of 1865. All but one of the first-class coaches fell into the bridge's

Aftermath of the Staplehurst railway accident as depicted in the Illustrated London News, from Wikipedia

gap…Dickens and his "Invisible Woman," the actress Ellen Ternan, and her mother Frances were in that one still-on-the-rails coach. Ten people were killed and 50 injured, some of whom, including Ellen Ternan, Dickens personally attended to. About this "terribly destructive accident" he wrote that "I remember with devout thankfulness that I can never be much nearer parting company with my readers forever, than I was then, until there shall be written against my life, the two words with which I have this day closed this book—THE END."

In mid May of 1866, two letters arrived at Dalton House addressed to "Mr. Edmund J. Croft"... one from Oxford University and the other from Cambridge University. When she saw these letters on the entry table, May immediately said to her father John. "We should open these letters and see what they say. Has Ted been accepted to either place or not?"

But John told her, "No, we don't open letters addressed to someone else in this family. We'll just take them with us to Ted's graduation ceremony at Eton on June 6th and he can open them himself. That'll be soon enough for us to know."

"What if he's accepted at both places? How will he choose?" May asked.

John had already thought of this question at some length. "First," he said, "Is the matter of the distances between these universities and London, and between these universities and our home here at Dalton House in Saddington. It turns out that the distances don't vary by more than six miles in either London's case (56 miles for Oxford and 62 miles for Cambridge) or from here (61 miles for Cambridge and 65 miles for Oxford). Cambridge does have the advantage that it is closer to the Garretts near Leiston (158 miles for Oxford and 75 for Cambridge). From these considerations of distance I'd have to pick Cambridge."

"I would think that the two universities' living arrangements for Ted would be more important. Do you have any information on what the student housing is like…or what it costs?" asked May.

"I'm still making inquiries about those matters, May. And I do agree with you that the living conditions, physical and financial, are even more important than the distances."

As for financial matters, John told Sarah, "I want you to be aware of just what our financial situation is. Too many wives are content to remain in ignorance about their husband's money…how much does he have and what is he spending it on."

Sarah answered, "I trust you in these matters, John, but I would indeed like to know how we are doing, so to speak…at least in general terms."

John paused to think for a few moments about how to abbreviate what he had planned to explain, then he related: "Well, when I arrived back here in England, having cashed out of all my Australian holdings and property, I had roughly £300,000 to my name in the bank at 53 years of age. The problem since is that I am spending a lot more of my money every month to fund our lifestyle than I am earning through my bank accounts' interest. I essentially retired at that age and have since no businesses to give us income, and no lucrative investments. The two named estates are appreciating, but you don't see that money until you sell...and I'm not ready to sell. These estates require extravagant furnishings and numerous hired help...and the food and travel costs... and the costs of education for the children have been steep. SO, the point is that although our lifestyle is indeed grand, so are our financial losses every month...which means that I now see my 1860 original £300,000 currently decreased to £200,000 after six years. That's been an average loss of £1390 per month...that's been our cost of living to now."

Sarah intelligently commented, "But that average includes those early-on extraordinary costs of the estates themselves. We won't have those costs any more...the monthly loss now is likely less, is it not?"

John answered, "Yes, that is true. But I now see the monthly loss at around £1000 per month. At that rate, my current balance of £200,000 will last me 16 years before it's all gone. In 16 years, in 1882, I'll be 74 years old. And if our plans to have children come to success our expenses will dramatically increase and we'll run out of money quite a bit sooner."

Sarah then asked, "What about the Fleckney Farm land tenants? Do they not give you some income that you should consider? Might we farm ourselves the land that isn't rented?"

John scratched his chin and admitted, "By God, I have not been reckoning that, you're right. That money is in a local bank and it is growing at the rate of about £300 per month. So that means that, totally, we are eating up 'only' £700 per month... let me see now...so as to last us not 16 years but 24, until 1890. I'll be 82, God willing. But YOU will be then 52 and there'll be no more money to sustain us."

Sarah continued, saying, "We'll just have to make some profitable investments. You know that my 1000 shares of stock in Garrett & Co. are now part of "OUR" estate. They are currently worth £30,000, but they have steadily increased in value in recent years. We could invest in more Garrett & Co. stock...and in other stocks as well. No one knows more about stock investments than you, a former stock exchange stockholder. Our income from the invested money will soon exceed our losses and costs put together. I have faith in this."

Sarah, you are right as usual. I'm proud of you," John said. "And indeed I've already started a stock exchange investment that I haven't reckoned in these calculations either. That's Robert Wright's High Quality Homes stock which I bought 100 shares of at £2 per share in early 1863. Last time I looked it up it had doubled in value. I daresay we could buy some more of that stock also."

On the 6th of June, 1866, John, Sarah, May, and Harry were in Windsor, Berkshire, to attend Ted's graduation from Eton. The Eton campus adjoins the royal family's Windsor Castle to the immediate north across the River Thames. The graduation was an impressive ceremony with traditions going back to the founding of the school in 1440 by King Henry VI. Seated in a large crowd, the Crofts had to crane their necks, hoping to see Ted in his cap and gown accept his diploma. When his name was shouted out by the Eton Marshall, they all clapped their hands politely without calling out anything vocally, following the school's tradition. Afterwards they made a visit to Ted's residence where the housmates posed for a group photograph in their jackets and ties.

Edmund J. Croft and his Eton housemates in 1866, from alamy.com by license. Edmund is second from the right end of the third row from the front.

When they were at last alone together, John and May hugged Ted while Harry slapped him on the back repeatedly…all saying, "Well done, Ted," and "Congratulations!" Sarah waited for the hugs and back slapping to end and then said, "What a wonderful achievement in life, Ted, to take a diploma from Eton. A great future awaits you now, we are all sure."

John had, through numerous inquiries, discovered the very ideal place for his entire family to share a meal after Ted's graduation. He personally drove their rented four-seat coach from Windsor fifteen miles west to the Village of Lacock in Wiltshire near the Avon River. In Lacock was "The George Inn," established in 1361 and still providing its customers with quality food and drink over *five hundred years* later.

A photo taken in 2019 of "The George Inn" still in operation after 658 years in Lacock, from CFA.

John asked to have his family seated in front of the restaurant's fireplace where the meat was being roasted over an open fire on a spit which was being turned by a specially-bred "turnspit dog" inside a side-mounted cylindrical wheel.

This is the George Inn's fireplace with its turnspit dog wheel on its left side. Photo from 2019 by Lesley Hoyt Croft. From the CFA.

As they ate an excellent meal of roasted beef with steamed ears of corn, John observed, "It's hard to imagine all the history of our country that the customers here have been a part of. Good and bad times, rich and poor times, happy and sad times. But I'd say few had here such a fine time as we are today enjoying together. Indeed I could not be prouder of this family than I am right now."

"Huzzah!" said Ted, raising his glass of light ale, "I propose a toast…TO US! Long may we live as we now are!"

The others all raised their glasses…Harry of water…and repeated, "Long indeed!"

Harry asked, "From here can we go to the Stonehenge? I've read that it's an interesting place to visit. It's older than the pyramids in Egypt."

Ted answered, "Once I went on a tour to Stonehenge from Eton. It was very interesting and I even have a hand-sized stone I picked up there as a souvenir. BUT, it was a two-day trip by coach. So, although it's only another day's coach ride to it from here in Lacock, it'll take all of us another 2 days by coach to get back the 65 miles from Stonehenge to Windsor where our train connection to London is. I think that would be too long and costly a trip for us. And I'd like to get back home sooner than that. I'm expecting letters from Oxford and Cambridge about my applications any day now. I have friends at Eton who have already received their letters which were addressed to them there."

John, looking significantly at May, asked Ted, "Have any of these friends of yours been accepted?"

Ted answered, "One to Oxford, one to Cambridge, and three to neither, getting rejection letters instead."

"Well, let's see what your letters say," said John, withdrawing the two letters from his jacket pocket. He handed both of them to Ted, who took several deep breaths and used his table knife to slit the wax sealed envelope flaps of both. The others waited breathlessly for him to read the first, the Oxford, letter.

In a few seconds Ted gave an anguished look upward toward The George Inn's ceiling, and announced, "It's a no from Oxford. I won't be going there."

John groaned in disappointment and suggested, "What does Cambridge say?"

After only a brief glance, Ted almost shouted, "I've been accepted into Cambridge's Trinity College. I start in the fall. I'm asked to send in my housing request. There are several possibilities. All likely scarily expensive."

"Education is priceless, but we can afford it," answered John. "Congratulations, son! Your hard work at Eton has paid off for you."

Harry was excited about his older brother's success, but he asked, "So now can we go to Stonehenge?"

John explained that the people at the coach rental stable were expecting him back the next day. And he had no way of communicating with them about any extension on the time, conjecturing that if he took another three days without telling them they might be seriously inconvenienced. Harry took this rejection well, saying, "Oh well, it will be nice to get back home."

Twenty-four days later, on Sunday afternoon 30 June, 1866, the Crofts received an unexpected visit at Dalton House from Sarah's youngest brother, Frank Garrett. John noticed that Frank had grown a beard and that he seemed quite serious, even sad. Right away to Sarah, he said, "Sarah, our father has passed away. He died four days ago of a heart attack on the 26th and they're burying him in St. Peter's Cemetery today at just about this time. I decided that I didn't need to attend his funeral and that I should come here right away to tell you. Mother says we should come back together for the reading of his will on Friday July 6."

Sarah didn't take in any of the information after Frank's words of "our father has passed away." She burst into tears and screamed, "Noooo, Nooo, Nooo! It can't be!" John grabbed her and hugged her tightly as she started burbling incoherently. John calmly told her, "Sarah, just take a few breaths, dear…take a few breaths, please. Let's all sit down in the parlor."

Frank Garrett, Sr. in 1866, from CFA.

May was dabbing her eyes with a handkerchief in sympathy. She came over to the divan where John and Sarah were sitting and offered another handkerchief to Sarah, saying, "Take this. It's no shame to cry at such a time as this, dear Sarah. A good cry will help you get past the shock of it."

Sarah took the handkerchief and said, "Thank you, May." Then she held it to her nose and sniffled as she continued crying for a few minutes. Then she asked Frank, "How did he die?"

"Mother said he just did not wake up Tuesday morning as usual," said Frank. "His heart had stopped in his sleep. She had the doctor summoned and he came quickly, but there was nothing he could do. Mother is taking it pretty well, saying that he did not suffer at all, but just went away. She said that it was apparently 'his time to go'."

Ted asked Frank, "How old was he?"

Frank answered simply, "Fifty-nine."

At this Sarah burst back into crying and tears. She turned to John and said, "He was the same age as you are now. We should pray to the Lord that he doesn't take you any time soon. What would I do without you?"

John commented to Sarah and Frank that "Your father, my friend Richard Garrett, had a grand and fruitful life. He is survived by nine loving children and already ten or more grateful grandchildren. He died wealthy from a successful business that will continue his legacy. He will be remembered as a prominent benefactor of diverse causes, churches, and charities. He and I were born in the same year, and I have always endeavoured never to waste my time…but your father has done more. I hope you are proud of him."

Frank shook his head in agreement and replied, "We are very proud of him."

So, where will the reading of his will take place?" asked John.

"It will be at the Leiston Works at noon on Friday. I'll have to leave here on Tuesday to get back there on the day before, as I think I should."

"We'll all go together, Frank," said John. "We will pay your father our respect by doing so, and offer what consolation we can to your mother Elizabeth. She was always such a godsend to him and a mother without parallel to all of you."

Frank Garrett had taken two days by train via London to get to Saddington where he had rented a horse and 2-seat coach to get himself to Dalton House. But as a group of SIX they needed to travel the 95 miles to London by train (6 hours), stay the night in a London hotel, then change rail lines to travel the 100 miles (8 hours) to Leiston the next day, which was Thursday, July 5th.

Frank invited May to ride with him to turn in his rented coach in Saddington before taking a cab ride to the station…and then to sit with him in the train's first-class coach for the trip to London. In the London Hotel's restaurant she sat next to Frank at the dinner table and at the breakfast table the next morning. And she sat next to him on the train from London to Leiston too. John and Sarah observed that they obviously got along, as John said, "famously."

At the Leiston Works administration building at noon on Friday the 6th, a buffet-style lunch of sandwiches and tea was served to over 40 family and close friends, who commiserated with each other about their mutual loss of an important figure in their lives. Mother and now widow Elizabeth Dunnell Garrett (cf. p. 62) sincerely expressed her deep gratitude over and over to all those there for their emotional support.

When it was time to present Richard Garrett's will, his personal and corporate attorney, Eduard Hoare of the C. Hoare banking family and partner in the prominent London law firm of **Taylor** (James Wells Taylor), **Hoare** (Eduard Hoare), **Taylor** (James Parkinson Taylor), **and Box** (William Box, scribe), announced that only Richard Garrett's wife, his children, and his grandchildren were to be present when the will was read because of privacy concerns. They were the only people, he said, who were listed in the will as his heirs. "I'm sorry, but no spouses, friends, or acquaintances are allowed at the reading," he said. "Grandchildren yet to be born will be included as are those now living."

So the heirs all assembled in a separate room to hear Eduard Hoare read the will. John had to wait for Sarah's account of it later.

Sarah related that her father's will was attested by Attorney Hoare to amount to £473,000, not including real estate and some foreign investments which the will's executors, her brothers Richard, John, Henry, and Frank, would be responsible for selling and distributing the proceeds therefrom within three years time. For serving as executors her brothers were awarded an immediate £250 each. They were primarily charged with administering a separate trust, the Elizabeth Dunnell Garrett Trust, in the amount of £100,000, for the purpose of taking care of their mother in her accustomed style of living at Carlton Hall (which was exempted from the executors' real estate sales) through the remainder of her life…any residual funds to be distributed to the other heirs as the executors would then specify. In addition, each of Richard Garrett's nine surviving children (Richard, John, Betsy, Sarah, Ellen, Jane, Henry, Clara, and Frank) including the executors, were to be given an immediate £30,000 each. All Richard Garrett's grandchildren, both the eleven living and those yet to be born (two of the children's wives were pregnant at the time of the reading), were to be given £100 each to help them get a financial start in life.

"So we will be able to add £30,000 to OUR estate, John," explained Sarah, "There will be more to come within three years…and a bit more yet with each child we have."

"And who will be running the family company?" asked John.

"It will be run by Richard, Henry, and Frank working as a committee," answered Sarah. "I don't know why my brother John is not included in the committee. Perhaps he declined to serve… We'll have to ask Frank when we get the chance."

"It doesn't really matter," said John. "I'm sure the Company will be continuing its profitable operations with your three brothers in charge. They seem to get along well."

Frank Garrett came out of the room where the reading of the will had taken place and immediately went to find May Croft in the larger room where the others were congregated and waiting. After a minute or two conversing, both Frank and May came to talk to John and Sarah. Holding May's hand at his side, Frank asked, "John, would you allow me to court your daughter May…to write her letters and to arrange visits with her for now, but with an intent to become engaged to marry while still in this year?"

John recoiled backwards in a startle as if he had been pushed. He glanced at May and saw that she had a look of trepidation on her face…but she nodded affirmatively at him, and said, "We both think it was meant to be, Dad."

John protested, "But you're both so young, May…so young."

May answered, "We're older than you were when you first married. We've both completed our education. Frank is well employed and in command of significant wealth. We think we are ready to marry and start raising a family of our own."

There was a pause as John looked at Sarah and saw that she was looking expectantly at him. Then May said, "Please, Dad…give Frank your permission to court. We are in love."

Ted and Harry, seeing their father and sister May in conversation with Sarah and Sarah's brother Frank, sensed that something of importance was apparently happening and came over to join them. Ted, looking at how Frank was holding May's hand, asked John, "What's going on, Dad?"

John sighed and answered to them all, "I'm giving Frank here permission to court May. That's what's going on."

Ted turned to face Frank and asked, "Do you promise to always treat her well?"

Frank right away replied, "I do."

Ted offered Frank his hand to shake and said, "Then, as her brother, I don't object."

Harry, following his older brother's lead, added, "And neither do I."

John's voyages to and from the Anglo-Burmese War and Australia affected the topics of interest to him in his reading of the newspapers and the *Gentlemens' Magazine* so that he stayed informed of the events of the Austro-Prussian War in Europe and the construction of the Suez Canal in Egypt, which promised to shorten British sea voyages to the Indian Ocean by 3750 miles.

The Austro-Prussian War lasted only 1 month and 8 days, from June 14th to July 22nd of 1866, but the Prussian victory decided the exclusion of Austria from Germany, the northern states of which included Mecklenburg-Strelitz where John had sought his deceased brother Nicholas's widow in 1862.

London had an epidemic of cholera in 1866 which centered on the east end, where work on the sewage system and water treatment sites was not yet completed. The epidemic killed over 5,000 Londoners, and caused John and his family in Saddington to avoid traveling there for a time.

One of the heroes of the epidemic was Elizabeth Garrett (cf. p. 67), Newson and Louisa Garrett's daughter, who had, through outstanding study and persistence, been admitted as the first woman licensed to practice medicine by the British Society of Apothecaries in 1865. She opened St. Mary's Dispensary for Women and Children on Seymour Place in Marylebone. It was the first place where women and children could find medical services practiced only by women. In the first year since its founding, her dispensary treated 3,000 patients who made 9,300 visits to it.

John read aloud a newspaper article about Elizabeth Garrett's success to Sarah, May, Ted, and Harry at breakfast one morning in August, boasting to them that he had once advised Elizabeth Garrett to "LEARN EVERYTHING, and DON'T GIVE UP" on her dream of becoming a practicing physician. "I knew she was going to make it. I somehow just knew it," he told them.

That August John traveled on his own to see Hyla and then-pregnant Jane Elkington in Birmingham. He told Hyla he wanted to investigate the possibility of purchasing commercial quantities of powdered cocoa from the Cadbury Company that was headquartered there. He and Sarah had discussed adding a dairy to their Fleckney Farm and drinking chocolate was a product they wanted to feature.

Hyla told John, "I do know all three of the Cadburys…the retired father and founder John, and his two sons Richard and George. They have an office on Bridge Street here in Birmingham…there I could introduce you to Richard and George. I would think George might be the one most appropriate for you to talk to. Richard is dealing primarily now with their retail business, which started out as a grocery. I think George is leading the chocolate business."

As they were in Hyla's coach on their way to the Bridge Street Cadbury office, Hyla warned John that the Cadburys were Quakers and strongly pacifists and abolitionists. "So don't mention that you are a veteran of the Anglo-Burmese War," he advised. "You won't find any commonality with them in that."

Only George Cadbury was at the office when John and Hyla arrived. But George seemed happy to see Hyla. He welcomed them both into a private conference room and asked, "What can I do for you gentlemen?"

When John informed George Cadbury that he was looking to arrange a source of powdered cocoa to make drinkable chocolate at his planned dairy, George immediately frowned and said, "Our own source of cocoa from our British Gold Coast colony in West Africa is not at all reliable now. The Ashanti people who run our farms there near Accra have been in rebellion. We are trying to find alternative sources, but this effort does not look good at this time. We've now even lost touch with our British Governor of the Gold Coast, Edward Conran…we only hope he's still alive."

Despite receiving such a negative prospect, John felt drawn to George Cadbury personally. In his subsequent conversation with John and Hyla Elkington, George impressed them with his heartfelt concern for people, even those Ashanti people who were endangering his business's supply. When they were departing, he gifted John a five-pound bag of cocoa powder "for his family's personal use." When John was leaving Birmingham to return to Saddington, he remarked to Hyla, "This George Cadbury is a truly extraordinary man."

George Cadbury (1839-1922), from quak-ersintheworld org.

John took an interest in the Great Tea Race of 1866, a contest of clipper ships to see which one could, starting together in May from Foochow in China, be the first to deliver a full load of Chinese tea back to England. He found out where he could place a wager on his favourite clipper, *Ariel*, but Rev. Alfred strongly advised him to "Wager not, and bet not, lest you diminish your lot in life." As it turned out, *Ariel* docked second at Gravesend to *Taeping* by only 28 minutes on the same tide after 99 days and more than 14,000 miles of a sailing race that found them in sight of each other several times.

When the result was published in London's year-old *Pall Mall Gazette* after the 6th of September, John wrote a letter to Rev. Alfred that he was happy that he had "heeded his sound advice about wagering on the Great Tea Race."

Clipper ships Ariel and Taeping in the Great Tea Race of 1866 by Jack Spurling, from Wikipedia. Note the stunsails aloft.

Before Ted left Dalton House to enroll in Cambridge University's Trinity College in September 1866, his father John entrusted to him a large camphor-wood trunk that he had purchased a decade before when they still lived in their Mount Adelaide home on Sydney, Australia's, Darling Point.

John told Ted, "The only thing I've used this trunk for here in England is to store photographs and my correspondence on our family history. I'll empty it and we'll get it shipped to you in Cambridge by train."

The actual trunk in author Lee B. Croft's office in Phoenix, Arizona, 2022. From CFA.

"Dad," Ted wanted to know, "what family history are you corresponding about, and with whom?"

"For six years now I've been writing to people, mostly church vicars, who have access to birth records and baptisms, marriages and funeral ceremonies in an effort to detail our family's connection to other Crofts in England," John explained. "I want to know just how we are connected to the Crofts of Croft Castle in Herefordshire, and the Crofts in Claughton Hall."

"Are you sure we ARE connected to these Crofts?" asked Ted. "There are a lot of Crofts in the world."

"In my study of the matter, I have concluded that ALL the Crofts of England, from which the other Crofts of the world derive, descend from a single individual called 'Bernard Barbu," meaning 'Bernard the Bearded' who was a commander in the army of William the Conqueror of Normandy when he crossed the channel, defeated and killed our Anglo-Saxon King Harold II at the Battle of Hastings in 1066, now roundly 800 years ago."

"But how did this Bernard get the name Croft?"

"The Normans spoke a kind of French, as did William the Conqueror. As the victor at Hastings and our new King, William replaced King Harold's nobles with his own. His commander Bernard the Bearded was awarded a desirable property in Herefordshire…the site where he built the Castle… which was described by the place name Croft…a word meaning "*a sheltered plot of arable ground.*" So in French its Lord became 'Bernard de Croft,' meaning 'Bernard of the place called Croft'. It wasn't until the Norman nobility in England adopted the English Language by the fourteenth century that the French preposition 'of' ('de') was dropped and the phrase 'of Croft' became the surname 'Croft'."

"How do you know all this, Dad?" Ted asked.

"I got this knowledge from some very learned people…the very kind of people you will be learning from at Cambridge's Trinity College…especially those faculty members in your chosen major—'History and Modern Languages'." answered John. "I have here in this trunk a whole series of letters from the Reverend W. B. Grenside, the Vicar of Melling in Lancashire…a man educated at Cambridge twenty years ago. He has sent me his '*Memoranda Relating to the Familie of Croft, County Palatine of Lancaster.*' If you want, I'll leave it in the trunk for you to read. It's full of the family's historical information…the development of our coat-of-arms and such."

"So we have a coat-of-arms?"

"Indeed we do," answered John.

Letters from Ted in the next three months were a joy to John and his family. They were filled with stories about life in Cambridge, his classmates, his teachers, his subjects—especially French, which he joked "I never will get the better of."

Edmund Croft, off to Cambridge in September 1866 at age 18 (cf. p. 222 also). Script is in father John Croft's hand. From the CFA.

Ted reported on his accomodation as a "fresher" in a small individual bedroom with a desk within the College itself. The toilets and showers are "down the hall," he said. "But the other freshers are a great bunch. I know two or three from Eton."

On December 4th, 1866, Ted was allowed to leave the term's classes three days early to attend the wedding of his sister May to Frank Garrett (cf. p. 228) at St Margaret Church in Leiston on the next day, Wednesday December 5th. He had to return right after the wedding to take his course examinations and finish the term.

The wedding was a grand affair. And the reception afterwards at Carlton Hall (cf. p. 52) was as convivial as ever, attended by almost everyone in the family and everyone they knew.

Frank and Mary Anne Croft Garrett on their wedding day, December 5th, 1866. From CFA (cf. Frank on p. 228 also).

At the reception, May got a moment alone with her father and told him, “Dad, this is the happiest day of my life.”

John replied, “That’s what your mother told me the day you were born.”

CHAPTER FIVE: The Main Thing— CHILDREN.

So, in the year 1866 a father and a daughter (John and May Croft) marry a sister and a brother (Sarah Louisa and Frank Garrett). Both these couples (John and Sarah Louisa Garrett Croft and Frank and May Croft Garrett) are very wealthy, living in named estates (Dalton House in Saddington, Leicestershire for the Crofts and Carlton Hall near Saxmundham, Suffolk for the Garretts) and having more than ten household staff members in each household to support them as they began to have children.

John Croft's sons Ted and Harry discussed the kinship terms of this situation.

Harry said, "Dad's children with our step-mother Sarah will become our half-brothers and half-sisters."

And Ted retorted, "And our sister May's husband Frank will be our brother-in-law and their children will be our nieces and nephews. And they will all be Dad's grandchildren. That means he will be adding children to his family as his daughter, our sister May, adds grandchildren to it. I guess that's not really so strange."

Harry added, "but both we and our Croft half-sisters and half-brothers will be the cousins of our Garrett nieces and nephews. It will be interesting to see whether we wind up having more Croft half-siblings or more Garrett cousins."

And here then is the CROFT and GARRETT childrens' birth list in order of birth dates. Given also are facts known about their subsequent adult lives. ..with the women's married names and children and subsequent issue if known.

1.) **MARGARET CROFT COHEN** (b. April 14, 1867 in Saddington, Married Adolphus Cohen (1 Mar., 1857-6 Sept. 1933) in 1892…two sons Nicholas and Adolphus John…d. 18 Dec., 1914).

Margaret Croft Cohen in a signed photo in 1912. From CFA.

This is a June 1912 photo of Margaret Croft Cohen's son with husband Adolphus Cohen, Nicholas Croft Cohen (b. ca.1893). CFA.

2.) **ELIZABETH M. "Mabel" GARRETT** (b. 23 Oct.1867 in Leiston -d. ?).

3.) **JOHN WILLIAM CROFT, JR.** (b. Mar., 1868 in Saddington- well educated in England, emigrated to America, married a Canadian Lady, but became a U.S. Army physician who practiced as a veteran in Detroit, MI, divorced in 1899, visited his half-brothers Harry in British Columbia and Ted in Tacoma, Washington, before passing away in California on 13 November, 1912).

Margaret, age 5, and John Croft, age 4, at Dalton House in Saddington, from CFA.

4.) **EVELYN "Evie" GARRETT** (b. 21 Dec. 1868 in Leiston- d. ?)

Evie, age 3, and Mabel Garrett, age 4, at Carlton Hall in 1871. From CFA.

5.) **FRANK GARRETT, JR**. (b. 9 Dec.1869 in Leiston, and died in Leiston on 19 March, 1952). He married Evelyn Rosa Brooks (6 May 1868-28 Dec. 1951) 1 June, 1899, and they had FIVE daughters: Evelyn (b. 10 Sep., 1900-d. 19 Apr., 1969); Helen Mabel (b. 6 May, 1902-d. 11 Jan., 1992); Irene Elizabeth Garrett Richardson (b. 2 May, 1903-d. Jan., 1986); Dorothy Garrett Marwood (b. 1 Aug. 1904-d. 1992); and Phyllis Clifton Garrett Craig (b. 16 May, 1912- d. 9 July, 1944 in Woodbridge).

From Frank Garrett, Jr.'s daughter Irene (called "Betty") and her husband Jack Richardson (b. 23

Dec., 1892-d. 22 Jul., 1940 in Sudan) was born oldest son John Richardson (b. 26 Sep., 1933- d. Oct. 2020) and two daughters, Elizabeth and Penelope. That son John and his wife of 60 years Felicity Gardiner Richardson (b. 24 Sep., 1937…m. 9 May 1959…living) were met by me (LBC) and wife Lesley Hoyt Croft (b. 31 Mar., 1953-living) at the **Parrott and Punchbowl** near Aldringham for a nice family dinner on 29 April, 2019.

Aldringham's Parrot and Punchbowl Pub. Photo by the author in 2019.

Author Lee B. Croft (b. 19 Sep., 1946 in Cut Bank, Montana, USA—living and writing) with Cousin John Richardson in 2019, who died in 2022. Photo by Lesley Hoyt Croft.

From Frank Garrett, Jr.'s daughter Phyllis Clifton Garrett Craig (called "Poppy") (b. 16 May, 1912-d. 9 Jul., 1994) and her husband Daniel MacKinnon Craig (b. 20 Mar., 1907 in Finchley…married 1 Jun., 1935 in Leiston..d. 23 Mar. 1982 in Woodbridge) was born Dorothy Margaret Craig Young, the family genealogy scholar we know as Margaret Young (b. 4 Jun., 1936 in Framlingham, Suffolk-living) who is also shown below with her husband Dr. Stewart Young (b. 20 Mar., 1937 in Esher, Surrey…married 26 Aug., 1961-living to see Suffolk locations named after him).

Dr. Stewart and Margaret Young with author Lee B. Croft (L) in 2019. Photo by Lesley Hoyt Croft.

Here below is Margaret Young's grandfather Frank Garrett, Jr., shown as a young man with his younger brother Alfred Stead Garrett:

Frank Garrett, Jr. and his younger brother Alfred Stead Garrett, ca. 1888. From CFA.

6.) **ELEANOR "Nellie" CROFT RANSON** (b. Feb., 1869, in Saddington. Marries Edward Ranson of Norwich on 9 May, 1888…has 3 daughters and a son Richard Ranson, a physician, who died in France in WWI as a Canadian medic).

Here I simply wish to copy for the reader a quite long fine-print newspaper article detailing the wedding of "Miss Eleanor Croft and Mr. Edward Ranson" in the year 1888. I cannot be certain which newspaper the article is printed in... either the *Suffolk Times* or the *Aldeburgh, Leiston & Saxmundham Times* or the *Lowestoft Journal*, or the *Ipswich Times*...all were being published in the Aldringham area in 1888. Attempts to search their archives online with snippets of the text, however, did not turn up an issue. So here is the copy:

"Marriage of Miss Eleanor Croft and

Mr. Edward Ranson

The little ivy-clad church of St. Andrews, at Aldringham, was the scene of a very pretty wedding on Tuesday. The contracting parties were Mr. Edward Ranson, of Lowestoft, third son of J. Farrar Ranson, Esq., Heathside, Norwich, and Eleanor, youngest daughter of the late John Croft, Esq., of Dalton House, Saddington, Leicestershire, and niece of Frank Garrett, Esq., Aldringham House, near Leiston. The relationship of the bride to Mr. Garrett, in whose family she has for some time resided, naturally created much popular interest in the neighbourhood, and flags and bunting were displayed at Leiston and on the road leading to Aldringham House and the church in honour of the happy event. At the junction of the Leiston and Thorpe roads the landlord of the **Parrot and Punch Bowl** (cf. p. 251) had erected an evergreen arch, decorated with flags, and wishing, by an inscription, '*Long life, health, and happiness*.' Some time before the hour appointed for the ceremony the church was crowded by friends and others, whilst the path from the gate to the porch, which was covered with matting, was lined with villagers, who patiently awaited the coming of the bride, in whom all seemed to take a deep and affectionate interest. The bridegroom, accompanied by his best man (Mr. J. D. Sims of Ipswich), took up the usual position at the altar. He was soon joined by his graceful bride, who entered the church leaning on the arm of her uncle, Mr. Frank Garrett, who gave her away. Her dress was of ivory corded silk, trimmed with Horniton lace, Medici collar, long train profusely adorned with orange blossoms, and a Brussels net veil. She carried a magnificent bouquet of orange blossoms and white exotic flowers, and wore a pearl and diamond crescent brooch, the gift of the bridegroom. She was attended by four bridesmaids—Miss Evelyn Garrett, Miss Mabel Garrett, and Miss Bessie Grimwood (cousins of the bride), and Miss Grace Ranson (sister of the groom). These young ladies were charmingly attired in French pink, trimmed with corded silk, and shoes, gloves, and etc. to match; hats of French tulle of the same colour, and they carried beautiful bouquets of Marechal Neil roses and maidenhair ferns, and wore lovers' knot brooches, encircling pearl and coral hearts, set in gold, the gifts of the bridegroom. There was but little music set into the service, the only hymn sung being the well-known one of '*The Voice that Breathed O'er Eden.*' The nuptial knot was tied by the Rev. B. W. Raven, M.A., Rector of Leiston, assisted by the Rev. C. DuGard Makepeace, M.A., vicar of the parish, and at the conclusion of the ceremony the Rev. B. W. Raven delivered a short but impressive exhortation to the newly married pair upon their future life.

The party left the church to the strains of Mendelssohn's '*Wedding March*,' played by the organist, Miss Agatha Peskett. The wedding guests included Mr. and Mrs. A. Hayward, Mrs. and the Misses Key, the Rev. E. and Mrs. Thelwall, Mr. Walton Turner (Ipswich), Mr. F. Turner (Ipswich), Miss Anna Turner (Ipswich), Mr., Mrs. and Miss Wallis, Mr. and Mrs. Farrar Ranson, Mr., Mrs., and Miss Garrett, Mr. G. Garrett, Mr. N. Garrett, Mr. and Mrs. A. Collins, Mr. and Mrs. Mathias, Miss Marian Turner, Rev. B. W. Raven, Mrs. and Miss Flick, Mr. Wilson Ranson, Rev. T. S. and Mrs. Curteis, Mrs. and the Misses Johnson, Mrs. Grimwood, Rev. C. DuGard and Mrs. Makepeace.

A reception was afterwards held at Aldringham House. The bridecake, a magnificent specimen of the confectioner's art, was supplied by Messrs. Buszard, of Regent Street, London.

A fine artist's conception of a posh English wedding reception with an ornate cake.

During the afternoon a merry peal was rung on the bells of Leiston Church, and later on the newly married pair left for London, en route for Scotland, where the honeymoon will bc spent. The bride's traveling costume was tailor-made Scotch tweed, with jacket to match, and dove grey bonnet, trimmed in white heath.

The presents included: Dessert knives, Mr. and Mrs. A. Brooksbank; flower vases, Mrs. Gerard Barton; silver cigarette case, Mr. H. J. Barton, R.E,; biscuit canister Mr. and Mrs. Beasley; silver salt bowls and spoons, Messrs. G. and B. Croft; Maltese lace d'oylys, Mrs. Cowell; Indian handkerchief case, Miss Cowell; a silver dessert service, Mr. and Mrs. Hyla Elkington; crumb spoon, Miss Francis; sofa couvre, Miss Garrett; silver sugar bowl and cream jug, Mr. and Mrs. T. R. Grimwood; Minton dinner service, Mrs. Grimwood; Elkington silver teapot, silver coffee-pot, silver sugar basin, and silver cream jug, Mr. and Mrs. Frank Garrett; butter dishes, Mr. Frank Garrett, Jr., and the Misses E., W., and L. Garrett; set of silver teaspoons, Capt. E. Gabriel; family Bible and Family Prayers, Mrs. Johnson; silver gilt sugar sifter, Mr. and Mrs. Keith W. Murray; cabinet album, Mrs. H. H. Master; books, Rev. C. and Mrs. Makepeace; paintings, Mr. F. Miller; oak dining-room chiming clock, Mrs. F. Peck; drawing-room folding screen, Mrs. Gurney Pease; copper and iron newspaper rack, Capt. Peskett; copper and iron flower- stand, Mr. and Mrs. Postans; cheque, Mr. and Mrs. Farrar Ranson; bread server, Mr. and Mrs. Farrar Ranson; worked screen, Miss Ranson; tablecover, Miss Grace Ranson; brass tea- kettle, Miss Annie Ranson; crocodile skin, Mr. Robert Ranson, Florida; brass candlesticks, Messrs. W. and W. H. Ranson; grape scissors and nutcrackers, Mr. Harry Ridgers; mirrors, Mrs. Robinson Ridley and Miss Grimwood; silver butter knife, Mr. and Mrs. A. F. Rayner; silver knife and fork, Mr. and Mrs. Roberts, card case, the Misses M. and O. Ransome; silver basin, the Misses Sanderson and Bidwell; standard lamp, Mr. J. D. Sims; silver Cupid vase, Mrs. Sultzer; toast rack, Mr. and Mrs. T.

W. Southey; flower vases, Master G. and the Misses E. and G. Southey; butter dish, Miss Stanford; tea service, Mr. and Mrs. W. M. Tapp; silver waiter, Mr. Walton Turner; cheque, Mr. and Mrs. E. R. Turner, cheque, Mr. and Mrs. A. J. Turner; cheque, Mr. Frederick Turner; Shakespeare and three volumes books, the Misses Turner, Lowestoft; silver frame, Mr. and Mrs. E. A. Tewson; flower vase, Mr. and Mrs. J. F. Wilson; pipe, Mr. Gilbert Winslow; salad bowl, Mr. and Mrs. Wallis, and etc.

A present from the employees at the Lowestoft, Norwich, and Yarmouth timber yards was accompanied by a congratulatory address."

COMMENTARY: It is indeed wonderful to read carefully through this newspaper wedding account. How lovely it certainly was! It's interesting that the bride, Eleanor Croft, is almost the sole Croft mentioned, except for the "G. and B. Croft" who are not mentioned as being in attendance, but gifted the pair "silver salt bowls and spoons." Eleanor was born to Sarah Louisa Garrett Croft and John Croft in 1869 and was 19 years old at this wedding. Her closest-in-age brother Frank Garrett Croft (1872-1889) is not mentioned, but her cousin Frank Garrett, Jr. (1869-1952), in whose household (i.e her Aunt Mary Anne Croft Garrett and Uncle Frank Garrett, Sr.'s household) at Aldringham House near Leiston she lived after the deaths of her stepmother Sarah Louisa (in 1874) and her father John (in 1883). The "B." Croft is likely her youngest brother Benjamin Croft (1874-1918) but the "G" Croft is not clear, possibly a mistake by the article's author and should be "P" for brother Peter Croft (1873-1947) as they also were then living in the Garrett's Aldringham House. After the wedding this picture was taken at Frank and Mary Anne Garrett's Aldringham House:

RANK Snr (43) FRANK Jnr (19) WINIFRED (17)
ILIAN (16) MARY ANNE (44) KATHLEEN (15)
9 May 1888

This photo from the CFA shows (L-R) Lilian Croft Garrett (b. 1872, married John Douglas Broad 19 December, 1900 in London, d. 1963) at age 16; this is a rare photograph of leading British industrialist Frank Garrett, Sr. with family (6 May, 1845 —24 August, 1918) at age 43, he's taking something from his son Frank Garrett, Jr. (1869-1952) at age 19; then sitting is the really extraordinary Mary Anne (called also "Mother May") Croft Garrett (b. 12 February, 1844 in Sydney, Australia—d. 31 January, 1897), wife of Frank Sr. and mother of his eleven Garrett children. Then, after the death of her father John Croft's wife Sarah Louisa Garrett Croft in 1874, surrogate mother of seven of John and Sarah's children,...see her earlier photo at age 16 in 1860 with her two younger brothers Edmund and Henry Croft (cf. p. 79) here at age 44. Then in the photo above is sister Winfred Garrett (1872-1925) in back at age 17, and in front is sister Kathleen Penelope Garrett (1873-?) at age 15.

John Croft's oldest, his daughter Mary Anne Croft Garrett, wife of Frank, Sr., and resident in Aldringham House after 1876, was from 1874 to her death in 1897 (i.e. for 23 years), the *de facto* mother of her own two brothers (Edmund and Henry Croft…cf. p. 79), her own eleven Garrett children with husband Frank, Sr. (Elizabeth, Evelyn, Frank, Jr., Winfred, Lilian Croft, Kathleen Penelope, Alfred, Mary Ruth, Stephen, Mary (died in birth 16 Dec., 1883) and Victor Richard), AND her seven surviving Croft half siblings, the children of her father John Croft (1807-1883) and his wife, her husband's older sister, Sarah Louisa Garrett Croft (1837-1874) (Margaret, John, Eleanor (being married herein), the twin Richard (whose brother Nicholas had died in 1870), Frank Garrett, Peter, and Benjamin). This means that she was, to some degree or other, caring for as many as TWENTY of the Croft-Garrett family's children (and while pregnant herself much of the time), housing them in the Aldringham House near Leiston after 1878. Another consideration of interest is the FINANCIAL aspect. ALL these children were privileged to attend the best schools...Eton, Harrow, Rugby...and attend the most expensive and prestigious universities...Oxford and Cambridge and London. Both Mary Anne's father, John Croft, and her husband, Frank Garrett, Sr., were very wealthy and could afford this...and leave appreciable estates behind as well.

I here apologize for revealing in the preceding included text some life, marriage, and death facts about this biography's principal characters ahead of where we are in the "natural order" of their lives' narrated events. But now I will return to the list of children born to John and Sarah Louisa Garrett Croft and to Frank and Mary Anne ("May") Croft Garrett after their marriages in 1866. The list continues after John and Sarah's daughter Eleanor Croft Ranson, who was born in 1870, with:

7.) and 8.) twins **NICHOLAS and RICHARD CROFT** (both b. 23 May 1870 in Saddington... twin Nicholas dies of scarlet fever 7 Sept. 1879 and is interred with his parents at St. Peter's in Carlton-Saxmundham, but Richard marries "an English Lady," becomes a Doctor of Medicine, dies of pneumonia in Victoria. B.C., Canada, on 15 Jan., 1901, after, like older brother John, Jr. (cf. p. 249), visiting his half-brother Henry "Harry" Croft who by then lived there).

L-R Twins Nicholas and Richard Croft on the plush chair in Dalton House in Saddington at 8 months of age in January 1871. CFA

9.) **WINFRED MAY GARRETT** (b. 24 Apr., 1871 in Leiston–d. 1935).

10.) **ALFRED CROFT** (b. ?1871 in Saddington-d. ?).

11.) **FRANK GARRETT TERTIUS CROFT** (b. 22 Jan,1872 in Saddington…dies a prominent athlete at Rugby School, allegedly from eating bad clams, on 7 Dec. 1889). The name "Tertius" means "the THIRD in Latin…he was named after his uncle Frank Garrattm, Sr., and was thus "the third" Frank Garratt after his cousin Frank Garratt, Jr. (born earlier in 1869…cf. pp. 250 and 253) and Frank Garrett, Sr. (cf. 228, 260)

Frank Garrett Tertius Croft at Rugby School in 1888, From CFA.

12.) **LILIAN CROFT GARRETT BROAD** (b. 8 Sept.,1872 in Leiston-marries Douglas Broad and has children: Vera Broad (b.1901-d. 1989), Doris Broad (b. 1903-d. ?), Kenneth Broad (b. 1904-d. 5 Aug., 1929) John Broad (b. 1906-d. 5 Aug., 1929…why Kenneth and John die on same day is a ?), Lt. Col. Richard Broad (b. 1910…becomes a

Douglas and Lilian Croft Garrett Broad ca. 1910. From CFA.

prominent soldier in WWII, meets my (LBC) parents in the 1970s, has children with wife Dora: Sandra Broad Dudley (d. 2000) and Michael Broad (b. 1935…marries wife Jacqueline, has daughter Laura), and Hazel Broad (b. 1913-d?). Lt. Col. Richard Broad dies in 1990). Lilian Croft Garrett, who died in London 13 Feb., 1963, is shown at age 16 on page 260 also.

13.) **PETER CROFT** (b. 30 Jan., 1873 in Saddington, a Boer War soldier and sire of the Croft family in South Africa with wife Julia Nettie Underwood of Boston, USA, whom he marries Sept. 27, 1902 in South Africa…they have children Edmund "Ted" Croft who marries wife Villeria, and a daughter who marries a MacFarlane and has a son Ian MacFarlane (b. 1927…a hunter in the Okavango Delta whom we (LBC and LHC) hosted at our Phoenix, AZ, home when he came to visit the notorious gun aficianado, Col. Cooper in Paulden, AZ in ca. 1995, d. 2005?). Peter Croft died in Bloemfontein, Free State, South Africa in 1947.

14.) **KATHLEEN PENELOPE GARRETT** (b. 20 Dec.,1873 in Leiston..d.?).

15.) **BENJAMIN CROFT** (b. 17 Jan.,1874 in Saddington…marries Margaret Elizabeth Perry, has son Alfred Croft in 1899 who married Irene Victoria Blanch McAvoy (called "Terry") in 1920 and has a daughter Marilyn Croft Gill (b. 1932) who, with James Francis Gill had two daughters Jacqueline Ann Gill and Juanita Gill (b. 1954) and a son William Douglas Gill (b. 1955)...Benjamin's mother Sarah Louisa Garrett Croft died ten days after his birth on 27 January 1874, causing extreme distress to his father John Croft...Benjamin grows up to become a Major in the British Army and dies as the last combat casualty of World War I on 10 November, 1918, in Marvenot, near Mons in France. He was 36 years old, leaving wife and son bereft. He has more than one church memorial plaque in Suffolk

Major Benjamin Croft, killed in WWI action on Nov. 10, 1918 leaving wife Margaret Elizabeth Perry Croft and son Alfred Croft (b. 1899-d. 1977). From Croft Family Archives.

16.) **ALFRED STEAD GARRETT** (b. 28 Feb., 1875, in Leiston, married Winfred May Chalmer (Winfred "Win" born 7 Jul. 1877…marries Alfred on 25 Apr, 1900, dies ?) and has children: Alfred Boteler Garrett (3 Apr.1901 in Leiston, dies a 20-year-old Lieutenant of the 92nd Regiment of P.W.O. Punjabis, Indian Army, falling in action on 25 Nov. 1921 near Barshor in Baluchistan and is buried at Quetta), Lt. Col. James Stead Garrett, OBE, (1903-1948), who served in the 8th Punjabi Regiment in India and, with wife Angela Clare Withers Garrett (1911-1937) had 3 daughters Diana Garrett Marchant-Smith (b. 1939), Jill Elaine Garrett Garnett (b. 1941), and Roseanne Garrett Bradley (b. 1945). Alfred and Winfred May Garrett also had a daughter, Angela Clare Garrett (1911-1968). Alfred dies in Suffolk in 1953. There is a picture of young Alfred Stead Garrett with his older brother Frank Garrett, Jr. on p. 253 above.

The Garretts' children to this point are listed as being "born in Leiston," because from their 1866 marriage until 1876 Frank, Sr. and May Croft Garrett lived in the "Dinsdale House" opposite the Long Works House on their factory property in Leiston. But in 1876 Frank, for reasons later revealed, purchased the larger Aldringham House near Saxmundham, within only slight distance from the Garrett family's Carlton Hall (cf. p. 52), from Lord Rendlesham's estate, for £27,000 and their subsequent children were born there. Here is a photo of that incarnation of Aldringham Hall

Frank, Sr. and Mary Anne Croft Garretts' Aldringham Hall from 1876. From CFA.

17.) **MARY RUTH GARRETT** (b. 11 Mar.,1877 at Aldringham…marries Reginald Lee James on 17 Jan. 1899 and has children Marjory James, Mary James, Hugh James, and Phillip James, who has a son Richard James with wife Doris…dates unsure, as is date of Mary's death.)

18.) **STEPHEN GARRETT** (b. 6 Sept., 1878 in Aldringham…marries Mary Marples (19 Nov. 1877-1958) on 19 Sept. 1905 and had children Stephen Denis Garrett, who with Jane Perkins (10

Nov. 1914 married 17 Dec. 1934, dies 2006 in Cambridge) had children Rachel Garrett Davy, Lucy Garrett Hornsby Abubakar Lee Housden, Catherine Berry Garrett Sweeny, Michael Garrett (who with wife Joan Hooper (b. 30 Oct. 1917 and had children Stephen Garrett (b. 1947 living with wife Monica Mary O'Brian) and son Mathew James (b. 1977) and daughters Justine Clare (b. 1981), Seana Garrett (19 Nov., 1950), and Mollie (Mary Brenda) Garrett Zak (1910-1985) who with husband Wily Zak had son Joseph (Zak) Garrett (retention of Garrett name was deliberate) who with wife Margaret had a daughter Samantha Garrett who had sons Stanley and Charles Hargreaves with husband Martin Hargreaves and a son Paul Garrett who with wife Maria has a son Alfie Garrett (b. 2002), and daughters Mimi Garrett (b. 2004) and Poppy Garrett (b. 2008).

STEPHEN GARRETT (i.e. he born in 1878) became a Captain of the 4th Battalion of the Suffolk Territorial Army and was killed in action at the World War I Battle of Neuve Chapelle on 12 March, 1915 at age 36, and he is buried at Estaires in France. He and his father Frank Garrett, Sr. were very close and, after Stephen's death, Frank Garrett, Sr., became a bit withdrawn…took up wood carving, etc.).

A photo of Captain Stephen Garrett from a Garrett & Co. brochure.

19.) **MARY GARRETT** (b. 14 Dec. 1883 and died the same day in Aldringham…is buried with her parents in St. Andrew's Church Cemetery).

20.) **VICTOR RICHARD GARRETT** (b. 21 Oct. 1887 at Aldringham…married Gladys Fisher (1890-1961) and had one child, a son, Richard Strang Garrett (b. 15 Jan. 1920, d. 29 Jul., 2008 at St. Leonards on the Sea, Sussex). Richard Strang Garrett married Margaret Anne Selves (b. 11 Apr. 1921) and had three children: Anthony "Tony" Richard Garrett (b. 2 April, 1947…married to Valerie Young (b. 7 September, 1947). They have a son, Samuel Rupert Garrett (b. 12 July 1982), who married Shikha Sharma on 30 March, 2019. They have met my younger brother Wayne Steven Croft (b. 21 August, 1953—living now in Missoula, Montana, USA), his wife, Judith Pleunneke Croft (b. 23 December, 1951) and their younger son Daniel Edmund Croft (b. 14 December, 1989) when Daniel came to study for a year at Oxford University in 2010. They also met my parents, Bill and Norma Croft, when Bill and Norma visited England in the late 70s and on a visit that Anthony, Val, and Sam made to the United States in 1996. Richard Strang and Margaret Anne Selves Garrett's second son is Simon Samuel Garrett (b. 10 October) who, with wife Judith (*neé* Haynes) (b. 1954) have a son Alexander Richard Garrett (b. 30 April, 1990, who married Olivia Parkes on 25 June 2022) and a daughter Isobel Philippa Garrett (b. 19 January, 1993) now living in Melbourne, Australia. And Richard Strang and Margaret Anne Garrett have a third child, a daughter, Margaret Jane "Jane" (b. 25 June 1956) married to John Kevin Divall (b. 1951) and they have four children: Sarah (b. 1981), Patrick (b. 1983), Timothy (b. 1986), Katherine (b. 1991), and, at present, seven grandchildren. Victor dies in London in 1980.

Family genealogist Margaret Young records that Victor Richard Garrett, as the youngest of the Frank Garrett, Sr. children and the grandfather of living-in-Hastings cousin Tony Garrett and wife Valerie, was extraordinarily stressed when his mother, Mary Anne Croft Garrett or "May," passed away when he was only 10 years old in 1897. And Victor was reportedly not pleased when his father, Frank Garrett, Sr., only two years a widower, took as his second wife his former wife May's older spinster first cousin, Emma "Barbara" Stead (cf. p. 50) on 15 April, 1899.

This photo from the collection of his grandson Tony Garrett is of Victor Richard Garrett with his 1905 Alldays & Onions 4 cyl 6 hp motorcar made in a Birmingham Factory and costing £130. It has

the BJ registration license plate for Suffolk and is missing its brass radiator and grill (?).

So, listed-above in this chapter are the 18 CROFT or GARRETT children born in the given order to JOHN AND SARAH LOUISA GARRETT CROFT and FRANK and MARY ANNE CROFT GARRETT from 1867 to 1887…20 years.

Even before my (author LBC) 70s of age I began to read the obituary columns in the daily *Arizona Republic* at our Flagstaff heat-retreat or at home in Phoenix. Once a month or so I would read of someone's death listed there and the photograph or description of their lives' events would reveal that I personally knew them. I began to scrawl in pen on the obit how many people there were in their "issue," that is how many children, grandchildren, great grandchildren or, sometimes even, great great grandchildren they welcomed into the world during their lifetimes…this constituting at least the biological legacy of their lives. My all-time champion…a woman of 102 years of age… had 229 such "issue" across 4 generations (children, grandchildren, great grandchildren, and great great grandchildren). I'm sorry that I don't now recall her name, but she died in 2022 or 2023.

So, it occurred to me to get some measure of what my biography subject here, John William Croft (1807-1883), achieved in the way of a biological legacy, expressed by the number of his direct descendants. This caused me to do some counting from my cousin Margaret Young's really remarkable "Outlines of Descendants." Their time period covers **seven generations** spanning **150 years** (from 1867 when John and Sarah Croft had their first child, Margaret Croft Cohen, until 2017 when Margaret Young compiled her outlines of descendants). Both Margaret (born in 1936) and I (born in 1946) are of the 5th generation of descendance from John Croft.

Of the names on Margaret Young's descendants' outlines…those descendants of John Croft and Sarah Louisa Garrett Croft and those descendants of Frank Garrett, Sr. and Mary Anne Croft Garrett…one might expect that half the total number should have last names of Croft or Garrett, and the other half (representing the names changed by female Crofts or Garretts of the family when they married and had children with men of other names).

So here begins the count. The families composed of the Croft and Garrett descendants is precisely **four** in generation 1 in 1867, i.e. John, Sarah, Frank, and Mary Anne. For generation two they add **22** children (I am counting John's earlier sons Edmund (who had four Croft sons with Alice Downing) and Henry, called Harry, who married

Mary Jean Dunsmuir but had no issue). so now we have **26**.

The number of descendants of John and Sarah Croft from generation 3 to generation 7 is **423** by 2017…and is growing apace. 106 of these still bear the last name Croft. The other 317 have 102 different last names: (alphabetically) Abubakar, Arnold, Bailey, Bradley, Broad, Brooks, Brown, Burvik, Catford, Chalmer, Cohen, Connoly, Conway, Craig, Cran, Davy, DeLaTerre, Divall, Dobson, Doyle, Dudley, Duell, Gardiner, Garnett, Gill, Gomez, Gould, Gower, Grierson, Frank, Fisher, Frost, Hargreaves, Hall, Haynes, Hobbs, Hooper, Horner, Hornsby, Hunt, Hutton, James, Jones, Kirchner, Lambert, Lee, Ling, Lloyd, MacFarlane, Maguire, Marples, Marwood, Marchant-Smith, McAvoy, McCoy, McKee, Merritt, Morrison, Mullen, Nelson, Needham, Newnham. Osborne, Penny, Perkins, Perry, Prince, O'Brien, Ranson, Ratsey, Readman, Reid, Reid (2x), Richardson, Rodrick, Ross-Elliott, Sandals, Sanders, Selves, Sennet, Snowden, Soffe, Springle, Stewart, Sweeny, Sweeny-Soffe, Tomlinson, Underwood, Walmsley, Waghorn, Wall, Watson, Waters, Webster, Wheeler, Whittaker, Willets, Withers, Wren, Wyncoll, Young, and Zak (102 here listed).

AND, the number of descendants of Frank and Mary Anne Garrett from generation three to generation seven is **352** by 2017. There are 114 names other than the 238 Garretts: (alphabetically) Ainsley, Allender, Anderson, Anthony, Arch, Barringer, Bate, Beasley, Beauclerk, Beck, Birgitta, Boucher, Bousfield, Bardnack, Breden, Burns, Cater, Coates, Cunnngham, Davis, Dougherty, Easton, Elgood, Faulks, Faviell, Fenwick, Fernberg, Findlay, Fox, Gardner, Gee, Gomme, Goodwyn, Gow, Grace, Grieg, Griffiths, Guildford, Hamlin, Hardin, Hartley, Harvey, Hawkins, Hayward, Henry, Holden, Hodges, Leopard, Newman, Lockett, Lomer, Louise, Lovett, Luttrell, MacLean, Marin, Mayers, Mayne, McClean, MCullocy, McIntosh, McKay, McPeek, Middlethon, Mitchell, Moore, Moorecroft, Morton, Mulchay, Murphy-Grimshaw, Newberry, Newman, Newschild, Olivier, Paterson, Pearse, Peck, Pollastri, Powell, Rae, Readman, Reeves, Richards, rush, Samson, Sanders, Sauvarin, Sennett, Shearer, Skipper, Slade, Smith, Smyth, Stephenson, Stinton, Streeten, Sybil, Symns, Tapp, Taylor, Tewson, Thal, Tomlinson, Trow, Unit, Vans-Agnew, Walkowiak, Ward, Warkentin, Watts, Webster, Wendy, and Winser (114 here listed).

When you scan through these names, do you, perchance, recognize your own? Might you be found somewhere on the Croft-Garrett ancestry charts…i.e related to us? I would like to think so, especially inasmuch as, in ultimate fact, we humans on this planet are ALL related. And since Mary Anne Croft Garrett's descendants are also descendants of John Croft (through her), you can see that his biological legacy after 7 generations (2017) consists of **801** people (The generation 2 26 plus 106 Crofts and 238 Garretts and 432 other named descendants in generations 3-7) in his direct line living all over the world. In the time span covered in this book, four people became a family of over 800 bearing 218 last names (Croft, Garrett and 216 "others").

By the time of his death in 1883, John Croft had **nine** grandchildren from his daughter May and her husband, Frank Garrett, Sr.: (Elizabeth or "Mabel", b. 1867, Evelyn or "Evie," b. 1868, Frank Jr., b. 1869, Winfred May, b. 1871, Lilian Croft G., b.1872, Alfred Stead G., b.1875, Mary Ruth G., b. 1877, and Stephen G., b. 1878) AND **three** from his son Edmund John and his wife Alice "Mamp" Downing (Sydney Nicholas C., b. 1877, Edmund John, Jr. C. called "Miccie," b. 1880, and Henry William C. called "Lee," b. 1882). So that he died knowing of **12** grandchildren…and had many more to go. He did not live to see any of his many GREAT grandchildren.

John's oldest son Edmund, called "Ted," was my own great grandfather. I am therefore in the Croft tail-male line of John, Edmund, Lee, and my Dad, William Sydney C.…I'm the fifth generation…and I've contributed my son William (6th G) who has a son Christopher (7th G). My father

William Sydney Croft. b. 1919, who died in 2003 at 84, knew that he had **five** grandchildren from daughter Barbara Marie Casey Martin (10/3/1939-9/20/2009) who was his daughter with his married girlfriend Neva Marie Larson Casey (1919-2007) (and Barbara left him **six** grandchildren and, as of 2009, **16** great grandchildren); **four** grandchildren from me, his son Lee B. Croft. b. 1946, and my wives Betty Hill Croft Richter, b. 1945 (Cathy Lynn C., b. 1966, Christopher Wayne C. b. 1968, William Jerry C., b. 1970) and with present wife Lesley Hoyt C. b. 1953 (Hayden Lee Hoyt C., b. 1987), **three** grandchildren from son Jerry George C. b. 1947 and his wife Diana Lee Dudley C. (Jessica Erin C. b. 1981, Tyler Owen C. b.1982, and Jordan Elliot C., b. 1987), and **two** grandchildren from son Wayne Steven b. 1953 and his wife Judith Pluenneke C. b. 1951 (Michael Ross C., b. 1987, and Daniel Edmund C., b. 1989). That's **14** grandchildren that my Dad, William Sydney Croft, had at his passing in 2003. As of this writing there are also **four** great grands in this line. SO, from both spouses, Neva and Norma, my father, William Sydney Croft (1919-2003) now has at least **47 ISSUE** (5 children, 15 grandchildren, 23 great grandchildren, and 4 great great grandchildren)

My Dad was the first Croft sire in our lineage to know any of his GREAT grandchildren. He took joy in knowing: Cathy's daughters Josi Gloria C., b. 1988 and Sunny C. Daze, b. 1994…and Cathy's step-daughter Ashley Schwartz, b. 1987; Christopher Wayne's step children James Hendrickson b. 1985 and Amber Bianco b. 1991; and William Jerry's adopted daughters Azlyn C. b. 1989, Ayanna C. b. 1991, and natural children Elisabeth Madison C. b. 1998, and Christopher Jerry b. 2003). That's **nine** great grand children known to my Dad, William Sydney Croft (1919-2003) before his death.

I (author Lee B. Croft), William Sydney Croft's oldest son, am also personally acquainted with some of my great grandchildren—first in that my daughter Cathy Croft Kirchner Schwartz Schade's step-daughter Ashley Schwartz has two daughters (Michaela Anne Marie Robbins, b. 2007, and Samantha Marie Osborne, b. 2012) who are therefore my "step great grand daughters, AND Cathy's daughter Sunny Kirchner Croft Daze has a daughter, my natural great granddaughter, Bonnie V. Daze b. 2021, whom I have met more than once and hope to see much more of in my life. So, at age 77, I have **THREE** great grandchildren and hope to have more.

Here I am inserting the first few pages of a document I wrote on Christmas Eve, 2014, entitled "**The Croft Line Back…Way Back**:"

"I am going to record here a survey of my own Croft 'Tail-Male' line. Contrary to the above, this line essentially begins in the present as 'generation one,' and lists direct progenitors going back in history seven generations.

Let's start with my youngest Croft grandson CHRISTOPHER JERRY CROFT as "generation ONE" in this Croft line back. Note that this list gives ONLY THE CROFT-NAMED FATHERS AND SONS and some siblings from the listed wives.

Gen. 1: **Christopher Jerry Croft** (b. 20 Feb., 2003 in Spokane, Spokane, WA, USA-living), now a medieval history student at Eastern Washington University.

Gen. 2: **William Jerry Croft** (b. 23 Mar., 1970, in Tucson, Pima, AZ, USA-living). Wife is Rhonda Frank Croft (b. 12 Dec., 1968, in Billings, Montana, USA-living).

Spokane Attorney William Jerry Croft (left) with wife Rhonda (left front), daughters Elisabeth (rear left, '98), Ayanna (front right, '91), Azalyn (back right, '89), and son Christopher Jerry Croft (right)

Gen. 3: **Lee Bliss Croft, Ph.D.** (b. 19 Sep., 1946, in Cut Bank, Glacier, Montana, USA--living). First wife was (1965-1979) Betty (neeé Hill) Croft Richter (b. 20 Dec., 1945…mother of daughter Cathy L. (b. 1 May, 1966-), and sons Christopher W. (b. 21 Aug., 1968-), and William J. (b. 23 Mar., 1970-); current wife (m. 6 Jun., 1981-) is Dr. Lesley Hoyt Croft (b. 31 Mar., 1953-), mother of son Hayden L. H. (b. 5 Oct., 1987-living).

Prof. Lee B Croft (Author)

<u>Gen. 4</u>: **William Sydney "Bill" Croft** (b. 11 Nov., 1919 in Tacoma, Pierce, Washington and d. 15 Nov., 2003, in Great Falls, Cascade, Montana, USA). Wife from (m. 12 Oct., 1945-) is Norma Rose (neé Dingeldein) Croft (b. 15 Jul., 1927, Bronx, NY, USA-d. 22 Feb., 2022 in Great Falls, Montana, USA), mother of sons Lee Bliss, Jerry George (b. 22 Oct., 1947-), Wayne Steven (b. 21 Aug., 1953-), and daughter Nancy Julia Croft Jacobson (b. 23 Nov., 1963-). See p. 280 for more.

William Sydney "Bill" Croft (US Navy, WWII, 1942-5). Founder of CROFT PETROLEUM, an oil business in Cut Bank, Montana (1968-).

Gen. 5: **Henry William "Lee" Croft** (b. 22 Sep., 1882 in Boisfort Prairie, Lewis County, WA, USA- d. 14 Dec., 1951 in Tacoma, Pierce County, WA, USA). Wife (m. 24 Dec., 1918) was Pearl Irene (neé Bliss) Croft (b. 2 Aug., 1896-20 Mar., 1984), mother of William S., Lt. Col. Bliss H. (1921-2009), and Gloria R. (1926-1979).

Henry William "Lee" Croft (Alaskan Gold Rusher, Pacific Coast Heavyweight Boxing Champion (1908-1910), Hotel Croft owner and Pierce County Sheriff, Tacoma, WA, 1942-1950)

Gen. 6: **Edmund John "Ted" Croft** (born 31 May, 1848 at Wooloomooloo Hill Estate, Paddington, Sydney, New South Wales, Australia-died 22 Dec., 1925, in Tacoma, Pierce, WA, USA). On July 5, 1876 in London, England, he married Alice "Mamp" Downing (5 Jun., 1846-20 Dec. 1917), mother of Sydney N. (1877-1941), Edmund J. "Miccie" (1880-1933), Henry W. "Lee", and Jeremiah "Jerry" (1884-1934). Edmund's younger brother **Henry (called Harry) Croft** (b. 15 Jan., 1856-28 Jul., 1917) whose wife was Mary Jean Dunsmuir (b. 11 Feb.,1862 in Nanaimo, British Columbia, Canada- m. 29 Jun., 1885 in Victoria, B.C…and d. 15 Aug., 1928 in Esquimalt, B.C., Canada), and who became a mining magnate, served in the B.C. parliament in 1896 and founded the town of CROFTON, British Columbia, Canada (1902). Harry and Mary Jean had no issue.

Edmund John Croft (U. S. citizen from 1888, Washington State Legislator, 1906)

Gen. 7. **John William Croft** (b. 16 Jul., 1807 in Shoreditch, Middlesex, London, England-d. 3 Jan., 1883, in Aldringham House, near Saxmundham, Suffolk, England). This, of course, is the one-time soldier in Burma, and Australian tycoon whose second wife Mary Ann Stead (b. 21 Feb., 1812 in Islington, Middlesex, London, England- d. 7 Mar., 1857 at Darling Point's Mount Adelaide Estate, Sydney, Australia) whom John Croft married 21 Mar., 1843, in Islington, England, is buried there in Sydney-Newtown's Camperdown Cemetery with four children (of 7, 3 survived: daughter Mary Anne Croft Garrett (b. 12 Feb., 1844 in Paddington, Sydney, New South Wales, Australia-d. 31, Jan., 1897, at Aldringham, Suffolk, England), Edmund John Croft, and Henry Croft (for both of these, see above). John was last married from 1866 to 1874 when his third wife Sarah Louisa Garrett Croft (b. 17 Sep., 1837 in Leiston, Suffolk, England…m. 5 Apr., 1866 at Leiston) died 27 Jan., 1874 at Saddington near Market Harborough, Leicestershire, England at age 36, 10 days after the birth of son Benjamin (cf. p. 267)."

John Croft (Veteran of the First Anglo-Burmese War (1824-1826), then Australian Tycoon (1843-1859), then English Gentleman with two named estates, in Hertfordshire and Leicestershire, England (1860-his death on Jan. 3, 1883). He survived three wives: Mah Men Le in Burma, Mary Ann Stead in Australia, and Sarah Louisa Garrett in England...but left the very large number of biological descendants, 801 of whom (cf. p. 278) in 7 generations across 150+ years have their names listed herein.

CHAPTER SIX: John's Last Years of Life.

John and Sarah Croft, who was largely pregnant and expecting to give birth in only two weeks, had invited most of their family members to a grand post-Christmas celebration on Saturday, December 27th, 1873, at their Dalton House in Saddington, Leicestershire. The parlor featured a grand fir tree decorated with colorful paper streamers and hand-made ceramic pendants and bulbs. At the top was an angel dressed in white and holding a golden cross. The immediate outside surrounding yards were decorated with candy-cane stalks sticking up out of the snow and connected by red and green ribbons.

"Yesterday we got a card in the mail informing us that Norman and Edna Gould are coming to our celebration from the Belmont House in Hoddesdon," said John. "I plan to increase their management payment there from £30/month to £50/month. They've done such a fine job staying on top of needed repairs and keeping the place attractive. We haven't had to deal with any problems at all, and the realtor Robert Flick tells me that the property is clearly continuing its very positive financial appreciation."

"John, don't forget that they have had a son while they've been in charge there," admonished Sarah. I think you should double their money to £60/month. They'll need it."

"You are right, Sarah," agreed John. "And they're bringing the son…whom they've named John after me…with them. He's now two years old, weaned, walking, and talking."

"It's a wonder," said Sarah. "I'll get the ladies to make sure there is a fine present under the tree for him."

"It's too bad Frank and May Garrett and their kids can't make it from their Dinsdale House in Leiston. Daughter May is due to deliver just before Christmas. I sent her back a note saying that we are praying for a safe birth," added John. "They are certainly well blessed with children so far… having FIVE already in seven years and expecting a sixth any day, as, even more, are WE, with our EIGHT including the twins in the same seven years."

"Well," smiled Sarah, "It has been quite a pace of family procreation. I'm still nursing baby Peter and will be nursing a NINTH child before I could possibly get him weaned. And what if it's twins again? My God!"

John just smiled and continued to talk about who was or was not expected to come to Saddington for their post-Christmas celebration.-

A photo portrait of John Croft, Master of Dalton House, Saddington, ca. 1873. From CFA.

"Hyla and Jane Elkington (cf. pp. 96-97) are coming with all five of their children from Birmingham," he said, "You'll have to help me remember the names…another namesake John is the oldest…then Bertha, David, Hyla Junior and…and…"

Sarah helped him, adding "Grace is the youngest, now almost three years old. Since only cousin Barbara (cf. p. 50) is coming from the Rev. Steads (cf. pp. 46-47) in Ovingdean, we're giving her the bedroom next to the stairs which adjoins the three we're giving to Jane and Hyla and the kids. She can be of help to them, as well as to us, in keeping track of all the children. Including ours, there will be two dozen here in all. But seven are those of our Saddington neighbors who don't need bedrooms."

"Do we have gifts for all of them?" asked John.

"We're gotten them all psalm books with their names engraved into a gold gilt cover, saying "From John and Sarah Croft, December 27, 1873," answered Sarah. "These have already been delivered to us and the servants have completed the gift wrapping."

"When I was a kid," commented John, "I would have been happy with a simple rubber ball."

A photo portrait of Sarah Louisa Garrett Croft taken at the same setting (note the chair) as the above photo of her husband John Croft, ca. 1873. CFA.

The Croft family celebration was chaotic, with children running around everywhere, but very joyous. Before the grand afternoon meal, served as a buffet, John gave a short prayer of grace and then raised his flute of champagne and called for a toast. "TO THE CHILDREN" he exclaimed, "May they be long so blessed in their lives hereafter!" The guests all resounded, "HUZZAH!"

That night, when John and Sarah were side by side in their bed, John hugged her and said, "We are now experiencing life as I always dreamed it would someday be. Our blessings very clearly abound, and for that I am grateful to God. But I am also grateful to you, dear Sarah. Without you, I'd still be dreaming. That's for sure. I love you beyond measure."

Sarah answered, "And I love you, John," patted her swollen belly, and fell into a peaceful sleep.

On Friday afternoon the 16th of January, 1874, Sarah's water broke and she went into labor. John, as previously arranged, sent for Dr. Graham Hannity of Saddington to come to Dalton House to attend to the birth. The labor went through the night and into the morning of Saturday, January 17th, when a baby boy, whom John and Sarah had decided they would name Benjamin, was brought into this world.

Dr. Hannity, a handsome man of about 50 years of age, told John that "It all went well. The labor was not the trial some of Sarah's have been in the past and she is now resting comfortably. The baby seems healthy. He's in the bassinet with Mrs. Killick watching him. He's been crying and moving his arms and legs well. I can proceed with the circumcision right away if you wish."

John affirmed "I do," then watched Dr. Hannity perform the circumcision on baby Benjamin, whose crying took on a screaming nature for a minute or two afterwards. John was able then to pick him up for the first time and hold him close, patting his back very gently and murmuring to him "there, there…you'll be all right…let me take you to your Mama."

John took baby Benjamin over to the bed and gave him to Sarah and her maid Laura Killick who helped Sarah wrap the boy in his swaddling clothes. It was then that both Laura and John noticed that the bed sheets under Sarah were stained with an appreciable amount of blood.

John asked Dr. Hannity, "Is this amount of blood normal for a delivery?"

Dr. Hannity said, "It's a tolerable amount. I've seen more or less after the placenta is removed as it is here. The main thing now is for Sarah to get rested. She'll need to start nursing the boy right away…but she knows this well. I have to leave now and get some rest myself. But I'll be by tomorrow to check on her and the baby."

The next day Sarah felt stronger and was encouraged by baby Benjamin's successful session at her breasts. Dr. Hannity observed that the "postpartum hemorrhaging," which he attributed to Sarah's uterus not tightening as it should because of her high number of previous births, was apparently lessening a bit. He wanted Sarah to stay as motionless in bed as she could and try to keep her feet elevated on pillows so that they were higher than her head for a day or two. He also took some time to tightly pack her vagina with gauze to "staunch the flow." She definitely did not like that, but Dr. Hannity insisted that it was necessary. And he told her and John too that this should be her last pregnancy. "It's all about regulating the intimate relations with the menstrual cycle," he suggested.

In THREE days, Sarah said her bleeding had stopped and that she wanted to get out of bed to "get things done, and see to the other children." John and Laura Killick and Dr. Hannity all advised her to stay in bed several more days. Dr. Hannity said she could "take a nice long soak" in a warm bath if she felt up to it, and so she did this, covering herself up to have the other children…Margaret, John Jr., Nellie, the twins Nicholas and Richard, Alfred, and two-year-old Frank…come into the bathroom to "see that she was all right." On her own she removed some of the vaginal packing. But that evening the hemorrhaging clearly increased and Dr. Hannity returned to the house to redo it. "So, it's back to bed for you, dear," he told her.

At six days, Sarah, who was breast-feeding both baby Peter, then just a year old, and the new baby Benjamin, seemed weaker to John. "It's now almost a week since the birth, and you aren't recuperating as we would all like," he told her. "I want to send Laura to London to ask your cousin Elizabeth (cf. p. 67) to come here to consult with Dr. Hannity. She's achieved just renown, you know, as a women's physician and has her own large medical practice there now. Perhaps she knows therapies other than Dr. Hannity's that we might try."

"She's had a child of her own, daughter Louisa, this past 1873 year," said Sarah. "And now, I've heard, she and James are pregnant again. So, she may indeed have some helpful insights."

Early on the morning of Friday, January 24th, 1874, John helped their maid, Laura Killick, board the Saddington train to London. He gave her a letter he had written to Dr. Elizabeth Garrett Anderson and told Laura to "do what you can to convince her to come here right away to help our Sarah."

Laura Killick returned to Saddington the next day, reporting to John, that "Dr. Elizabeth is coming." And, Dr. Elizabeth Garrett Anderson arrived at Dalton House before noon on Sunday, January 26th. With her was a neatly dressed woman of about thirty years of age, a Mrs. Mercy Hadley, whom she introduced as a "wetnurse from our registry," and Mercy's two-year-old son Matthew. "I think you will want to take Mrs. Hadley and Matthew into your household staff, Uncle John," said Dr. Elizabeth. "Her husband is a gunnery officer in Her Majesty's Navy and is somewhere far away for the year or more, and she has nowhere better to live in the meanwhile…and is in need of income. She has weaned her son Matthew here, but is still lactating healthily. She can be of help to you in many other ways as well. I strongly recommend her in this situation. I now employ a wetnurse of my own and without her I wouldn't be able to carry on my medical practice as I do."

When Dr. Elizabeth first saw Sarah in their Dalton House's large bedroom, she immediately sprang to her side and hugged her closely. Then she took Sarah's pulse, asking grimly, "Still bleeding, eh?"

Sarah responded, "Yes. It's a wonder I have any blood left."

In the afternoon after church, Dr. Hannity came for his daily visit. He had heard of Dr. Elizabeth Garrett Anderson, and announced straightaway that he had no objection to women physicians as many of his colleagues did. "I welcome your consultation in this case," he told her when they spoke in private. "I gave her a dose of ergot powder two days ago, and she did not vomit it up or have other adverse symptoms, but the bleeding was not lessened. I just don't know what else we might try. Sarah Croft is getting near the end, I truly fear. Tomorrow will be ten days of hemorrhaging and you know that's a rarely survivable threshold to cross. My feeling is that surgery is not an option here either…any incision will further deplete her critical blood supply. The ether anaesthetic could kill her in such a weakened state."

"My plan is to try a blood infusion," Dr. Elizabeth related. "I have met and studied the work of the London obstetrician Dr. Joseph Blundell, who in 1818 successfully arrested an apparently terminal case of postpartum hemorrhage by injecting four ounces of the woman's husband's blood into her. In the ten years afterwards he recorded five other successful hemorrhage cessations as a result of ten other similar transfusions…that's a fifty-fifty chance of success."

Dr. Hannity commented, "I have heard of this. But whose blood will you use…her husband John's?"

"No," explained Dr. Elizabeth. "My research indicates that the best chances of a blood transfusion working to the patient's benefit is a transfusion from a close blood relative. Sarah and I are first cousins, daughters of full brothers, and are only fourteen months apart in age. I'll transfuse my own blood into Sarah…and twice more than Dr. Blundell's 4 ounces. I have the appropriate syringes and gear here to accomplish this. The addition of my blood will hopefully not only bolster her current weakened supply but aid in her blood's clotting ability as well."

Dr. Hannity rubbed his chin in thought and then said, "That sounds good. How can I help you?"

"Well, you could be the one to use my syringe to suck 8 ounces of my blood out of my arm. That would be of help indeed. I don't fancy having to do that myself."

The transfusion process went smoothly, with Dr. Hannity extracting half a pint of Dr. Elizabeth's blood out of her left arm at the elbow joint. Then Dr. Elizabeth used the same syringe to push much more slowly its blood content into a selected vein in Sarah's left arm. In a half hour, Sarah said she was feeling a bit stronger and Dr. Elizabeth had largely overcome a declared "light-headedness" of her own. Dr. Hannity left Dalton House thinking that Dr. Elizabeth's strategy may have done some good, but Dr. Elizabeth noticed later that evening that Sarah's bleeding had not perceptibly lessened and that Sarah was on the brink of losing conciousness. She did inquire of her cousin about how her babies, Peter and Benjamin, were responding to Mrs. Hadley's attempt to breastfeed them. Dr. Elizabeth assured her that "Both are doing well."

John shared the bed with Sarah for the final time that night. He hugged her close and told her that he loved her as she was going to sleep, but just after midnight he noticed that she was no longer breathing. He jostled her to no response, asking "Are you awake, Sarah? Are you still here?" But Sarah had died and could not stir. He then broke into more than an hour of convulsive sobbing before lighting the candles and getting dressed. He noticed on the bed that Sarah's face had an expression on it that he could only later describe as "calm and serene." Her eyes were closed.

When John told Dr. Elizabeth that morning that his wife, her cousin, Sarah, had passed away during the night, she responded mainly with compassion for him although she used a handkerchief to wipe away her own tears. She said that she wanted to be with him when he told the children. "I'm quite experienced now at telling children about their parents' death."

So at the breakfast table that January 27th morning, John did not say his usual grace, but asked the five of his now nine children who were sitting there (Margaret at almost seven years, John Jr. at almost six years, Eleanor or "Nellie" at five years, the twins Nicholas and Richard at almost four years) to listen to "something important" that their "Aunt" had to say.

Dr. Elizabeth asked the children to put their palms together in prayer and showed them how to do it herself. Then she said, "Children, your mother Sarah has left us and gone to heaven where she will be waiting some day for you. God asked her to come there to help him take care of the children already there. She wants you to know that she loves you all and that you should all do your best to get to heaven where she is so you can see her again. Do you understand this?"

Margaret, the oldest, began to cry and asked John loudly, "Daddy, did Mommy die?"

John answered, "Yes Margaret, she has died."

"Why did she die?"

And John answered according to what Dr. Elizabeth had said, "God needed her in heaven and she went to help him."

"Can you get her back here where we are?" asked Margaret. "We need her here."

Fighting back tears, John answered simply "No, I can't. But I'll do whatever I can to help you live your lives so that you see her again in heaven."

Later, when Dr. Hannity returned to Dalton House to hear the bad news, he told John that he would sign a death certificate listing the cause of death as "postpartum hemorrhage." John was a bit more composed then and was able to express his desire that Sarah be interred in a temporary grave…awaiting him…at St. Peter's at Carlton in Suffolk (cf. p. 95) where he and Sarah had been married in 1866.

When Dr. Elizabeth was preparing to return to London, she asked John if he would indeed add Mrs. Mercy Hadley as a wetnurse for his now motherless nursing babies and as a staff member of his Dalton House household, and John assured her that he would. She then asked, "John, I know your daughter May from your late wife is now married to my cousin Frank Garrett and has had several children already. But what are the other older children doing?"

John answered, "I've now lost THREE wives in my life. In Burma as a young soldier, I married a

Burmese Christian convert I called "Mena." I was only 17 when we married and was just 20 when I lost her when she was only 28 to tropical fever… losing also my adopted daughter "Mimi"…to murderers… and our own son John too, to fever. They are all three buried in Burma. I married Mary Ann Stead here in England in 1843 when I was 35 and took her with me to Sydney, Australia. She died of rheumatic fever at age 45 in 1857, leaving me at age 49 with three children alive from the seven we had together. She and the other four are buried there in Sydney's Newtown Cemetery. And now at age 66 I'm bereft of my third wife Sarah who has just died at age 36 leaving me the eight children we have had together here. My older children are now adults… May, now 30, is, as you say, having children as the wife of your cousin Frank Garrett in Leiston. But son Edmund, called Ted, now 26, has left Cambridge University to roam the world…Europe, Egypt and the pyramids where he was badly bitten by a camel, and through the new Suez Canal back to his birthplace of Australia and also to New Zealand. And son Henry, called Harry, now 18, has finished with honors at Rugby and is enrolled in the Derby School of Mining Engineering."

Throughout the remaining months of 1874, John Croft became problematically "apart" from his accustomed daily house and business dealings as a result of his being unable to recover his equanimity after Sarah's death. He was, in fact, crippled by his grief. For days at a time he did not leave his Dalton House bedroom. He would only get dressed in the late afternoon to come to the main family dinner and say grace for his children, who were tended to in their development by his staff—mainly Mrs. Mercy Hadley, who nursed the babies, Mrs. Anna Smythe, who tutored the preschoolers, and Mrs. Laura Killick who kept track of the older ones' schooling.

John had to be reminded to get his staff properly paid at both his Belmont House estate in Hoddesdon and his Dalton House in Saddington by sending signed drafts to the bank with Belmont House's Norman Gould or Dalton House's Laura Killick. John had to sign special dispensations for them to represent him to the local banks. Two of John's Fleckney Farms' tenants stopped paying their rent and the men who provided the labor for John's own lots in the Fleckney Farms simply stopped working for him as they were not being paid and took jobs elsewhere.

That summer John received a written notice from his stable foreman, Mr. Abel Giddons, informing him that the Fleckney Farms' Croft lots' hay crop for the horses' fodder was not being cut and that they would have to arrange to have others paid to provide it lest their horses start to starve. He ignored this notice until Mr. Giddons came to the house to tell him this in person, whereby John gave him £200 in cash and told him to "take care of it."

At Sarah's funeral service at St. Peter's near the Garrett's Carlton House on Saturday, February 14th, 1874, John struggled through a eulogy stressing how loving and caring Sarah had been to him all their days together and about what a wonderful mother she had been, not only to their eight children together, but also to his older children, especially the sons Ted and Harry as they grew to adults in their home. The gathering in St. Peter's, mostly Garretts, stood up in support when he finished.

On the train back to Saddington, John was dozing a bit in his seat when he suddenly heard Sarah speaking to him, saying "You're on your own now, John. But I want to tell you some things…to help you as I can."

John snapped to full consciousness and, looking around at his fellow passengers, replied aloud, "Sarah, where are you?" One man across the aisle to his left asked, "What? Are you talking to me?"

John nodded negatively to this man and said, "No, excuse me, sir."

Sarah's voice continued clearly then, adding "I'm where you will some day be also, John. Already here I have met your two dear wives past, Mena and Mary Ann. They would like to speak with you also. I hope that is all right with you."

John made a coughing "Harumph!" and answered shortly "It is."

After that the voices of his three deceased wives would come to him unpredictably. And they would respond to his spoken retorts as if they were in his physical presence. They all had various pieces of personal advice to give him. Mah Men Le, whom he called "Mena," told him to send some money to the American Baptist Missionary Union in Boston, Massachusetts', Ford Building, and that he should specify that his donation was to support the development of their Rangoon Baptist College ("The enrollment there will surprise you"). Mary Ann wanted him to send letters to their Australian friends…the Morts, Tooths, and Mannings… And to "Tell our son Teddy to send a letter to his Eton friend Robert Tooth in Sydney congratulating him on his marriage last year to his cousin, Fred's daughter whom you know, Helen Tooth," she said. And Sarah advised John to find a way to invest more of their money into the business of Robert Wright ("The High Quality Homes stock should be at least tripled"), George Cadbury ("The chocolate magnate is doing better now"), and the Elkingtons' gilding business in Birmingham ("Hyla will be of help to you in this, I'm sure"). To these insistent, apparently omniscient, voices, John could only respond with "Yes, dear. I will. Don't worry, I'll do it."

John had only slight reluctance to admit to his friends and relatives…and the children too…that he was carrying on conversations with his deceased wives. And he did really make some efforts to follow their advice. He easily tripled his amount of stock in Robert Wright's High Quality Homes, Ltd., noting that the price per share on the London Stock Exchange had increased from £2 per share to £20 per share from 1863 when he bought 100 shares to this year of 1874 when he purchased another 200 shares for £4000. When he told Robert about doing so on the spoken advice of his dead wife Sarah, Robert asked his wife Caroline if she thought that her "One-time brother-in-law John Croft" had "slipped his tether and needed some medical help."

Both George Cadbury and Hyla Elkington told John that their family businesses were private enterprises and that only the family members held any stock… that their stock was not publicly traded at all. But George Cadbury told him that he appreciated his intention of donating his money to the Cadbury family business and that he would recommend to his brothers that John henceforth be retained as a financial confidant and advisor…and that this was a PAID position. George asked John, "would £100 per quarter be sufficient?" Having heard about this offer, Hyla Elkington offered to recommend John to his brothers to serve in an equivalently paid advisory position with Elkington Gilders, Ltd., adding, "You'll have to make it to Birmingham more now, John."

In the last months of 1874 and first months of 1875, John became more and more withdrawn from his accustomed world of family and business, causing him disapprobation and interpersonal problems of diverse kinds. This was because he was listening to dialogue from the beyond, where his past wives now resided. And it was not only the wives, but his deceased former children too, meaning Mena's twelve-year-old daughter Mi Kaw Le, called"Mi Mi," and their infant son, John Edmund Croft, whom John could only hear to laugh or cry while being held by Mena or Mi Mi. Also being held at different times in these dialogues were his babies with Mary Ann from Australia: the second John, Jr., James Nicholas, Alice Jane, and Alfred.

Once, during a peaceful hour or so in his Dalton House Estate's Carriage House (cf. photo p. 89), John listened to a dialogue in which wife Sarah observed to her companions, "Here we all are in Heaven, the Lord's paradise. I fancy it's because we all lived our lives purely in the Lord's eyes.

None of us ever killed anyone during our lives on earth."

Mena immediately commented, "But John was a soldier in Burma, and he killed countless enemy Burmese soldiers in the war there. He may even have killed my own brother, U Le Byu, who was a leading elephant Mahout for the crazy King Bagyidaw."

Mi Mi added, "And he killed those agents of King Bagyidaw who killed me!"

Mena continued, "So John's killings were righteous killings, of people who were the servants of evil. Such killings in the Bible were forgiven by the Lord upon the perpetrators' repentance so that those who committed these killings were able to be admitted to our company in Heaven. And that's why Mi Mi and I have not seen here in Heaven King Bagyidaw nor any of his soldiers…not my brother U Le Byu… nor any of the King's evil agents."

Mary Ann engaged quickly into this discussion, adding, "John did kill a man during our marriage. It was a deranged criminal named Ian Farley, in our Sydney Mount Adelaide kitchen near Christmas time in 1851. Farley was an embezzler who had become a lunatic in prison and was seeking revenge on John for firing him from his job at

John's workplace. Farley had already killed his wife and her father in the days before he came to our estate to attack us with a knife and kill us. John saved other lives for sure by shooting him dead. The Lord will surely reckon this in his consideration of admitting John to join us here."

Sarah put in: "I'm quite sure that John didn't take anyone's life during the almost 8 years of our marriage…and that he has many times offered the Lord his repentance in prayer for the lives he had to take while he was married to the two of you, Mi Mi and Mary Ann."

At this statement, John told the whole group, "Yes, I have many times asked the Lord for repentance in prayer. Many times."

Also among John's heavenly conversationalists were his older brother John James, who had died of smallpox at age 22 in 1820 when John was 13, and his brother Nicholas, born on 14 January, 1813, who had died in St. Petersburg, Russia, during a cholera epidemic on 7 March, 1845 while he represented Garrett Industries there and was married at that time (m. 16 Sept., 1835 in Moscow's English Church) to still-living in John's acquaintance Caroline Fink Marsow Croft Wright (b. 1807 like John), current wife of Robert Wright (b. 1805), founder of High Quality Homes, Ltd…and step-mother of Robert's son, India service officer

David Wright. David's wife was Caroline's daughter Catherine (b. 22 Sept., 1845 in her mother's hometown of Streletz, Germany), with whom Caroline was pregnant when her husband, John's brother Nicholas Croft, and her first two daughters all died.

In their conversations, John's younger brother Nicholas had with him his two deceased daughters, Mary (b. in Moscow in Fall 1840) and Martha (b. in Moscow in 1843), who had both died of cholera in St. Petersburg before him in March, 1845.

Older brother John James expressed his gratitude to John for providing his widow Elisabeth Wallace Croft with monthly funds from their father Nicholas's estate after his death in 1837, and for helping his daughter Elisabeth with a dowry arrangement enabling her to marry William "Billy" Atkinson in that same year. "You really helped me out in taking care of my widow and daughter, John. And finding a good job for my daughter's husband Billy at Croft Cask, Keg, and Barrel was beyond all expectations."

Brother Nicholas asked John, "Do you remember that tavern fight we got into together back in 1836 before I went to Russia?"

John answered, "Yes, I recall it pretty well. It was essentially an argument about who could swing the tavern's hanging rings onto a nail in the wall. You were uncanny at it and couldn't miss. Our opponents thought you were cheating somehow, but they couldn't really say how. Punches were thrown… and it was just us against five of them."

"That's it," exclaimed Nicholas, "And WE WON IT. You were a wonder to watch in that skirmish to be sure. Two of those guys were left lying on the floor and the others bolted out the door to get away."

"They were drunk, and I had had considerable practice working as a magistrate's apparitor," explained John. "But you more than held your own."

"Girls," said Nicholas to his two little ones, Mary and Martha, whom John could now "see" in his mind as brother Nicholas spoke, "This is your Uncle John. He was my hero when I was your age…and he's still my hero now."

One morning in May of 1875, two of John's young stable hands, the brothers Ralph and James G. Whichelo, came to the Dalton House to report to John that they had seen 75-year-old William Tarrant, one of the Fleckney farm's hay farmers, walking toward his plot carrying a musket. "We think he means to shoot our bull Titan, who has gotten through a gap in our fence into his alfalfa field. He's threatened to do so if we don't fix the fence and keep Titan in our own pasture…and we just haven't had time to get that done."

When John, still in his bedtime bath robe, and the Whichelo brothers got their one-horse flat-bed utility cart to the road gate into Mr. Tarrant's field, they could see that their bull Titan was happily munching Mr. Tarrant's still young crop of green alfalfa in the diagonally opposite corner of his field a quarter mile away. It was easy to see the fence gap only yards from the entry gate through which Titan had entered the field. And half-way to the bull in the center of the field was Mr. Tarrant limping toward Titan with an old military "Brown Bess" flintlock musket.

James jumped from the bed of the cart to open the gate, and Ralph drove the cart through it. From the cart seat John yelled at the top of his lungs, "Bill, don't shoot my bull! Stop where you are!"

In two minutes John and the brothers Whichelo had driven the cart right up to where Mr. Tarrant had stopped. Getting down from the cart seat, John approached him and said, "Bill, just hand me that musket right now. If you don't, the three of us will take it away from you by force. You've only got one shot."

Mr. Tarrant turned the musket directly toward John only steps away and said, “What if I were to just shoot you, John. It’s your bull who is eating and trampling my crop, threatening my livelihood. Your workers can’t seem to get the fence fixed as I’ve asked them repeatedly to do. It’s time now for some more decisive action on the matter.”

John looked with a frown at the two stable hands, but again demanded, “Give me the musket, Bill. I can’t let you kill my bull Titan… He’s a breeding champion worth more than your whole crop. And I’ll pay you for what damage he’s done, anyway. Just hand me the musket.”

But Mr. Tarrant still did not surrender the musket, responding, “I wasn’t planning to kill your bull, John. I’ve loaded the weapon with rock salt chips and shooting him with it would likely teach him a painful lesson about staying out of my field, fence or no.”

At that point John lunged at Mr. Tarrant and grabbed the musket’s long barrel. But the older man was surprisingly strong in trying to wrest it away from John. While they both struggled for control of it, John noticed that the musket’s pan guard had been pushed upwards. So, he gathered up a large gob of saliva in his mouth and spat it onto the skiff of gunpowder on the musket’s flash pan. “You can’t fire it now,” he said with a grimace, “So just let me have it.”

Ralph and James moved in quickly to seize the stubborn old fellow and pry his hands off the musket so John could take it away from him.

“I’ll just be taking this home with me, Bill,” John said, “And I’ll let you have it back after the crop is harvested in the fall. Meanwhile, I’ll ask my fellows here to chase my bull Titan out of your field and fix the fence by the end of the day.”

But Mr. Tarrant answered, “I’m not letting you steal my musket, John. It’s the only protection weapon I have at home. I’ll be seeing the new Sheriff right away about it. He’ll have you taken in for theft, and you’ll wind up paying a fine as well as paying me the cost of damages I reckon to be at least £100.”

THREE days after this disturbing incident, Leicestershire Sheriff Thomas C. D. Whitmore, appointed that March by the Duke of Cornwall’s “pricking” process to serve the 1875-6 term, came at noon to the Dalton House to see John personally. He was wearing his blue uniform coat and had his Sheriff’s badge hanging on a ribbon around his neck. And he had two burly apparitors with him. In the house’s entry Sheriff Whitmore asked John straightaway, “Did you and two accomplices forcibly remove Mr. William Tarrant's musket from his possession and are you keeping it still in your possession here within your premises?"

John, still wearing only his robe over his underwear, answered forthrightly, "Yes, I took Bill Tarrant's musket into my possession…and that took a bit of a struggle. He was going to shoot my prize bull Titan with it for getting into his alfalfa field. I told him he could have it back after the alfalfa was harvested…and that I would pay him for any of the damage done."

"Hmmm. I see. But Mr. Tarrant wants you in jail for theft pending a magistrate's hearing. Do you have a solicitor?"

"I am a licensed solicitor myself," answered John. "And I'm hoping to avoid both jail and a magistrate's hearing. If Bill Tarrant had shot my bull, it's he who would be facing jail and a hearing. My actions indeed prevented such trouble for him. Might you get him to understand this? As for his musket, I'll gladly give it to you right now and you can return it to him immediately instead of his having to wait for harvest time to get it back from me. Maybe that will appease him. What do you think?"

Sheriff Whitmore looked significantly at his two apparitors and said, "That sounds reasonable to me, Mr. Croft. I'll talk to him about it and let you know."

John then turned to the apparitors and said, "I worked as a magistrate's apparitor for a couple of years in Hoddesdon before I was licensed as a solicitor. It was a stressful job to be sure. So I can easily wish you well from that experience."

Sheriff Whitmore then suggested, "If you will retrieve Mr. Tarrant's musket for me right now, I will return it to him and try to convince him to drop his charges against you."

"I've got his musket in our barn. If you'll accompany me there just now, I'll give it to you. Bill told me he had loaded it with rock salt so as not to kill my bull…just wanted to teach it a lesson. I haven't checked the weapon to see if that is so. If it is loaded with rock salt, I'd like to know. It would mean to me that my tenant farmer Tarrant isn't really such a bad fellow…had no intent to kill at least."

Sheriff Whitmore asked, "And what should I tell this tenant farmer of yours you will pay him for your bull's damages to his alfalfa crop?"

"He mentioned £100 to me actually. But I would pay him double that if he agrees to drop his charges against me. That is surely more than the damages actually are, I think you'll agree."

"Before we came to see you, we inspected Mr. Tarrant's field and its now intact fence," explained Sheriff Whitmore. "And I would certainly agree. Your bull didn't eat or trample much alfalfa and even left some fertilizer on the scene to Mr. Tarrant's benefit."

The two apparitors broke into laughter at the Sheriff's description of the "crime scene," but John didn't even crack a smile. His THREE deceased wives had begun to suggest to him courses of remedy for his legal predicament and he was answering them aloud as he walked in his bedtime robe and slippers with the Sheriff and his apparitors to the barn.

"Gumley Hall…the Sheriff is the owner of Gumley Hall in Market Harborough?" John exclaimed at information from Sarah. "So what?"

The Sheriff and the apparitors all looked at each other with quizzical expressions on their faces, but they did not say anything in response as John continued his apparent monologue.

"So the Sheriff's a member of Saddington's just rebuilt St. Helen's Anglican Church? And it has a Baptist chapel attached to it from 1848? So I'm to mention that I was baptized into the Baptist Church in Burma? I don't think so, Mena."

Sheriff Whitmore asked John, "What's that, Mr. Croft? I don't understand…" But John did not answer him and continued to speak as they walked.

"And today, May 26th, is Sheriff Whitmore's 36th birthday? A Captain of the Royal Horse Guards he was? Daughters Mildred and Ethel and a son Francis who will become a soldier too and live to age 90? Our son was at Eton too, and I was also a soldier, Mary? And I should mention that I was wounded in the service of the crown? Likely he wasn't wounded at all as a Royal Horse Guard…unless he fell off a horse."

"Who are you talking to, Mr. Croft?," asked Sheriff Whitmore. "And how do you know these things about me? How could you know it's my birthday today? And about my residence, my church…and my children? And, strangest of all, to say that my three-year-old son Francis will become a soldier and live to the age of 90? How could you possibly know this…HOW?"

John told his wives to "please be quiet," and answered when they had done so, explaining directly to Sheriff Whitmore, "I could tell you I dreamed it, but the truth is that my three deceased wives are, from heaven, suggesting ways to me that I might use these factual commonalities between you and me in order to influence you to decide not to arrest me or have me legally prosecuted for a crime."

The two young apparitors, who had witnessed John's apparent one-way "conversation" with his heavenly wives, looked at each other and shook their heads as if to say, "This guy is definitely a lunatic."

Sheriff Whitmore was clearly disturbed, and said curtly as they arrived at the Dalton House's barn door, "Just get me the musket and we'll get out of here. I think you should see a doctor, but I don't know what kind."

John retrieved the musket for Sheriff Whitmore and watched him and his two apparitors drive away in their jail transport wagon. The next week he drove himself to the Market Harborough jail to sign some papers and remit through the Sheriff to Mr. William Tarrant a check in the amount of £200 for his bull's damages to Tarrant's alfalfa field in the Fleckney Farms tenant lot he rented from John.

In early June of 1875, John's wives informed him of the addition to their relatives in heaven of John's namesake, John Croft Wright, the 11-year-old son of British Foreign Service officer David Wright and his wife Catherine Croft Wright who were living in the British princely state of Rampur in the Uttar Pradesh region of India. He had died tragically in a fall off a horse he was learning to ride. His father, David Wright, an Oxford graduate, had been working as an advisor to the Rampur State's "Nawab," Kalb Ali Khan Bahadur, who ruled under the protection of British Governor-General and Viceroy of India Thomas G. Baring, 1st Earl of Northbrook.

Having received this sad news about a young relative he had never actually met, John took the time to write a note to his daughter May, who had briefly been friends with the boy's mother, Catherine Croft Wright, after her dual marriage to Robert and Caroline's son David in London's German Lutheran Church in April of 1863 (cf. pp. 162-168).

In his note, John wrote: "Dear May…Sarah, your mother Mary, and my first wife Mena in heaven have informed me of the death in India of David and Catherine Wright's son John Croft Wright who died in a fall from a horse this past week. I know that you have been in some correspondence with Catherine and I can only imagine that she will be notifying you of this great sadness by mail soon…"

This message upset May mightily, especially when she did receive in the mail a card from

Catherine in India informing her of her son John's tragic passing. When she asked her husband Frank Garrett about how her father was able to know about the boy's death in India before a letter sent by the grieving mother could so inform her, Frank reminded her of the "existence of telegrams."

Frank told her, "Your Dad is, as a friend and investor in David's father Robert Wright's company, likely privy to information that Robert had already received by telegram from India about his grandson's death. "That has to be it. But I worry about your Dad telling people that he's being informed of such events by his dead wives from heaven. We ought to advise him to stop telling people this right away before it causes real problems for him."

On Thursday, July 8, 1875, John Croft's brother-in-law Hyla Elkington (cf. p. 97), paid a surprise visit to Dalton House and patiently waited until John dressed appropriately and came down to greet him.

"I've been told that you are having some problems in your grieving, John," he said. "Your daughter May told Jane that you are telling people that you are talking with your wives who have passed. Is this true?"

John answered firmly, "Yes, it is. I didn't make them up. They contact me give me advice and information."

"Hmm, I see," said Hyla, nodding his head negatively. "And people at large, as well as neighbors and family, are saying that you rarely leave your bedroom…not the best way to have a hand in raising your children. I know you aren't going to church, and that your servants are taking the children to Sunday School for you. You aren't paying your bills or your staff promptly, and you've had some troubles with your tenants…and even the Sheriff. This kind of news, unfortunately, spreads far and wide, independent of your intent. I've come to tell you that you have to get this situation under control right soon. I've come here to help you if you'll let me."

John frowned severely and answered, "How will you do that?"

"I'd like to provide you with some simple distraction from your grief, which has turned pernicious on you now."

"Distraction? What kind of distraction?"

"I want you to return with me tomorrow by train to our Newhall Street electro-plating factory in Birmingham. On the way there we can talk about anything else but your dead wives. Jane and I and the children will do our best to host you in our home as family while you stay with us. And at the office there you can give me and my brothers investment suggestions as we will now be paying you quarterly to do."

"I don't want to be a bother to Jane and the children," John answered. "And I can just send my financial advice to you by mail."

"I think it's important that you get out of your house and come with me to Birmingham, John. We're having an interesting event you might enjoy…a visit from the Sultan of Zanzibar…definitely not something you might experience every day."

John was indeed struck by Hyla's mention of this "interesting event," and asked, "Zanzibar? Isn't that an island off the east coast of Africa in the Indian Ocean? Why would their Sultan want to come to Birmingham? Who is he anyway?"

"Sayyid (Sultan) Barghash bin Said al-Busaidi is just 39 years old, and is the son of the Omani Sultan and an Ethiopian concubine. He succeeded his older brother Majid as the Zanzibar Sultan after Majid's death in 1871, and agreed upon our British demand to abolish, with our naval help, Zanzibar's lucrative slave trade two years ago in 1873. So to us he's a kind of hero."

Barghash bin Said al-Busaidi, Sultan of Zanzibar (b. 1836, ruled 1871-d. 1888). From Wikipedia.

"But why does he want to visit Birmingham?"

"A delegation of our diplomats and interpreters will bring him to our gilding factory on Saturday morning. He wants to have the plaster death masks of his father and brother gilded in gold. And we will do this for him as he watches the process. So,

I plan to present you to him personally as one of our 'financial advisors.' I know you've met many important people in your life, but have you ever before been presented to an actual head of state?"

John became thoughtful and answered, "No, I haven't. And I didn't imagine I ever would."

"Well, this is your once-in-a-lifetime chance. Are you with me?" asked Hyla encouragingly.

John made up his mind and complimented Hyla with his response, "Hyla, I'd follow you anywhere. Count me in. I'll gladly come with you to meet the Sultan of Zanzibar in Birmingham."

So, John's trip to Birmingham was a success in many ways…not the least of which was his agreeing, at Hyla and Jane's ardent request, to strongly request his dead wives to leave him alone in his travail…and to stop telling others about his communication with them. And, on Saturday, July 10, 1875, at 11:00 am, in the Newhall Street Factory, he bowed deeply to Barghash bin Said, the Sultan of Zanzibar, as Hyla presented him as "Mr. John Croft, Esquire, Gentleman, Solicitor, and the Elkington's 'financial advisor'.

An unknown artist's sketch of the Sultan of Zanzibar (taken aback on the right, with John Croft holding his arm) witnessing the Elkingtons' Electro-plating process in Birmingham on July 10th, 1875. From CFA.

Here, from the *South Wales Daily News* article entitled "*The Visit of the Sultan of Zanzibar to Birmingham*" (author unnamed) of 10th July, 1875 (cf. www. 925-1000. com) are excerpts concerning the Sultan's visit:

"On Saturday, the Seyyid of Zanzibar visited the famous silver and electro-plate works of Messrs Elkington & Co. in Newhall-street. His Highness was accompanied by his suite and Alderman Biggs (ex-mayor), Dr. Badger, Dr. Kirk (agent and Consul-General at Zanzibar), and Mr.

Clement Hill (Foreign Service attache)…A large number of persons awaited the arrival in front of the works, and greeted the Seyyid with a hearty cheer as the carriages drew up before the portico entrance. Passing up the noble staircase, with an imposing array of bronze figures and statues of the Kings of England on each side, the distinguished visitors were ushered into the show rooms. The sight which meets the eye on entering this spacious apartment is most striking….Time would only permit of a cursory glance at the most prominent things, and the chief features were pointed out to His Highness through Dr. Badger, who interpreted to the Seyyid…There were also a large number of beautiful and useful articles in the course of manufacture for the use of his Royal Highness the Prince of Wales during his tour of India. Glancing at cases filled with silver and gold cups, dessert services, and other ornamental articles of electroware, including a splendid service, after the style of the one made for the King of Siam, the Seyyid passed by a covered way to the various workshops of the manufactory. He appeared much interested by the electro-depositing process. In the room where this process is conducted are large vats, and one of the largest electro-magnetic machines in England. The enormous strength of the machine was shown by the burning of thick iron and copper wire, at which the Seyyid was highly amused, for he laughed heartily when he saw the effect (see illustration above) produced by the connection of the wire with the battery…On reaching the department where plating and gilding are conducted, the Seyyid was shown the process, and His Highness gilded several coins of the realm, in the same vat in which a vase was gilt by the Princess of Wales. He took the coins away with him, and was so delighted with this process that he remained some time watching the gilding operations, and on leaving the department he exclaimed to Dr. Badger that Birmingham was like 'Bir-Minham' in Arabic, which Dr. Badger explained was the Seyyid's meaning to express that Birmingham was a source of great wealth. The party then returned to the show-room, where, in addition to the coins which he had gilt, a copy of Messrs Elkingtons' Fine Art Catalogue was presented to the Seyyid. He then wrote his name, 'Barge-hash-bin-Said,' in Arabic characters in the visitors' book, and Dr. Badger, Dr. Kirk, Mr. Hill, and Alderman Biggs (and John Croft…LBC) also entered their names. The Seyyid, before departing, expressed himself highly gratified with his visit."

When John and Hyla were riding back to the Birmingham railroad station, Hyla asked John if he would also accompany him to Leiston to attend a meeting with May and Frank Garrett and the lawyers James Parkinson Taylor and Edward Hoare of the London firm of Taylor, Hoare, Taylor, and Box. "We hope you will assent to our establishment of some kind of guardianship of your financial estate, threatened as we all think it is by the recent deterioration of your mental condition."

This request angered John appreciably, and he said, "Hyla, I understand that you, as my brother-in-law and friend, have only my best interests at heart. That is why I have agreed to your insistence that I curtail my communications with my wives and cease mentioning them to others. But this simply goes too far. There is nothing wrong with the state of my finances. My management of them is still such that you and your brothers are paying me to advise on the status of your own financial management. Just yesterday I advised your board members to invest in Robert Wright's High Quality Homes Ltd.…an investment which has tripled in value for me in the past ten years."

"Your financial estate may be increasing in value, but you are not responsibly paying your growing number of bills: groceries and home maintenance supplies and animal feed, school expenses and university tuition, church tithes…even your subscriptions to newspapers and journals have elapsed. Nor are you paying even your estate staff in a timely fashion. A competent financial guardian would take care of these disbursements for you… and you wouldn't have to worry about who may be bringing suit against you," Hyla then invited, "So let's go to Leiston together and draw up a guardianship. I assure you that both your family and your trusted attorneys strongly recommend this now before things get any worse."

"Hyla," answered John most firmly, "I will be going directly back to Saddington and home. NO ONE BUT ME is going to manage my finances. Tell that to Frank and May and the lawyers."

A photograph of John Croft from 1875. From CFA.

On Tuesday afternoon, July 13, 1875, a pair of strong young apparitors appeared at the door of

Dalton House and demanded to see "Mr. John Croft, Esquire, Gentleman of the Residence."

It took twenty minutes for John to come to the front door to meet his "visitors." He was still wearing his bedtime robe and slippers. Yet he asked forthrightly, "What can I do for you young fellows?"

The lead apparitor answered, "You can sign this form indicating your receipt of a subpoena we are serving you with which requires your personal presence at a Court of Lunacy hearing in the Hoddesdon courthouse at 11:00 am on Wednesday, July 21st, of this year. If you do not sign, we are to physically arrest you and transport you to the Market Harborough jail for further processing."

John exclaimed, "Me!? To a Court of Lunacy?! Who is ordering such a travesty?"

The apparitor answered, "The subpoena names the UK's Lord High Chancellor Hugh Cairns and his appointed Commissioner of Lunacy, Lord Anthony Ashley Cooper, the 7th Earl of Shaftesbury. They are the responsible parties, but your case will be heard by Inner Temple Barrister Samuel Warren, who is one of their registered 'Masters in Lunacy.' He will be adjudicating your case at this hearing. Documents and personal affidavits will be placed in evidence for your response."

At this, the other apparitor said, “We hope that you, sir, will sign our form. We don’t really want to place you under arrest.”

So John invited the apparitors inside, escorted them to his office room, picked up a feather pen on the desk, dipped it into the inkwell, signed the attestation of his subpoena receipt, and gave it back to them.

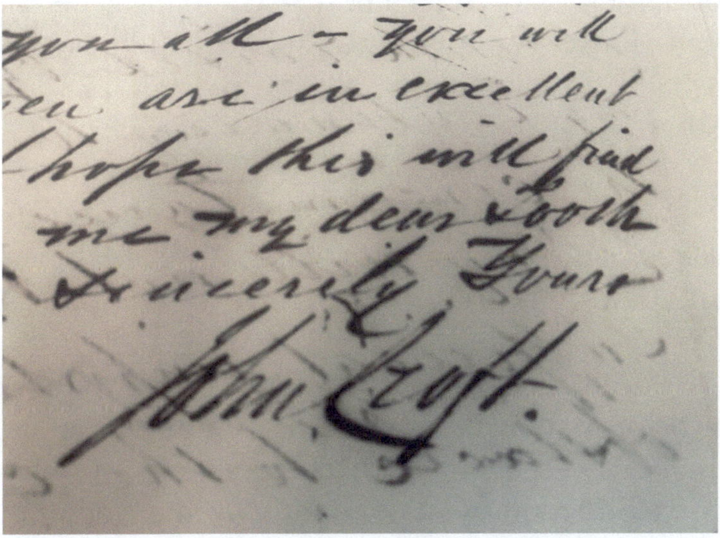

A sample of John Croft’s handwriting (to family friend - “I hope this will find me my dear (Robert Lucas) Tooth”), and signature in 1880), from CFA.

Despite the subpoena, John did not go to the Court of Lunacy in Hoddesdon on the 21st of July, but he took the precaution of escaping instead to his Belmont House closer to the Lunacy Court in Hoddesdon after sending a courier to inform his senior solicitor, James Parkinson Taylor, of his situation. He told his Belmont House managers, Norman and Edna Gould, not to tell anyone else about his presence there, and was pleased that in the week after the 21st of July no authorities had come there seeking him.

On Sunday afternoon, August 15th, 1875, Solicitor James P. Taylor came to see John at his Belmont House. With him was John's daughter May's husband, Frank Garrett, Sr (cf. p. 207, 228, 245, 260).

"James," asked John right away after greeting the men and shaking their hands, "What happened at my lunacy hearing?"

"Well, you've been declared a **lunatic in absentia and you're now being sought as a fugitive**," answered James. "But Frank and I think we can avoid having you committed to the Bedlam lunatic asylum in Southwark. All you have to do is sign some documents we've brought with us."

Drawn by Tho. H. Shepherd. Engraved by J. Tingle.

NEW BETHLEM HOSPITAL, ST. GEORGE'S FIELDS.

Southwark, London's, "Bedlam Lunatic Asylum" in 1828, from Wiki.png.

"What documents are those?" asked John, looking at both men with a serious frown.

James concisely related: "The documents attest that you will immediately transfer the control of your financial estate…**all** your funds and holdings whatsoever and wherever…to your son-in-law Frank Garrett. To accomplish this you will agree to put both your present estates up for sale by auction, and you and your minor children will take up residence in the household of Frank and May Garrett. They are promising to acquire or build an estate residence large enough to make this feasible."

John was outraged and said, “There’s no way I’ll agree to that. Whoever ordered this is the lunatic here, not me.”

But James remained calm, and replied, “Let me read to you the official order of the Lunacy Court’s presiding Master, Samuel Warren.”

John answered, “This is that same Samuel Warren who wrote the book, *Ten Thousand a Year,* back in 1840 or so? I’ve read it and think it evidence that he is himself indeed a lunatic. His main character in it, a forger and fraud trying to claim a vacant earldom, he gives the name ‘Titbat Tiddlemouse.’ That should have gotten him committed to the Bedlam asylum long ago.”

Portrait of Samuel Warren (1807-1877) by John Linnel, ca. 1865. From Wikipedia.

"I assure you that Samuel Warren is adjudicating this matter soundly," continued James. "Even charitably, given the evidence considered."

Frank Garrett put his hand assuringly on John's shoulder and added, "Let's listen to the man's official decision."

James held the document in his hands and began: "It is dated and filed on the 12th of August 1875 in the matter of *John Croft, a person of unsound mind.* It reads: 'To the Right Honourable, the Lord High Chancellor of Great Britain… Whereas by an order made on the 21st day of July, 1875, the custody regulation, occupation, disposition and receipt of the Estate of the said lunatic have been committed and granted to Frank Garrett of Leiston Works in the County of Suffolk, Engineer. And whereas by my certificate made in this matter on the 29th day of July 1875 I directed that the said Frank Garrett in lieu of giving security by bond with sureties as the Committee of the Estate of the said lunatic was to be at liberty to transfer into Court to the Credit of the matter of 'John Croft, a person of unsound mind,' to an account to be entitled 'Security Account to the Committee of the Estate' the sum of £4000 new £3 per cent Annuities. 1) Now I certify that the said Frank Garrett has as appears by the Office copy Certificate of the Paymaster General dated the 5th day of August, 1875, which has been produced before me, transferred into Court to the credit of 'John Croft, a person of unsound mind,' 'Security Account of the Committee of the Estate' the said sum of Four Thousand pounds new Three pounds per cent Annuities pursuant to my said Certificate. 2) And I further certify that the security of the said Frank Garrett and the grant to him of the Custody of the Estate of said Lunatic are completed. All which I humbly certify to your Lordship'. This certificate was addressed to Great Britain's Lord High Chancellor Hugh Cairns, but it was sent through Commissioner in Lunacy, Anthony Ashley-Cooper."

Realizing his son-in-law Frank Garrett's willingness to post a large financial security bond of Garrett Industries stock in his behalf and to provide him with another place to live, John was abashed. He asked, "who thought of all this?"

Frank answered, "It was mostly May's idea… with the help of Hyla and Jane Elkington…and James P. here, of course. It was he who suggested this course of action to Samuel Warren in chambers. And Samuel Warren then decided the matter in our favor, despite credible affidavits prescribing your immediate committal. And you should know that we have strategies in mind so that you will recover your financial control in a year or two…and our real estate master Robert Flick thinks you will be able to avoid selling your estates too. Only will you and the children have to live with us for a while. May and I have got our eyes on a house in Aldringham that should be large enough for this purpose."

James Taylor added, "All you have to do is sign the papers we have with us now. We'll take care of the rest. It is our belief that you will regain your soundness of mind in a short time while you get the better of your troublesome grief. When this is clearly demonstrable we'll get you back in control of all your accumulated wealth."

A photo of Frank Garrett, Sr. (1845-1918) at 30 years of age in 1875, from CFA

Your author (LBC) did some research in 2018 to impart an appreciation to the readers of Frank

Garrett's provision of a security bond worth £4000 in appreciating stock. According to Eric Nye, a currency researcher at the University of Wyoming in the USA (cf. uwyo.ed/numimage/currency), 4000 British pounds in 1875 had the purchasing power (salary, real estate, etc.) equivalent to $406,482.32 2018 United States' dollars. My thought is that Frank Garrett should have been nominated for son-in-law of the century!

Frank Garrett's strategy to avoid the sale by auction of John' s two estate properties involved his arranging with Messers Fisher and Sons, prominent realty auctioneers, to sell John Croft's properties at auction…and to schedule such auctions. The auctions' sale advertisements and prospectuses date from 1876 to 1881 and mention a property "overseer" at Saddington of one "J.G. Whichelo" (cf. pp. 312-313). But although these advertisements and prospectuses were sent to the Court of Lunacy as evidence that John Croft's designated property custodian Frank Garrett was complying with the terms of John's signed agreements with the Court to sell these properties, he was able through registered real estate appraiser Robert Flick to register an auction *reserve price* with Messers Fisher and Sons that was well beyond what any sane bidder would offer. These reserve prices were £48,000 for the Belmont House property in Hoddesdon, Hertfordshire, and £58,000 for the Dalton House and Fleckney Farms property in

Saddington, Leicestershire (cf. p. 86). Samuel Warren, the Lunacy Master of the Court in John's case, died in July 1877, and the Court's jurisdiction area was thereafter changed, occasioning some lack of enforcement continuity that was beneficial to John. Frank successfully petitioned the successor court in January 1879 to return to a "clearly recovered from his unsoundness of mind" John Croft direct personal control of his finances. And later that same year Frank was able to recover control of his appreciated to £4240 worth of his Garrett Industries company stock. Frank made mention to others that the total worth of John's financial holdings had increased markedly in value during Frank's court-mandated management of them, though John claimed that he had made the key profitable investment decisions that enabled the increase even while Frank was his money's "court custodian."

It took a year for Frank and May Croft Garrett to complete the purchase for £27,000 of the deceased Lord Rendlesham's Aldringham House Estate in 1876. So John Croft's life in Saddington's Dalton House was still occasionally awkward financially as Frank Garrett's accountants started paying his bills. But when the Aldringham House was at last remodeled and ready in May 1876, John, his children and most of his Saddington household staff, including stable foreman Abel Giddons, cook Beatrice Stamper, household staff head, Laura Killick, the tutor Anna Smythe, the nanny Mercy Hadley, and eight male resident stablemen and shop hands. Fortunately, John's mental state during all the tribulations of such a distant and large-scale house move, definitely improved after he regained control of his money in 1879 even though he was also saddened severely by the loss of his twin son Nicholas to scarlet fever in September of that year.

Even after John regains active control of his money at age 72 in 1879, he still continued to reside at Aldringham anyway. This was because of his clear realization that, due to his daughter May's wonderful role in the care and upbringing of his children there, he would be setting them all back in life if he returned them to his sole care of them in the Dalton House in Saddington. No matter that he thereafter listed Belmont House in Hoddesdon as his address…he and his children with Sarah Louisa Garrett Croft actually resided in the Aldringham House near Saxmundham and the Garretts' historic Carlton House Estate. At Aldringham House he had a first floor bedroom, his own toilet room, sat at the head of the table at all family meals, and was regarded by all…that is, by Frank and May and by what by the time he moved into Aldringham House in mid 1879 were **SIXTEEN** Garrett (9) or Croft children (7), as a kind of "Pater Familias."

Through the law firm of Taylor, Hoare, Taylor, and Box, John Croft wrote his will in November

1879, two months after the death of his son Nicholas. A copy of his will, hand-scribed by law clerk William Box, currently resides in the camphorwood trunk (cf. p. 240-2) that John Croft purchased in Australia in the 1850s and gave to his son Edmund J. "Ted" Croft when he went off to Cambridge University in September of 1866. Below is a photograph of a copy of this will on top of this same 170-year-old trunk now sitting in my (LBC's) home office in Phoenix, Arizona, USA, in this year of 2023:

*A hand-scribed copy of John Croft's will on the family's camphorwood trunk. Inscriptions read from the top: "Dated 11th November 1879. Copy... **WILL** of John Croft, Esq. Taylor, Hoare, Taylor & Box, 28 Great James Street, Bedford Row W6."*

The will begins traditionally with "I, John Croft of Belmont House, Lord Street, Hoddesdon in the County of Hertford Esquire hereby revoke all Wills, Codicils and other testamentary dispositions heretofore made by me and declare this to be my last Will and Testament..." He then bequeaths £2000 each to his children with wife Mary Ann Stead Croft..that is to his daughter Mary Anne and sons Edmund and Henry. He then appoints his estate's executors with collective power of decisions concerning his residual financial estate. These are FOUR: Sons Edmund and Henry Croft, son-in-law Frank Garrett, and "Hyla Elkington of Selby Oak near Birminham in the County of Warwick, Esquire." Each of the four trustees is to receive £100 per annum as long as they serve.

John does not forget his promise to his deceased older Sister Surrey Martha Croft Metcalf to "take care" of her son, his nephew Thomas Edmund Metcalf (cf. p.190). He bequeaths to him "and his wife and children (if any at the time of my death) the sum of £100 per annum paid quarterly in March, June, September, and December," but only

IF said Thomas Edmund Croft "has not then been outlawed nor become an uncertificated bankrupt."

John appoints his daughter Mary Anne "May" Garrett to be the legal guardian of any of his minor children who survive him. He also specifies conditions under which his appointed executors may be discharged of their duties to serve, and that it is the responsibility of the other executors to decide if the discharged executor be replaced or not, and, if so, by whom. A discharge may be given to executors who die, move to reside abroad, become bankrupt, or criminal, or are (as he had been four years before) declared lunatics.

Here is the last known photograph of JOHN CROFT, from CFA…taken at Aldringham House (cf. p. 269) on his 75th birthday, July 16th, 1882, after he had taken back control of his finances and written his will. He dies at the Aldringham House the next year on 3 January, 1883 (cf. pp. 286-7), after a short illness, listed on his death certificate as pneumonia. He was 75 years, 6 months and 18 days old, an age I (LBC) passed as I was writing this, the last of three volumes of his eventful biography.

A photo of John Croft on his 75th Birthday, July 16th, 1882, taken at Aldringham House. From CFA.

And below is a photograph taken by Lesley Hoyt Croft in May 2019 of me (her husband and the author Lee B. Croft) with cousin Margaret Young at the grave of our mutual great great grandfather, JOHN CROFT in the Aldringham House adjoining cemetery of St. Peter's Church…his funeral site on 10 January, 1883…near Aldeburgh in Suffolk in sight of Carlton Hall, where he is interred with his last wife, Sarah Louisa Garrett Croft, and their nine-year-old son Nicholas Croft…and only a few steps away from the grave of Margaret's triple-great grandfather Richard Garrett III (1807-1866) and his wife Elizabeth Dunnell Garrett (1806-1884).

Author Lee B. Croft and cousin Margaret Young at John and Sarah Louisa Garrett Croft's (and twin son Nicholas Croft's) grave at St. Peter's Church Cemetery near Saxmundham, Suffolk. Photo by Lesley Hoyt Croft.

The inscription on John's side of this gravestone reads: "In Loving Remembrance of JOHN CROFT of Dalton House, Saddington, Leicestershire, formerly of Mount Adelaide, Sydney, New South Wales, born July 16th, 1807, died January 3rd, 1883. '*There remaineth therefore a rest to the peo-*

ple of God.' Hebr. 4:9 vrs'." On the other side is "In Loving Remembrance of Sarah Louisa, Second Daughter of Richard Garrett of Carlton Hall and the Lamented Wife of John Croft, of Dalton House, Saddington, who died January 27, 1874, aged 36 years. '*In Thy presence is fullness of joy. Psalm XVI.ii.'."* And on the triangular west end of the grave's top is the inscription: "*Also Nicholas, son of John and Sarah Louisa Croft, born 23 May, 1870, died 7 September, 1879."*

CHAPTER SEVEN: Family Stories After John Croft's Death.

After her father John Croft's death in 1883, Mary Anne "May" Croft Garrett gave birth to two more children: a daughter named Mary Garrett who was tragically born and died on the same day, December 14th, 1883, and a son four years later, Victor Richard Garrett, on October 21st, 1887. "Mother May" was highly esteemed not only by her large number of Croft-and-Garrett family members and their relatives, but by the entire community centered around the city of Leiston in Suffolk near the Garrett Industries "Long Shop."

When May died on 31 January, 1897, Frank Garrett, Sr. and everyone he knew were deeply grief stricken. She was unanimously revered for her caring nature and her constant encouragement and inspiration of them all. So Frank took an idea that he had long admired from his deceased father-in-law, John Croft, who, forty years before in 1857, had paid for the creation of a stained glass window memorializing his wife, May Garrett's mother Mary Ann Stead Croft, in Sydney, Australia's, St. Andrew's Cathedral. So Frank asked several experts in the field of this art who was "the number one man in stained glass church windows," and was most often given the name of CHARLES EAMER KEMPE (cf. pp. 76-7), since John Hardman Powell had died in 1895 (cf. p. 99 and pp. 194-5).

Charles Eamer Kempe (b. 29 Jun., 1837-d. 29 Apr., 1907) was a wonderful and prolific (his stu dio produced over 4000 stained glass windows) master of the stained glass art and he had a very grand home called "The Old House" in Lindfield near the Kemp family mansion called Ovingdean Hall in Ovingdean near Brighton in East Sussex where the Rev. Alfred Stead, Mary Ann Stead Croft's brother, had served as St. Wulfran's Church rector from 1844 to his death in 1889. Charles Kempe had decorated St. Wulfran's Church ceiling years before. As a child he had been in Sunday

School classes at St. Wulfran's with Rector Alfred Stead's eldest daughter and May's first cousin, the one-year-younger-than-he Emma Barbara Stead (cf. p. 50), *whom two-years-a-widower Frank Garrett married in London* on Saturday, April 15th, 1899, to the consternation of some of the Garrett's family (notably May's youngest son Victor).

This is a photo of Frank Garrett, Sr., after his April 15, 1899 marriage to Emma "Barbara" Stead (18 Jul., 1838-21 Dec., 1916). From CFA. See other photos of him on pp. 207, 228, 246, 261, and 339.

Charles Kempe was a strange man with an interesting biography. He added the "-e" to the end of his name to differentiate himself from his father's other "Kemp" family members, who were highly privileged members of English society. He shares a gravestone with his father in St. Wulfran's Church cemetery (where also is the grave of my (LBC's) triple great grandfather James Stead) that labels him "…Charles Eamer, Fifth Son of Nathaniel Kemp," omitting Charles's preferred spelling of the family name.

And Charles had a Latin motto: "*Qui seminant in lacrymis in exultatione metent*" ("They that sow in tears shall reap in joy"). He was an admirer of the early Welsh-born, Cambridge educated, religious poet George Herbert (1593-1633), who wrote: "A man who looks on glasse,/ On it may stay the eye:/ Or, if he pleaseth, through it passe,/ And then the heav'n espie." I have included here, on p. 76, a photo of Charles Eamer Kempe. But other photos of him, despite his fame, are quite hard to find. The only other later photos of him that I can find are in the recently published books about him and his studio's work by the wonderful stained-glass art scholar Adrian Barlow. These books are: The Life, Art and Legacy of Charles Eamer Kempe (2018) and Espying Heaven: The Stained Glass of Charles Eamer Kempe and His Artists (2019), both published by the Lutterworth Press of Cambridge, England.

Money was no object of concern for Frank Garrett, and so in 1899 Charles Kempe agreed to design, create, and place in Leiston, Suffolk's, St. Margaret of Antioch Church's east window an unparalleled stained glass window wherein 12 female saints are depicted with symbols of their lives' achievements…AND EACH SAINT IS GIVEN THE FACE (taken from photographs given to Kempe from different stages of her life) of MARY ANNE CROFT GARRETT.

I know of no other such stained glass achievement. It is simply unprecedented and magnificent. In studying the stained-glass art form while considering the windows dedicated to my great grandmother Mary Anne Croft Garrett (d. 1897) and her mother Mary Ann Stead Croft (d. 1857) by their grieving husbands, I have come to appreciate the beauty and depth of feeling these works evoke. And, though I admire Adrian Barlow's work, I can't help but be disappointed that Charles Eamer Kempe's Window of the Women Saints in St. Margaret Church in Leiston, Suffolk, is NOT MENTIONED among the hundreds treated and cited in his two recent books, nor is it listed in Kempe's otherwise impressive Wikipedia entry which Barlow's work clearly informs. This is an informational injustice I am trying here to correct. Let me show you in pictures the representational aspect of Kempe's St. Margaret Church window…a specific example of the facial likeness of Mary Anne Croft Garrett to the window panel representing St. Felicitas. First, here is the window itself.

Photo by author Lee B. Croft of St. Margaret of Antioch Church's stained-glass window by Charles Eamer Kempe and dedicated to the memory of Mary Anne Croft Garrett by the donation of her husband Frank Garrett, Sr.

First, notice that there are five columns of depictions of religious figures below the top "tracery" defining the shape of the window. The center column shows a haloed Jesus Christ, shown as the King of Heaven. The outside columns on each side show three "martyred women saints," who died because they faithfully abided by Christ's example of how to live in order to get to Heaven and live with him…three on each outermost column above an angel holding a message. Charles Kempe knew each of these martyred saints' stories from his religious education and his personal study. Now I can find these stories simply by typing their names in the Google search field. They are, from top left, up to down in each—SS. Apollonia, Perpetus, and Dorothy, then Margaret, Cecilia, and Euphemia, then across the center column Katherine, Lucy, and Agnes, and then in the right-side column Agatha, Prisca, and Felicitas.

When he rendered each one, Charles included in his "cartoon" (the term for the window's design sketch) a facial likeness of May Garrett from one of the many photos of her that her husband Frank

Garrett had sent to him. Let's see what kind of job he did in this. First here is the bottom right panel with the angel's message dedicating the window to Mary Anne Garrett, saying "Especially for Thy servant Mary Anne Garrett, who entered into rest 31st Jan: 1897, in whose memory this window is dedicated."

In this entire window's art you can notice Kempe's "trademark" peacock feathers, twinkling stars, his pelican, and his characteristic shock of wheat (at very top) in the tracey above…showing to the world his "signature." But just above this angel's message is the panel showing the signs and symbols of the oldest of the martyrs, St. Felicitas of Rome (b. ca. 101 AD-d. ca. 165 AD…reign of Marcus Aurelius, trial by prefect Publius). I conjecture that this likeness comes accordingly from a photo of Mary Anne taken later in her life…at an age Kempe thought might approximate that of St. Felicitas…who was executed because she refused to repudiate her Christian faith despite the torture to death of her SEVEN sons before her eyes. Her symbol is the sword she holds, representing the one that enabled her to join her executed sons in heaven. Seven little crowns dangle from the "Crown of Life" at the point of the sword. Here is the panel representing St. Felicitas of Rome. Focus your attention on her face.

This close-up photo of the bottom female martyr, St. Felicitas, was taken by author Lee B. Croft in May 2019 at St. Margaret of Antioch Church in Leiston, Suffolk, England.

Now here is a photograph of Mary Anne Croft Garrett when she was getting a little older in her life…this from the collection of my cousin Margaret Young. Be sure to compare her face…also looking to the left in this photo…to the face of Charles Eamer Kempe's St. Felicitas above.

I think that you will agree with me that THIS is the VERY PHOTO Charles Eamer Kempe used to depict St. Felicitas in Mary Anne Croft Garrett's Memorial Window of the Women Saints in St. Margaret Church in Leiston, Suffolk, England. The St. Margaret Leiston window is a work of both passion and world-order genius and deserves more prominent mention in the scholarship on such art.

The probate records show John Croft's personal estate at his death amounted to £29,505, but was resworn by his estate executors in March of 1884 at £41,505 well after the estate's proceeds were being distributed to the specified heirs. But this did not include the sales of the Belmont House estate, which brought in an additional £12,000 later in 1884, or the Dalton House and Fleckney Farm property, which added another £26,500 (cf. p. 86) in 1886. The main task of the four executors after John's death in 1883 was to see to it that John and Sarah Garrett Croft's 6 surviving children were well educated in the most prestigious places and were able to marry and start families in fine homes without financial difficulty. John's will mentioned his concern that his children with Sarah Garrett Croft and daughter May's children with Frank Garrett should be raised without financial differences, and the executors were committed to making that happen.

The four executors of John Croft's will communicated by mail, even though by the 1880s the two Croft executors, eldest son Edmund or "Ted" and Henry or "Harry" were no longer in England. They separately emigrated…Ted to the United States and Harry to Canada. Even though their father's will stated that executors who "moved to reside abroad" *may* be discharged of their responsibility, the "Garrett aligned" executors (Frank Garrett, Sr. and Hyla Elkington) and the Croft aligned executors (Edmund and Henry Croft) continued to operate as a group through their mail communications. When Hyla Elkington died in 1901, they decided not to name a replacement executor. And they did not name a replacement executor when Harry Croft died in British Columbia in 1916. So when Frank Garrett, Sr. died in 1918, Edmund "Ted" Croft was the only executor left to make continued decisions about what to do with the still considerable remainder of his father's money. He then became the main beneficiary, having the remaining funds deposited into his own U.S. bank accounts where he would use the money to support his own lifestyle and the lives of subsequent generations of his family members.

Edmund Croft (cf. p. 285-6 with photo) was my own (author LBC's) paternal great grandfather. After he and his wife Alice Downing Croft, called in the family "Mamp," came to the United States with their infant son Sydney Nicholas in 1878, they first settled in the town of Micanopy, the oldest inland settlement in the State.

This, from CFA, is a 1916 photograph of Alice Downing Croft, called "Mamp" (b. 5 Jun., 1846, m. in London on 5 Jul., 1876, d. 23 Dec., 1917)

Ted and Mamp always called their second son, born there in Micanopy and baptized "Edmund John," "Miccie" or even "Mike," after this place. But it was too hot and humid for them and they soon moved diagonally across the entire country to the Washington Territory, where they lived in several locales. Their third son Henry William., called "Hal" or "Lee," (b. 1882) and fourth son Jeremiah, called "Jerry," (b. 1884) were born in the hamlet of Boisfort ("Baw Faw") Prairie when Washington was not yet a state. In 1883 Edmund used his inheritance money to buy a large plot of land in the state of Oregon close to the coast. This plot of land bordered a lake now called Croft Lake, likely because of his one-time ownership. He subdivided the property legally and sold the lots for a sizeable profit. After this he was continually involved in buying and selling real estate.

Ted was positively impressed with the power and spirit of the United States and its citizenry, and his correspondence of letters to Frank Garrett in the Croft Family Archives clearly indicates that he became quite an ardent patriot of the U.S. In 1888 he and Mamp began the process to become a U.S. citizen. One of the first steps for them to make was formally to disavow their allegiance to Queen Victoria of England. Here is the form on which my great grandpa Ted, born in the British Commonwealth of Australia, did this:

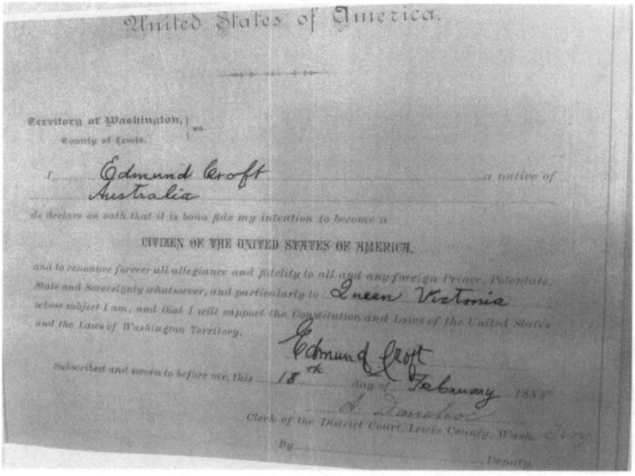
United States of America.

Territory of Washington, County of Lewis. } ss.

I, Edmund Croft a native of Australia

do declare on oath that it is bona fide my intention to become a

CITIZEN OF THE UNITED STATES OF AMERICA,

and to renounce forever all allegiance and fidelity to all and any foreign Prince, Potentate, State and Sovereignty whatsoever, and particularly to Queen Victoria whose subject I am, and that I will support the Constitution and Laws of the United States and the Laws of Washington Territory.

Edmund Croft

Subscribed and sworn to before me, this 18th day of Febuary 188[illegible]

[illegible]

Clerk of the District Court, Lewis County, Wash.

By ______ Deputy.

This form reads: "United States of America, Territory of Washington, County of Lewis…I (**Edmund Croft**) a native of (**Australia**) do declare on oath that it is *bona fide* my intention to become a **CITIZEN OF THE UNITED STATES OF AMERICA**, and to renounce forever all allegiance and fidelity to all and any foreign Prince, Potentate, State, and Sovereignty whatsoever, and particularly to **Queen Victoria**, whose subject I am, and that I will support the Constitution and Laws of the United States and the Laws of Washington Territory. (signed in hand-written ink script) **Edmund J. Croft**. Subscribed and sworn to me, this **18th** day of **February** 1888. (Signed) (**A. Danahoe**), Clerk of the District Court, Lewis County, Wash…"

Both Ted and Mamp became United States' citizens in 1889, the same year that the Washington Territory where they lived became a U.S. State. In 1904 Ted purchased a house in the southern part (twenty eighth political district) of the city of Tacoma to be their family home. And in 1906, Ted's fellow male citizens (women were not yet eligible to vote) elected him, Edmund J. Croft, to the Washington State Legislature as a congressman. He was very proud of this accomplishment and the trust that his fellow Washingtonians invested in him and his judgment in their behalf. He served a two-year term (1907-8).

In 1908 Ted bought a larger house for the family home at 609 S. I Street in the northern part (twenty seventh political district) of the city of Tacoma. And in April of 1908 Ted again bought land, 391 acres this time, around Oregon's Croft Lake, spending, according to his bank book with the "Bank of California" office in Tacoma, $2,840.00, …and again he subdivided the property into house lots and sold them for a nice profit, retaining ownership of a lakefront house and barn he called the "Croft Lake Ranch." He dreamed of making it into a hunting and fishing lodge. He had the lake stocked with trout.

The Croft Hunting and Fishing Lodge on Croft Lake in Oregon in 1909. Shown are (center) Edmund, "Ted," and Alice "Mamp" Croft with sons Edmund J. "Miccie," and Sydney. From CFA.

Oldest son Sydney and his wife Ida Mickle Croft lived there for a year or two, but their judgment was that not enough hunters or fishermen would pay to use it, so they moved to the Oregon town of Bandon. In those days it was difficult for Ted and Mamp to "get away" and travel the 400 miles from Tacoma by train to Portland and then by rented horse-drawn carriage to this "home away from home." In December 1917, Ted's wife Mamp died of influenza and he soon tired of living alone in their Tacoma house. He sold it and moved into the Tacoma home at 1218 S. Ainsworth of his son H.W. "Lee" and his wife since Christmas Eve of 1918, Pearl Bliss Croft (cf. p. 284). His grandson William Sydney Croft (cf. p. 283) was born there on November 11th, 1919. Soon after this, in 1920, he sold the Croft Lake property.

On May 6th, 1910, King Edward VII of the United Kingdom, died. Ted and Mamp decided to travel to the coronation of his successor, King George V, which was scheduled for June of 1911. Their purpose in making this journey (across the U.S. by train, across the Atlantic by steamship) was to acquaint their sons with the family "homeland" of England and their many relatives there. In the summer of 1910, father Edmund, "Ted," was 61, Alice, "Mamp" was 63, oldest son Sydney was 32, Edmund John, Jr., "Miccie" was 30, Henry William, "Lee," (my grandfather, later Tacoma

Sheriff…cf. p. 285) was 28 and had been since 1908 the Pacific Coast Heavyweight Boxing Champion (a career plan NOT appreciated by his parents), and the youngest son Jeremiah, "Jerry" was 27. All were mature men…though all were then still single. SO, Ted and Mamp openly expressed their plans to set the sons' sights on courting "proper English ladies" while they were introducing them to British society. This trip for six, planned to last most of a year and VERY expensive, was paid for out of Ted's bank accounts which included part of the remaining inheritance money from his father John Croft's 1883 estate.

They reached London in early December of 1910 and, on December 7th, were feted in the restaurant of the Liverpool Street Hotel (a hotel owned by the Great Eastern Railway…a Garrett Industries customer) by the family of Frank Garrett, Sr. and his second wife Emma Barbara Stead Garrett, whom Frank called "Barbara" (cf. p. 50) Here is a photo of the menu:

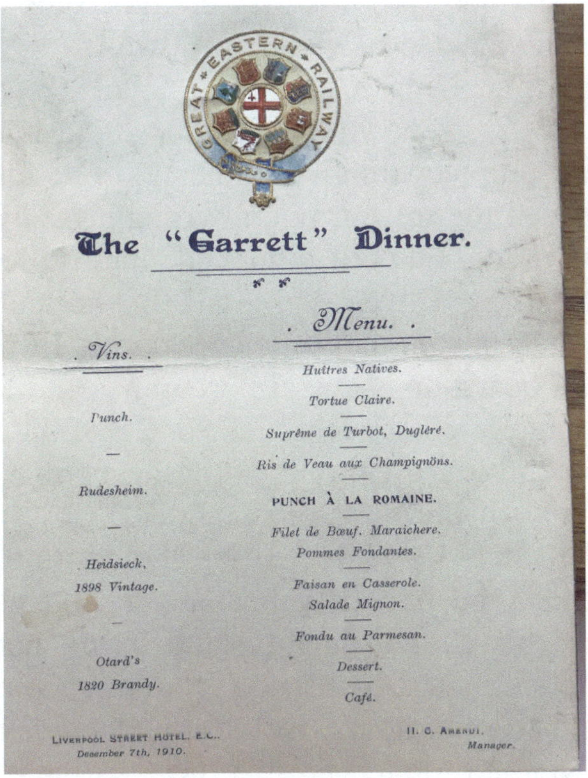

GREAT EASTERN RAILWAY

The "Garrett" Dinner.

. Menu. .

Huîtres Natives.

Tortue Claire.

Suprême de Turbot, Dugléré.

Ris de Veau aux Champignons.

PUNCH À LA ROMAINE.

Filet de Bœuf. Maraichere.
Pommes Fondantes.

Faisan en Casserole.
Salade Mignon.

Fondu au Parmesan.

Dessert.

Café.

. Vins. .

Punch.

—

Rudesheim.

—

Heidsieck,
1898 Vintage.

—

Otard's
1820 Brandy.

LIVERPOOL STREET HOTEL, E.C.,
December 7th, 1910.

H. C. AMENDT,
Manager.

*The Menu of "***The Garrett Dinncr***" at the Liverpool Street Hotel in London on December 7th, 1910 to welcome their Croft relatives to England, from CFA. Pretty posh fare.*

While they were in England, Ted and Mamp's family were royally entertained by their Croft, Garrett, and Stead relatives. Hunting and fishing were important in the entertainment of Ted and his sons. Ted records what we could only now consider the horrendous slaughter of game and fish in great numbers. In this they emulated the behavior of both the deceased King Edward VII and the succeeding King George V. King George was proud of his renown as a hunter and a marksman. On a trip to Nepal in December 1911 he felt he had to exceed the toll on tigers wrought by his predecessor King Edward who had once killed 23 of them during a two week visit. So he and his ten male guests shot and killed 39 tigers, 18 rhinoceroses, 4 bears, and several porcupines and leopards. The King himself accounted for 21 of the tigers, 8 of the rhinoceroses, one of the bears and a "good number" of the porcupines and leopards. In December of 1913 while visiting the estate of a Lord Burnham, he had fifty beaters driving pheasants toward his shotgun station and in six hours shot and killed over a thousand of them…one every 20 seconds for six hours. Even he is quoted as saying "we went a little too far that day." A fan of animal rights poet Ella Wheeler Wilcox (5 Nov., 1850-30 Oct., 1919) he wasn't.

A month before the Croft family's trip to King George V's coronation, poet Ella Wheeler Wilcox had published her animal rights anthem, "The Voice of the Voiceless," including these lines:

"I am the voice of the voiceless;
Through me the dumb shall speak;
Till the deaf world's ear be made to hear
The cry of the wordless and weak.

From street, from cage, and from kennel,
From jungle and stall, the wail
Of my tortured kin proclaims the sin
Of the mighty against the frail…

Oh, never a brute in the forest,
And never a snake in the fen,
Or ravening bird, starvation stirred,
Has hunted its prey like men.
For hunger, and fear, and passion
Alone drive beasts to slay,
But wonderful man, the crown of the plan,
Tortures, and kills, for play.

Now, this is the race as we find it.
Where love, in the creed, spells hate;
And where bird and beast meet a foe in the priest
And in rulers of fashion and State.
But up to the Kingdom of Thinkers
Has risen the cry of our kin;
And the weapons of thought are burnished and
brought
To clash with the bludgeons of sin.

The same Force formed the sparrow
That fashioned man, the King;
The God of the Whole gave a spark of soul
To furred and to feathered thing.
And I am my brother's keeper,
And I will fight his fight,
And speak the word for beast and bird,

Till the world shall set things right."

The Crofts visited Ovingdean in Sussex and Aldringham in Suffolk in addition to spending much of their time in London hotels going to balls, banquets, and horse races. The sons Syd and Lee were particularly bored and did manage to get away to involve themselves in some boxing activities even though Lee had solemnly promised his parents that he would not accept any paid matches or even sparring sessions while they were in London. But he and Syd, who was also interested in boxing and had served more than once as Lee's manager and training partner, went to the training camp of "Bombardier" Billy Wells (31 Aug., 1889-12 Jun., 1967), the 1909 Lonsdale Belt winner who was preparing to fight the British Heavyweight Champion "Iron William" Hague on April 11, 1911.

The Croft brothers ca. 1911, L-R: Sydney, Lee, Miccie, and Jerry, from CFA.

And here, from CFA, is a photo of "Bombardier" Billy Wells in 1911.

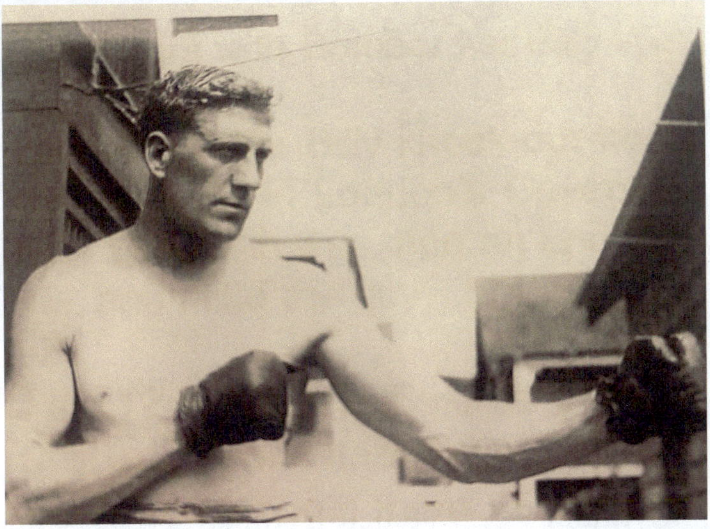

Wells was 6'3" in height and had a long reach. He weighed 188 lbs and had "a right hand like the kick of a mule" according to Syd, who, not having promised otherwise as brother Lee had, did engage in some sparring sessions with Bombardier Billy. Here is a photo that may have been taken by our Grandpa Lee in April of 1911 in London.

"Syd spars with Bombardier Billy Wells" from CFA.

Syd and Lee watched Bombardier Billy knock out Iron William Hague in the sixth round of a scheduled 20 round match in London's Covent Garden ring. Syd purportedly told his brother Lee, who was then an undefeated (54-0-2 actually…no losses but two draws) 6'1" and 180 lbs, "He's too good for me, and I like the guy…but I think you can take him."

The next month, on May 12, 1911, the Festival of the Empire opened at London's famous Crystal Palace. The exhibitions there were so fascinating that the Crofts spent as much time as they could there. The sports news was touting a world championship boxing match for Bombardier Billy Wells with the very controversial world champion…the African American sensation Jack Johnson (31 Mar., 1878-10 Jun., 1946) who had won the title in Australia against popular Tommy Burns in 1908. The news listed possible opponents for Johnson, calling them the "White Hopes" and Bombardier Billy Wells was among the foremost of these "White Hope" contenders. But Winston Churchill (30 Nov., 1874-24 Jan., 1965), then the British Home Secretary, had a match scheduled between them for October squelched, declaring it to be "il-legal" and "not in the best interests of the nation or empire."

A large portion of the Croft family's time in England was spent at Frank and Barbara Garrett's Aldringham House near Saxmundham in Suffolk. Ted's father John Croft had spent his last years in residence there when his daughter Mary Anne or "May" was the *de facto* mother of twenty Croft or Garrett children (if her mentoring her two young adult brothers are included) until her death in 1897. So by 1911 this grand and spacious estate was the center of the Garrett family's numerous grandchildren. Here is a photo of this five-level house from the time Ted and Mamp and their sons were visiting it.

Aldringham House in Suffolk in 1911. Photo by P. Drew from Rocky Media Archives, ebay ie.

And here is a photo from 1911 of the line of children, all but one are grandchildren of Frank and May Croft Garrett, ready to enter Aldringham House.

Cousin Margaret Young knows who they all are and who their parents are: L-R: Robin Walmsley (Elizabeth "Mabel"), May Garrett (Frank, Jr.), Marjorie James (Mary), Helen Garrett (Frank, Jr.), Boteler Garrett (Alfred), Betty (Irene) Garrett

(Frank, Jr.), Nancy Stamford (an unrelated friend), Jim Garrett (Alfred), Mary James (Mary), Joan Garrett (Alfred), Dorothy Garrett (Frank, Jr.), Hugh and Phillip James (Mary). Cousin Margaret's mother Phyliss Garrett (Craig) and Peter Garrett (Alfred) are not there in this 1911 photo because they had not yet been born. From CFA.

While the Crofts were staying at Aldringham in June of 1911, Frank Garrett Sr. and his wife Barbara Stead Garrett were planning a large banquet for the night of the actual coronation of King George V and his wife Mary of Teck as British sovereigns. The photo below shows that June 22, 1911 banquet in progress with the white bearded supervising senior butler Killick at the extreme left.

But the Croft lads all wanted to travel to London with some of the Garretts to witness the many marches and processions and appearances of the royals. So Frank Garrett, Jr. led a large group of revelers to London to partake in the actual ceremonies, and the four Croft sons went along.

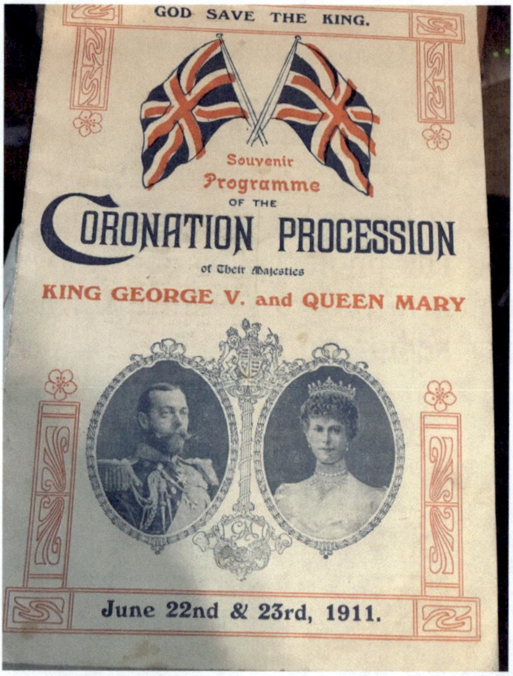

This is a photo by the author (LBC) of the actual "souvenir programme of the Coronation Procession" from June 22nd & 23rd, 1911, that was found among H.W. "Lee" Croft's possessions in the family ancestry trunk (cf. p. 241).

The family story is that son Lee Croft, our grandfather, and his cousin Lilian Croft Garrett Broad (cf. p. 260 in a group, also p. 265 with husband Douglas), ten years older than Lee and the well married mother of five young children who had stayed home at Aldringham, somehow got separated together from the others in the surging crowds near Westminster Abbey and did not return to find the others until late morning the next day. This caused cousin Frank, Jr. and Lilian's husband Richard "Douglas" Broad some concern. "Well, I couldn't very well have left her alone, could I?" explained Lee. "So I stayed right with her and she really showed me around. We had a wonderful time."

One of my (author LBC) discoveries…in August of 2019…in thc family ancestry trunk (cf. p. 241) was a man's dopp kit (toiletries kit) belonging to my Grandfather and former Tacoma Sheriff Lee Croft (cf. pp. 284, 370) who passed away in December of 1951. In this dopp kit were all kinds of fraternal order membership pins. Grandpa Lee had been a Moose, Elk, Eagle, a Mason, a Shriner, and etc. The dopp kit had his Sheriff's badges and his boxing championship medals…even the one naming him as the Pacific Coast Heavyweight Champion in 1908, three years before his visit to England and Aldringham House in 1910-1911.

When, 108 years after the Crofts visited England for the coronation of King George V, I was taking one of my Grandfather Lee's boxing medals out of its jeweler's box, I accidentally dislodged the underlying silk and cotton pad. From under the pad fell out a very small photo in less than a square shape as if it had been cut out of a larger group photo (I concluded). I easily recognized the woman in the photo to be Lilian Croft Garrett Broad (8 Sept.1872-13 Feb., 1963 cf. pp. 260 and 265). This, of course, is the woman mentioned above as being Grandpa Lee's partner in a mutual absence from their crowd of Croft and Garrett family members in London near Westminster Abbey the very night of King George V's coronation (cf. p. 375).

In 1911, Grandpa Lee was 28…Lilian Broad was 36, married and had five children with Douglas Broad (cf. p. 265) who was there to witness her absence from the group with Lee. Grandpa Lee married my grandmother, Pearl Bliss Croft (1896-1984, cf. p. 284) on Christmas Eve 24 December 1918, seven years later. He was 36 and she 22. But at some time, likely soon after the June 22, 1911, coronation celebration incident, he obtained and later secreted in one of his boxing medal boxes a portion of a photograph that contained the image of his alleged paramour, cousin Lilian. This shows, I conjecture, that he did hold a sense of affection and romance for her.

This photo from Grandpa Lee's dopp kit in the family ancestry trunk should be compared with the Garret group wedding photo on p. 260. Grandpa Lee's pocket watch is included to give the photo an indication of size. Photo by LBC.

The family of Edmund J. "Ted" and Alice "Mamp" Croft, with their sons Syd, Miccie, Lee, and Jerry, left England in early August of 1911. After visiting France (Paris), Luxembourg (Luxembourg), Belgium (Brussels), and the Netherlands (Amsterdam), they sailed back to New York City, and rode the railways back across the U.S. to their home in Tacoma, Washington, arriving in mid September.

While on the long train journey, Mother Mamp commented that she was disappointed that not one of her "highly eligible" single sons had managed engagements to any of those "proper English ladies" they had certainly met in abundance. But Syd summed up the sons' reaction, telling his Dad, "The English ladies were fine and proper enough, but we'd all rather marry one of our own kind. We prefer to find ourselves American girls to marry." And indeed they all did.

In 1912, Ted decided to run for a seat in the Washington state senate. Here is a copy of his "candidate's card:"

Notice that the card informs that he was "subject to Republican Primaries" which he did not win. But, on the back of the card he gives us a picture of his personal as well as his political views. The text reads: "I had the honor of representing the citizenry of the twenty-eighth district in the House of Representatives in Olympia 1907. In seeking your suffrage I stand for unswerving loyalty to the Government, just legislation, industrial tranquility, and enduring prosperity, powerfully assisted by the auxiliary of the Initiative, Referendum, and Recall. To strengthen the Moral Ethics of the State, I advocate the *Fifth*, *Sixth*, *Seventh*, *Eighth* and *Ninth Commandments* be placed on the interior walls of every Schoolhouse in the State." As a reminder these commandments from the Christian Bible are: 5) Honor your father and mother; 6) You shall not murder; 7) You shall not commit adultery; 8) You shall not steal; and 9) You shall not bear false witness against your neighbor.

In 1914, Ted became financially involved in an oyster company in Westport, Washington. He added $10,000 to the capitalization of an enterprise he and his three partners called the WEST POINT OYSTER COMPANY. The other three investors put in $30,000 each so that the company's capitalization was advertised to be $100,000. The company's "trustees" were listed as "C. W. Yana, President," "Arvid Rydstrom, Vice-President," "C.C.T. Clausen, Secretary-Treasurer" and "Edmund Croft, Trustee." The company's stationery states that the company owned and operated "Oyster Beds, 158 and 1/2 acres located at Grays Harbor" on the Pacific Ocean coast of the Quinault Reservation 90 miles west of Tacoma. The supervisor of the actual cultivation of oysters was an accomplished oysterman named S. Murikami, who lived in the nearby community of Ocosta-by-the-Sea.

A map of Grays Harbor and the communities of Westport and Ocosta (left bottom quadrant) from Wikipedia.

The papers and bank books in the ancestry trunk tell the story of the West Point Oyster Company's bankruptcy by the end of World War I in 1918, despite S. Murakami's reports of up to 40 shipments per month of amounts of 100-2500 sacks of oysters (at $1 for a burlap sack of a dozen in a November 1914 report) to 22 wholesale oyster companies, the Washington Hotel, and the Northern Pacific Railway. Transportation of the oysters in unrefrigerated vehicles was a major problem, causing many refunds for reported "bad oysters upon arrival." Still, Ted told people that in the four years of this company's operations his investment had returned double his money back to him. His bank books do not show this.

In 1914, executor Ted used more money from his long deceased father John Croft's estate to help finance his sons Miccie and Lee's purchase of the 124-room Betz Family's Pacific Avenue Hotel at 1519 Pacific Avenue in downtown Tacoma. This cost him $22,000. His son Lee had been working as a forest ranger tasked with managing the forests of the national parks in the U.S. northwest, and had spent time on the Blackfeet Indian Reservation adjacent to Glacier National Park in Northern Montana in that capacity. Glacier National Park was our country's 10th National Park, having been established in May of 1910. Lee had also been two years in the Washington National Guard so that the hostilities that would become World War I in Europe were a bit of a concern to him. He and Miccie decided to change the name of the hotel to HOTEL CROFT…see the signage below.

This photo, from Washington State Archives, shows the Hotel Croft in November 1915 a year after Miccie and Lee Croft purchased it with their father's help. The caption includes: " Rooms starting at 50 cents. The hotel, at 1519 Pacific Avenue was located between the Tacoma Implement Co. and the Beehive Restaurant."

Tacoma's Hotel Croft was primarily an accommodation for working men of all kinds: railroad workers, commercial sailors and fishermen, port stevedores, lumberjacks, and shipyard riggers and mechanics. A good number of these were staying at the hotel and paying by the month at the rate of **50 cents** per day. In 1917, Miccie asked Lee to buy him out of his interest in the Hotel Croft so that he could purchase a half partnership with a "Mr. Swanson" in the competing nearby Lewis Hotel. So their father Edmund advanced son Lee the $12,000 to give to Miccie so that both sons were now the sole proprietors of Tacoma Hotels. And in 1924 Miccie sold his half to Mr. Swanson and moved to California, dying there in 1933.

Lee met his wife Pearl Irene Bliss (cf. p. 284) when she was working as a waitress in the Beehive Cafe on Tacoma's Pacific Avenue next door to the Hotel Croft. They got married on 24 December 1918 and purchased a house at 1218 S. Ainsworth where their first son (and my father…LBC) William Sydney, called "Billy," was born on 11 November, 1919. By this time Ted had sold the house on I Street and moved in to live with son Lee and Pearl after his wife Mamp passed away of influenza on 23 December, 1917. And after Pearl gave birth to son Billy in November of 1919, she and Lee sold the Ainsworth house, buying another at 3914 S. 7th Avenue near the end of the 6th Avenue streetcar line. It was here that second son Bliss Henry was born on 16 June, 1921. Daughter Gloria Rose was born in a Tacoma maternity home on 10 December, 1926.

This is 3914 S. 7th Avenue as it appeared during a family visit to Tacoma in 2003. My Dad, William Sydney "Bill" Croft, said that the huge Port Orford Cedar in the front yard had been planted by his father Lee Croft to celebrate his brother Bliss's birth there in 1921. Photo by LBC.

The Hotel Croft on Tacoma's Pacific Avenue was still hosting visitors into the 1960s, when all the buildings on that block were condemned and demolished. In 1954 it celebrated it's 40th anniversary and bragged that it was the American hotel longest operating in one location. Here is a photo from 1932 of Lee Croft climbing onto the roof of a tour bus to put touring visitors' baggage on it:

Tour members wait under the portico for their baggage to be moved onto the bus-top by Hotel Croft owner Lee Croft in 1932. From CFA.

Edmund "Ted" Croft passed away in the 7th Avenue house (p. 386) on 22 December, 1925, and he is buried in the Croft family plot that he purchased in 1920 in the Tacoma Cemetery. I last visited his grave with others of our family with my Cut Bank, Montana, oilman father, William Sydney "Bill" Croft (1919-2003), in the 2003 summer before his death on November 15, 2003 at the age of 84 years and 4 days. In the cemetery he informed me that he did not want to be interred there in Tacoma, but preferred cremation, wanting to have his ashes await scattering together with the ashes of his wife Norma Rose Dingeldein Croft (cf. p. 283) at the family cabin on Ashley Lake near Kalispell, Montana. That happened in July 2023.

My father remembers how, in 1931, as a result of financial hardships attendent to the growing U.S. depression, his whole family of 5 (Lee, Pearl, he Bill, Bliss, and Gloria) had to PUT THEIR HOUSE UP FOR SALE AND MOVE INTO THEIR OWN HOTEL, which was the homesite of widowed and alone Grandma Pearl until 1959. The hotel was where all three children grew up and learned to work.

Here is a photo from 1945, showing Grandma Pearl Croft with her son Bliss's baby son Hugo Croft and her daughter Gloria's daughter Gloria Ann Wise:

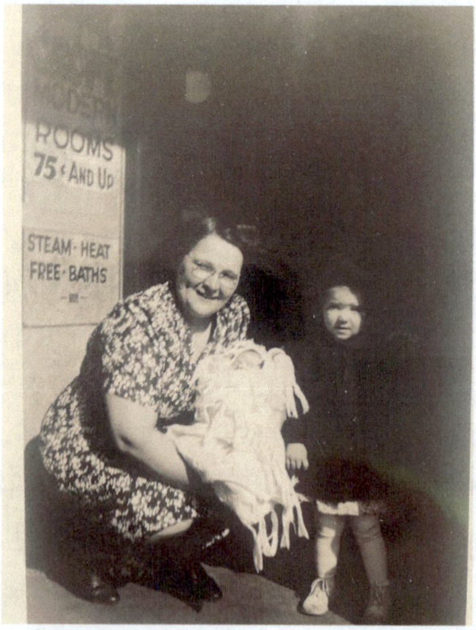

Notice that the sign at the left says "Hotel Croft, Modern Rooms, 75¢ And Up, Steam Heat, Free Baths." From CFA.

This poster is from after 1954 when the Hotel Croft celebrated its 40th year of operation.

Notice that this poster touts on the suitcase the "CROFT HOTEL" instead of the way the signs and stationery use the name "HOTEL CROFT." I have no explanation for this reversal. From CFA.

I personally (author LBC) stayed in the Hotel Croft more than once when I was a child in the late 1940s. In every room was a washstand with a sink…but the rooms had no bathrooms nor toilets. Each of the three stories of rooms had a hallway with a common bathroom…3 toilet stalls with a single bathtub…at the back end of the hall where you could enter a small landing of the black metal fire-escape staircase fronting onto the Tacoma railroad switching yard with its locomotives blowing off steam. My brother Jerry and I, then 4 and 5 years old, were told to get onto a chair so we could pee into the room's sink. On the sheets, pillow cases, and the paper-thin white bath towels were stamped a red heart with the words "STOLEN FROM LEE CROFT" on them. This was to prevent the guests from stealing them. To this day, I, Lee Croft, grandson namesake of the owner, have the "stolen from Lee Croft" stamp as a memento.

And here is a photo from 1950…a year before his death on December 14, 1951 (too soon gone at age 69 years, 2 months, and 23 days)…of Hotel Croft owner and my grandfather Lee Croft which appeared in the *Tacoma Tribune* newspaper. The newspaper writer focused his article on Grandpa Lee's outstanding boxing career.

This otograph of W.H. 'Lee' Croft was taken in December 1942 at the Croft Hotel, 1519 Pacific Ave., shortly after he was ected Pierce County sheriff. As a young man, Croft had been both an amateur and professional boxer. In his 54 bouts as an amateur and a professional, he never lost a fight.

RICHARDS STUDIO COLLECTION TACOMA PUBLIC LIBRARY 253-591

This photo's caption says it was taken at the "Croft Hotel" in December 1942. But the article about him was published by the Tacoma News Tribune in December 1950. Notice the caption's mention that "he never lost a fight." From CFA.

Reviewing here, Ted and Mamp and baby son Sydney moved from England to the United States in 1878…but by 1882 they were in the Washington Territory where they had sons Miccie, Lee, and Jerry. They became U.S. citizens in 1889 and moved to the city of Tacoma in 1904. Ted served a two-year term as a representative of a Tacoma district in the Washington Legislature from 1906 to 1908.

Ted's eight-years-younger brother Henry, called "Harry," was well educated in England at the prestigious Rugby School and at the highly regarded Derby School of Mining Engineering. But he emigrated to Canada in 1883 and wound up in the mining business in Victoria, British Columbia. There he became a renowned magnate, serving on railroad boards and founding a mining town named "Crofton" after him. I think (LBC) he is the only Croft of John Croft's numerous issue who has a Wikipedia entry today. In 1886 he was elected to the British Columbia Parliament's Legislative Assembly as the representative of the Cowichan Valley's district and served until 1894.

This photo is from Wikipedia, captioned "Henry Croft in 1885." This was the year of his marriage.

On June 29th of 1885, Harry married Mary Jane Dunsmuir, the fourth daughter of wealthy Industrialist Robert Dunsmuir (1825-1889), who insisted on providing the groom a $25,000 dowry. Wedding guests included William Smithe, the Premiere of British Columbia, and Theodore Davie, the Province's Attorney General. Her inheritance at her father's death four years later made Mary Jane one of Canada's wealthiest women, and Harry, already doing well in life, benefitted as well from the Dunsmuir family's practically limitless money.

This is a photo of Mary Jean Dunsmuir (11 Feb., 1862 -15 Aug., 1928) at age 18, before her marriage to Harry. From CFA.

Harry Croft was proud of his upbringing in Sydney, Australia...and particularly in his father's grand estate on Darling Point called "Mount Adelaide" where he was the only surviving Croft child born there. Here is a photo of this Sydney "Mount Adelaide" estate (cf. mention of it on John Croft's gravestone, p. 347) after it had been bought and transformed in 1886 into a exclusive young ladies residence called the "Ascham School."

The Ascham School building in 1892, formerly John and Mary Ann Stead Croft's estate at the highest point in Sydney, Australia's, exclusive Darling Point neighborhood, called from 1854-9 "Mount Adelaide." Harry Croft was born in this residence on 15 January, 1856.

So Harry Croft set out to build, on a high waterfront 19-acre lot in the Victoria, B.C., suburb of Esquimalt, a residence to surpass in grandiosity his father John Croft's "Mount Adelaide" estate as he remembered it from his childhood on Darling Point in Sydney. And he straight away decided to call his new Victoria estate "Mount Adelaide" as well. "I was born in a Mount Adelaide and I'll die in a Mount Adelaide as well," he told his wife Mary.

The house reportedly cost $28,000 to build and the construction took THREE years, being completed in 1889. Its interior furnishings are artistic wonders so that public tours were given there just to see them. Some of the walls feature STAINED GLASS WINDOWS, recalling the Croft family's commitment to using this art form for important purposes…memorials, for example.

This photo from CFA was taken in 1890 of Harry and Mary Jean Dunsmuir Croft's "Mount Adelaide" estate at 819 Dunsmuir Street, Esquimalt (a suburb of Victoria), B.C., Canada.

And here is a photo from the inside looking down the center stairs into the entry parlor .

Inside the Crofts' Mount Adelaide. From CFA.

Harry Croft stayed in contact with his older brother Ted by mail. These letters tell of the visits to both Ted and Mamp in Tacoma, Washington, and to Harry and Mary Jean in Victoria, B.C., of two of Harry's Croft half-brothers who had become medical doctors before emigrating from England and becoming citizens of the United States. First was Dr. Richard Croft (b. at Dalton House in Saddington, Leicestershire, England, a twin with deceased-at-nine-years-of-age Nicholas Croft, on 23 May, 1870…cf pp. 263-4). He came with his "English Lady" wife Sarah, who had also become a U.S. citizen, to visit Ted and Mamp for a week in the one-school hops-growing community then re-spelled "Boistfort" twenty five miles south of Chehalis, Washington, over Christmas in 1900. From there they traveled through Tacoma and Seattle north to visit Harry and Mary Jean who were living in the very impressive Mount Adelaide mansion in Esquimalt, Victoria, B.C. There Dr. Richard, even though only 30 years old, came down with an intractable pneumonia *and died* on January 15th, 1901. He was buried there in Victoria, with Harry and Mary paying for the grave and headstone. The devastated widow Sarah stayed on with Harry and Mary Jean another month after the funeral before deciding that she would "return to her family in England." She asked Mary Jean to advance her the money "to pay for the long hard journey home." Mary gave her a considerable amount of money, but a letter from Harry to Ted in 1914 relates that they had "heard nothing from Lady Sarah" since she left them.

The visits of Dr. John Croft, Jr. (cf. pp. 249-50) took place in the summer of 1908. He also first visited Ted and Mamp, who were then living in Tacoma. He had exciting tales to tell them of his time spent serving in the United States army during the 1898 Spanish-American War. With the 1200 men of the 34th Michigan Volunteer Infantry under the command of Col. John Peterman, he had been shipped to Siboney, Cuba, on the ship "Harvard," arriving on July 1, 1898. The very next day his unit participated in the famous Battle of San Juan Hill in which, by some "miracle," he said, no member of his unit was killed in the combat. "I only treated one man… Sergeant Jack Garner was his name…for a Spanish officer's sword slash which cleft his forehead and skull. But, to my surprise, he survived and returned home with the rest of us to Detroit in September of that year. All of our unit's deaths during the Santiago campaign were related to tropical fevers and other diseases."

Dr. John told Ted and Mamp that he had been married to a "Canadian Lady," but that she had been unfaithful to him while he was away in the war and that he had, therefore, divorced her in 1899 soon after his return.

When he was staying with Harry and Mary Jean in Victoria, Dr. John told them that it was his intent to travel thereafter to California and to begin his own medical practice there.

Harry and Mary Jean had been married for 23 years by the time of Dr. John Croft's visit. And they had no children. When Dr. John expressed his curiosity about this, they told him that they had "tried and tried, but just failed to bring about a pregnancy." Harry told him that Mary Jean always strongly desired to become a mother to children, and that he, Harry, was likely the physically impotent one. "She especially wanted to have daughters and then granddaughters so that she could indulge their every feminine whim. She puts on annual "fetes" in our garden in which dozens of grade-school-age girls…the daughters and friends of many of our neighbors and colleagues…dress up and pretend to be princesses and other entitled ladies."

Mary Jean Dunsmuir Croft's 1912 "Garden Fete" with more than 20 girls on the grounds of the Mount Adelaide estate in Victoria, B.C. From City of Victoria Archives through CFA.

Dr. John Croft, Jr. died in California in 1912 at the age of 44. In the letter correspondence between his half-brothers Ted and Harry both mention the fact that the brothers Richard and John had both become medical doctors in England, both emigrated to the U.S., both were dedicated to careers helping their patients…and both died "too young"… Richard at 30 and John at 44.

And Henry "Harry" Croft also died too young at 61 years, 7 months, and 13 days of age in his Mount Adelaide house in Victoria on July 28th, 1917. The doctor's diagnosis was a brain hemorrhage. The obituary cited his education at Rugby and the Derby School of Mining Engineering, saying that "he carried off many honors in examinations written on mining and other scientific subjects…no man of his profession obtained higher credentials in the Commonwealth…that his firm of Croft & Angus took an active interest in the development of the island's resources of timber, establishing a mill at Chemainus now operated by the Victoria Lumber Company… that he had served effectively for eight years as Cowichan's elected representative in the British Columbia Parliament's Legislative Assembly, and that he was the caring employer of hundreds of mill workers and miners during his long career."

This, from templelodge333 ca, is a photo of Henry Croft's grave at Ross Bay Cemetery in Victoria, B.C. I (LBC) visited it on May 23, 2018. The inscription reads, copying the style of Henry Croft's father John Croft's grave inscription at St. Peter's Church Cemetery near Saxmundham in Suffolk, England: "Sacred to the Memory of HENRY CROFT, born 15 January, 1856 at MOUNT ADELAIDE, Sydney, N.S.W., died July 28, 1917, at MOUNT ADELAIDE, Esquimalt, B.C.

So, my great grand uncle Henry "Harry" Croft did fulfill his intention, stated to his wife Mary Jean and recounted here on p. 394…to be born in a "Mount Adelaide" and die in a "Mount Adelaide."

And Harry's wife, Mary Jean Dunsmuir Croft, survived him by eleven years, living and also dying in their beloved Mount Adelaide on August 15,

1928 at age 66. She now rests in a grave adjacent to her husband Harry's in plot T-87E39 in the Ross Bay Cemetery pictured above.

The Mount Adelaide mansion in Esquimalt survived both Harry and Mary with other inhabitants until 1959 when it was demolished to make room for a number of luxury apartment buildings, some of which have other 800-numbered addresses on Dunsmuir Street…the major attraction of these apartments being their beautiful neighborhood.

A recent aerial photo of the Dunsmuir Street Neighborhood of the Dunsmuir Royale Apartments in Victoria, B.C. Mount Adelaide was close to the center of this photo. From capreit ca

Wikipedia has recently added an interesting section to the entry on "Henry Croft," informing that "Croft is featured on the *Netflix* series *Haunted* (Season 3, Episode 2…first aired on May 14, 2021) wherein the family of the depicted character "Wyatt lived in Croft's home and experienced hostile ghostly interaction with Croft. who is then seen smoking a cigar before terrorizing one of the family members further, such as pushing him down stairs and setting out fishing hooks as a trap to injure that family member—Wyatt. Croft is also suspected of causing the suicide of the previous tenant by his hostile actions."

If you then click up the Wikipedia site "Haunted (2018 TV Series)" you are informed of the falsehood of many aspects of the series' portrayal of Henry Croft…inaccuracies about having a grand house (putatively Mount Adelaide) not in Esquimalt but in the town of Crofton which, although it was named for him, was never his residence (he lived previously in Chemainus). But this *Netflix* series has made a kind of negative cult figure of Henry Croft. Just "google" him or "The Haunting of Croft House" and you'll see.

Edmund J. "Ted" Croft also wrote and received letters from his sister Mary Anne, "May's," husband Frank Garrett, Sr. back in England. This correspondence continued well after Mary Anne's death in 1897 and even after Frank's second wife,

May's older first cousin, Emma "Barbara" Stead Croft passed away in Aldringham on December 21st, 1916, of heart problems.

Here is a letter sent from Frank Garrett, Sr. to Ted Croft in Boistfort, Washington, only three weeks after Frank married Barbara Stead in London on April 15, 1899. You will see that he does not mention his quite recent marriage to Barbara in this letter to Ted.

"Aldringham House, Nr. Saxmundham
Leiston for Telegraph and Rail

7 May, 1899

My Dear Ted,

I am sending you a photograph of dear May, which I am sure you will like to receive. I hope it will reach you in perfect order and clear of all charges and that you will find it to be a pleasing likeness. I must say that I like it very much indeed, and I would not be without my own copy for any consideration.

I am having a white marble tombstone sculpted in Italy which I hope to see fixed in July. It is very simple and I hope it will not look too heavy. It is just a server for the inscription surrounded by an inclined border covered with sculptured flowers. The flat base below will be polished slate. I hope to send you a photograph of it bye and bye. I am also intending to put an "East Window" into Leiston Church, but the design for this is not yet completed. It should represent the King of Glory surrounded by St. Margaret and other 'virgin' saints—the Church being dedicated to St. Margaret. I am employing Mr. C. E. Kempe who is reputed to be the best man of the day for this work. Curiously enough when Kate Kingdon was visiting us a few weeks back she corroborated this and said she used to know him as a boy at Ovingdean Grange where his father was the predecessor of McNaughten. It would be very nice if you and Harry could come and see these things and spend a little time with us…

With best love to you and all yours, I am as ever Yours affectionately, Frank Garrett."

This letter shows that Frank Garrett contributed the basic idea for Charles Eamer Kempe's stained glass window design in Leiston's St. Margaret of Antioch Church (cf. pp. 353-8).

The letter below describes the situation of the Garretts during World War I.

"Aldringham
31 August, 1914

My Dear Ted,

Your two kind letters of July 20th and 31st reached me together. It is a painful task to answer them. The outcome for me, at the age of 70, is very dismal, although there is always a Rose looking in at the window. And the Rose that looks in at the window is hope that looks up to heaven!

Do you remember how sweetly my dear May used to sing this song? The greatest event in of my life is that I met her when I did, and I thank God that she is now spared this awful trial. Son Frank, as Colonel, and Stephen, a Captain, are with the 4th Battalion Suffolk Regiment and are under hard training for service abroad. Bridges has two sons with them—Butcher has one with Frank and one in Kitchener's army. Killick's only son has gone. About 20 men have gone from Aldringham. From Leiston 600 men altogether have left the works. Alfred and I are making extraordinary efforts to fill up the gaps—working something under less than half time, and under terrible financial pressure—Nine tenths of our business is with the Countries engaged in this wicked Armageddon and whereas huge sums should now be rolling in (Cash and Bills) we cannot collect one penny, and the bills we have negotiated and hold in portfolio must come back unpaid. The extent of our ultimate losses cannot be approximated.

Your dear old father used to say frequently; "From day to day to be good is to be happy" and that is what we must try to live up to!

Goodbye my dear Ted. With love to you all.
Yours affectionately,

Frank Garrett."

And this letter reports the death of Frank's second wife Barbara on December 21st, 1916:

"Aldringham
29:12:1916

My dear Ted,

I prepared you in my last letter for the sad news which I have to impart. My dear Barbara has passed away from us—after a fortnight of great suffering and restlessness, the characteristics of heart trouble. She died in a quiet sleep with her head resting in her hand. In her coffin she looked like the Emma Barbara Stead of 50 years ago when dear May and I visited Ovingdean Rectory on our wedding trip!

Surely no man was ever blessed with two such consecutive wives as I have been, and I am grateful for this great Blessing from the bottom of my heart. What a different man I might have been in other hands, Ted!

I shall miss Barbara's sweet intellectual companionship very much indeed, but my dear Children are simply splendid in my support. I often see my dear May's beautiful character reflected in them—and I mean to buck up and smile—as long as ever I can.

I have so many letters to write I must content myself with these few words to you and your dear

Alice. I pray that God may bless you both and all your children—for many years to come.

Yours affectionately, Frank Garrett

Barbara was 78 last birthday."

And this letter, about his personal memorial to Barbara and about the situation in the United States pressuring it to join in the war against Germany.

"Aldringham
Nr. Leiston
8 Feb 1917

My dear Ted,

Thank you, Old Man, for your kind letter of the 14th inst.

I can never sufficiently thank God for his mercy in having granted me the quite inestimable blessing of two such wives.

I can't think what I should have been without this blessing, and that of my dear children, who are rallying around me splendidly. I should be a real Brute did I not appreciate their loving considerations and attentions. I am awfully busy too.

It is necessary for me to make a new will—a most troublesome Business—an Mabel's business affairs have been occupying much of my time.

I am making a study for a carved tablet (mahogany) in dear Barbara's memory to be fixed in Aldringham Church—and I hope that you and Alice may come and see it some day. Who can tell? I am also giving to Aldringham Church a silver and cut glass Communion service, Elkington's best (it is still there and I have seen it…LBC). I am sure Barbara would like me to do this.

See this keeps me from morbidity.

I wonder what you will have to say now upon the political situation.

I am inclined to think that the U.S. is standing in need of "cleansing Fires"—But it appears that we may not truck much upon this subject in our correspondence. Goodbye my dear old Ted—may God bless and preserve you and all yours.

Yours affectionately, Frank Garrett."

Frank Garrett, Sr. passed away on August 24th of 1918. By that time the United States' President Woodrow Wilson had asked the U.S. Congress for a "war to end all wars" and the Congress voted to declare war on Germany on April 6, 1917. But World War I was hard on the Croft and Garrett families. Frank and May's son, Captain Stephen Garrett was killed in battle at Neuve Chapell in France (cf. pp. 271-4) at age 37, leaving a wife, Mary Marples Garrett and son Stephen Denis Garrett. John and Sarah's son, Major Benjamin Croft (cf. p. 267) was killed by a stray exploding shell on the very last day of WW1 hostilities, November 10, 1918, at age 36 in Marvenot, France, leaving wife Mary Elizabeth Perry Croft and a son Alfred Croft.

Ted's close friend from his Australian childhood and Eton School, Robert Tooth (cf. pp. 167-172), who had taken the name Lucas-Tooth in 1904 and had been given a hereditary baronetcy in England

A photo of Sir Robert Lucas-Tooth (1844-1915) from Wikipedia.

for his philanthropy by King Edward VI in 1906, had died of a cerebral hemorrhage on February 19th 1915. He and his wife, Lady Helen Lucas-Tooth, had entertained Ted and Mamp and their four sons at their English estate called Holme-Lacy when the Crofts and sons were on their 1910-11 visit for the coronation of King George V. Robert and Ted spent considerable time together hunting and fishing. But Robert and Helen had taken hard the WW1 deaths of their two oldest sons, Douglas Keith, who died as a Captain in the 9th Queen's Royal Lancers in combat in France at the age of 33 on September 14, 1914 being awarded the Distinguished Service Order (DSO) posthumously, and Selwyn, who died as a Captain of the Lancashire Fusiliers at age 35 in Flanders a month later on October 20, 1914.

After Robert Lucas-Tooth's death, he was succeeded by his third and only remaining son Archibald as the Baron of Holme-Lacy. And Archibald inherited Robert's financial estate, sworn in probate at over £905,000 in New South Wales and £276,000 in England. But Sir Archibald then also died in combat as a Major in the 2nd Battalion of the Honourable Artillery at the age of 34, leaving wife Mary as the Lady Lucas-Tooth. With no male successors, the baronetcy was then terminated, but in 1920 King George V re-created the baronetcy for the eldest son of Lucas-Tooth's eldest daughter Beatrice, the wife of Major Hugh Warrant, who then became Sir Hugh Lucas-Tooth.

Frank Garrett, Sr.,…John Croft's son-in-law and rescuer from commitment for lunacy and potential financial ruin…husband of both a Croft

(Mary Anne or "May") and then a Stead (May's and Ted's first cousin Emma "Barbara") and a major British industrialist died, possibly of the widespread influenza, at Aldringham at the age of 73 years, 3 months, and 18 days on August 24th, 1918. To some of his family's surprise he had changed his will and specified that he was not to be buried in Leiston's St. Margaret of Antioch's Church where was the Charles Eamer Kempe Stained Glass East Window dedicated to his wife of 30 years (1866-1897) Mary Anne "May" Croft Garrett (and where Mary Anne's remains had been resting in the family plot), but instead he was to be buried in the plot at St. Anthony's of Aldringham and Thorpeness where second wife Barbara's remains had been buried. It was his wish that ALL THREE of them…Frank and May and Barbara… should all be interred in the same grave there. The first to die (May) would be buried the deepest, then the second to die (Barbara), and then he, Frank, would be closest to the top. The gravestone was to be the one he had once described to Ted Croft in a letter from May 7th of 1899 (cf. p. 404).

My own (LBC...see the tennis shoe on my left foot at lower left) photo of the custom gravestone at St. Anthony's Church of Aldringham and Thorpeness's Cemetery of Frank Garrett and his wives Mary Anne and Emma Barbara. It reads: "In Loving Memory of MARY ANNE, For 30 years the devoted wife and affectionate companion of FRANK GARRETT, born 12th February, 1844, died 31st January 1897. "And we all bless Thy holy name for all thy servants departed this life in Thy faith and fear beseeching Thee forgive us grace so to follow their

good examples, that with Thee we may be partakers of Thy heavenly kingdom." Also, EMMA BARBARA (neé STEAD), the beloved second wife of FRANK GARRETT, born 18th July 1838, died 21st December 2016. Also FRANK GARRETT, born 6th May 1845, died 24th August, 1918."

When Edmund "Ted" Croft was staying by himself with his son Lee's family in Tacoma, Washington, after the death of his wife Mamp in 1916, his favorite occupation was telling young people stories about his life. Once, Lee's wife, Pearl Bliss Croft, asked him to write a few of his stories down so "We might all have them to read after you're gone. Your blessing us with stories doesn't have to end with you."

My father, William Sydney "Bill" Croft (1919-2003), lived his first six years in Tacoma, Washington, in the household with his "Grandpa Ted." He remembered how 'Grandpa Ted' always dressed in a starched collar, a tie, a vest, and a suit coat, and his sons used to brag that he was "the best dressed man in every company," even when he was working outside, or hunting or fishing. My Dad inherited his grandfather's custom fly fishing rod, inscribed as belonging to "Edwin (sic) Croft" and dated "1897," and it is stored with its more modern reel attached to a log ceiling beam in the Croft family's Ashley Lake cabin on the 'K-Trail' near Kalispell, Montana. Dad used to tell us that his father Lee and his three brothers were proud that Grandpa Ted had never in their experience had a "working job." He lived on his investments of the money he had inherited from his father, "John Croft of Mount Adelaide in Sydney Australia and Dalton House in Saddington England." He was, they then bragged, "worth thousands in pounds and dollars."

Here I feel I should include what Grandpa Ted, in 1924 or 1925 near the end of his life, wrote about his father John Croft's life and his own life. I am correcting the later typed version in places to account for certain quirky inaccuracies he includes that I attribute to some aged senility or dementia which his sons were accustomed to taking into account when he told stories they had been hearing change a bit during the course of the years.

"John Croft (part of a letter written in America, to his children and grandchildren to give them some insights into the life of his father and their life in Australia and in England).

My father, John Croft, was born at 45 minutes to 1 a.m. on the 16th day of July in 1807. He grew up to be a handsome, ruddy youth, 6 foot tall and 14 stone (196 lbs.) in weight.

He grew up in a large family in Hoddesdon, a suburb of London in Hertfordshire, where his father Nicholas founded a cooperage business named Croft Cask, Keg, & Barrel, Ltd in the same 1807 year father was born.

Father was sent to the 'Addiscombe Military Seminary' in Croyden when he was 14 years old and he graduated two years later, being commissioned an ensign in the Honourable East India Company's infantry. At age 16 in 1823 he was sent by ship, first to India, 'IN-jee-ya' as he pronounced it, where he and some friends witnessed a burning alive of two 'suttee women' near Madras, and then to Rangoon on the Irawaddy River in Burma, where he saw combat against enemy soldiers mounted on elephants in the first Anglo-Burmese War. In 1825, while a Lieutenant only 17 years of age, he married a native woman he called 'Mena' who spoke English, having converted to Christianity as a pupil of an American Baptist missionary named Adoniram Judson and his wife Ann. But Mena died of some fever before she could accompany Dad back home to England. He was seriously wounded in the war against the Burmese …almost lost his left arm he used to say…at a place called Donubyu. And he won a medal for his bravery under fire. He came home at Captain's rank to his family England in 1828, having been promoted by the overall Commander, Sir Archibald Campbell.

Dad worked for a time as an apparitor for the Hertfordshire court, and he worked in the family cooperage as well, but in 1831 he moved to a flat in London and read for the law in the first class of the King's College there. He got his solicitor's license in 1834 and went to work as an international business manager for the Sailcloths firm of Day, Son, and Hewitson in 1835 (in 1910 this firm was located on London's Victoria Street). His father Nicholas died two years later and Father sold the Croft Cask, Keg, and Barrel Company to a group of its employees…giving him and the other heirs considerable money for ten years thereafter.

After a few years, the Head of the Day, Son, and Hewitson firm asked Father to go to Australia and be their agent in their Sydney, New South Wales, office. This he decided to do after marrying his first cousin, Mary Ann Stead of Brixton, at the Islington Church on the 21st of March, 1843. They sailed for 6 months. Fellow passengers, with whom they made lasting friendships, were the Morts and the Tooths. Robert Tooth was later knighted by King Edward.

They arrived in Sydney later that 1843 year. The Mercantile & Sailcloth business proved so successful that John and a partner named Smith organized the Smith-Croft Company next door to the General Post Office on George Street in Sydney. Dad speculated in cattle, the Bathhurst Goldfields, and some sugar and sheep plantations, and was a partner with the Morts and the Tooths at

Twofold Bay on the Southeast Coast. He accumulated several fortunes and build a huge sandstone mansion called 'Mount Adelaide' at Darling Point, northeast of central Sydney.

Father was very adventurous and so he once took a voyage on the ship of a bank financier and 'blackbirder' named Benjamin Boyd out of Rushcutter's Cove on the Parramatta River to the Cannibal or Solomon Islands to trade barter items to the headhunter chiefs for groups of natives to come work on the Australian plantations of Croft & Tooth and others. The best items for barter were the large Londontown mirrors which the natives were fascinated by as they had never before seen their faces. The chief of the tribe would have two of his standard-bearers hold the mirror while he would admire the length of his privates in the nude. For such a wonderful looking glass the chief would sometimes give the ship's captain as many as 5 complete families to sail away to the 'land down under.'

One minor headhunter chief, a magnificent specimen, volunteered to go himself. He was named 'Chief Dickybird' as he was always in trouble. After a year this native ran amok in the native village on the plantation and killed four of his brethren. All of these were eaten with great relish by their kinfolk, but poor Chief Dickybird was hung high on a eucalyptus tree before he could take part in the delicacy.

I was born in Sydney at 20 minutes past 10:00 a.m. on the 21st day of March in 1848. The other two surviving children were my brother Henry (Harry) and our elder sister Mary Anne. Dad and Mother had 7 children but four died of puerile (teething) fever. My dear mother died also of rheumatic fever in 1857 and lies with my brothers and sisters in the Camperdown Cemetery in the Croft plot. She passed away while under the treatment of Dr. Bellamy, a homeopathic practioner who had given her great relief in earlier complaints of minor importance. In the St. Andrew's Cathedral (Church of England) there is a stained glass window in memory of Mother, donated by my father. Each of the four main parts of the window depicts four separate parables in the New Testament. I attended the dedication ceremony in the Spring of 1858.

In 1859, two years after the death of Mother, Father decided to sell out lock, stock, and barrel and return to jolly old England. This he did, taking with him 150,000 pounds…a considerable fortune in those days.

Our family boarded the sailing vessel 'La Hogue' and began a 12,000 mile trip to England when I was 11 years old. It proved an exciting and dangerous trip. Six weeks out of Sydney one of the crew was attacked by smallpox, a very dangerous affair on a crowded ship. The sailor was placed in a lifeboat and slung over the side of the vessel. A cabin boy, whose face indicated he had previously had the disease and survived, was put in the lifeboat to look after the sick man. Fortunately, they both survived recovered in eight days and we were delivered from further outbreak. On the way we were beset by unusual storms and, going around the Cape of Good Hope, we lost six seamen overboard who were trying to reef the huge square sails which were torn to shreds on the yards during the storm.

Shortly after our ship reached St. Helena, scurvy broke out amongst the crew and lime juice was administered in large quantities. What proved even better was watercress, which had been loaded on board in good quantity before we left the island. After this hazardous voyage we finally hove-to at Gravesend on the 10th of May, 1859.

In England, my Father placed Henry and me in the finest schools. I began Eton in 1861. Whilst there I and my fellow students had our seats warmed many times while we bent spread-eagled over those famous 'birching stools.' I graduated from it in 1866 (cf. pp. 221, 226), having been accepted by Trinity College at Cambridge, where I began my university studies that year. Henry was a student at Rugby and then, from 1874 on, he was a student at the Derby School of Mining Engineering where he finished in 1878.

In the same year, 1866, that I graduated from Eton and entered Cambridge, our family intermarried with the Garrett family of industrialists in Leiston, Suffolk. That is, my Father John Croft married Sarah Louisa Garrett, second daughter of Richard and Elizabeth Garrett, on April 5th, and my older sister Mary Anne Croft married the youngest child of Richard and Elizabeth Garrett, their son Frank, Sr., on December 5th. So these two couples produced 20 children by 1887, four years after my Father's death. My sister and her husband Frank bought a house in Aldringham big enough to raise them all, and take care of Father too, who had been mentally incapacitated by his grief over his wife Sarah's death in 1874 and was declared a lunatic…so that he also lived thereafter at the Aldringham House until he died in it in January of 1883.

The man who later became Prime Minister and who married the richest girl in England, and who won the Derby THREE times, was a class-mate of mine at Eton. His name was Archibald Philip Primrose Roseberry and, in later years, Lord Roseberry. He later proved a brilliant statesman and a great benefactor of the Croft family. I always thought that 'Philip' was a little daft as he was always bragging about becoming rich and winning the Derby one day. His prophecy came true—he married the only daughter of the London family of the Rothschilds, one of the richest families in the world.

In March of 1868, just prior to my 20th birthday, I quit school at Cambridge University as I was eager to go back to Australia and perhaps seek my fortune. I was full of enthusiasm when I boarded the *SS Helvetia* at Portsmouth. This ship proved most unseaworthy and was uncomfortable to the last degree. The weather blew a gale all the way to Alexandria and the only respite was the two coaling stops at Gibraltar and Malta.

On landing in Alexandria we passengers were placed on board a large mastless scow or canal barge, shaped like a large doughnut. On this contraption we were towed up the Mahmoudieh Canal for 10 hours until we reached Atfieh on the Nile. From there we traveled by steamer to Cairo in 16 hours.

We stayed at the Shepherd's Hotel for Europeans for THREE days which I enjoyed immensely as it was my first sight of an Eastern city with its picturesque mosques, bazaars, and the curious Mohammedans being called to prayer. A trip to the pyramids and the great Sphinx proved both interesting and quite painful as I was bitten in the thigh by an evil-tempered camel, which bite became infected and bothered me all the way to Sydney.

From Cairo our route lay across the open desert for 90 miles and the road was a mere cut in the sand, which was extremely difficult to follow at night when it was cold and very windy. The journey was unbearably hot by day with the temperatures reaching 120 degrees F. at times. We rode in a wash-tub affair accommodating six persons and drawn by four mules. My fellow travelers were mostly Sandhurst graduates on their way to 'Inja's sunny climes.' This transit took 18 hours with only an occasional stop for refreshments. The luggage was carried on camels, as were the mails, cargo, and even the coal used by the Red Sea steamers. The camel is truly the lifeline of the desert peoples.

Upon arrival at Suez the ship *SS Malabar* awaiting us, and here I said goodbye to my Sandhurst friends who were to reinforce the Calcutta and Bombay constabularies for Her Majesty, Queen Victoria, Empress of India.

When we reached Sydney in August 1868, I visited many of Father's friends, including the Morts and the Tooths. Sir (sic) Robert Tooth gave me a job on one of his huge sheep stations near Christchurch in New Zealand where he kept 30,000 head. This farm lay in Canterbury Province, most beautiful at all times of the year, and here I decided that some day I would so settle. I had a jolly visit with some distant cousins, Henry and Harry Croft, sons of James Croft, at that time Archdeacon of Canterbury (1784-1869).

After 22 months 'down under,' I returned to England in 1870. On the train ride back to my family in Suffolk, I met Miss Alice Downing of Aldeburgh, Suffolk, who was to be my bride a few short years later. In August 1870 the French police in Paris imprisoned Alice, her sister Agnes, and her brother Alfred (later surveyor of the Columbia River, USA, under General Miles) while they were vacationing there. The French thought they were Teuton spies because of their blonde hair and blue eyes. Hearing the dread news, I hurried to see my old classmate Lord Roseberry and told him the sad news. Lord Roseberry immediately pulled the strings with Prime Minister Gladstone, who contacted the French government with a 'polite but decided communiqué' and kept the Downing sisters and Alfred from being shot as spies. Of course I would not be telling you, my children, these stories if my dear wife, your mother, had been shot as a spy in that Franco-Prussian mess.

Alice and I were married on July 5th, 1876, at St. Martin's Registry in London, and after our firstborn, Sydney—originator of the Sydney Croft Easter Lily in Bandon in Oregon—was born in London, we decided to become cattle ranchers in

America. We left England in the fall of 1878, two years after the Custer Massacre. It seems we Crofts are bitten with wanderlust. I trust that you, my sons, will keep these records for posterity. —- Emund J. 'Ted' Croft."

Ted Croft died on December 22nd, 1925, in the Tacoma home of his son Lee's family (cf. p. 386). He had so worded his own will that his entire remaining financial estate be put into a trust after his death...thence to be distributed equally to *all his* ***grandchildren*** *living after the death of his last-to-die son.*

Ted's "last-to-die son" was my own grandfather, Henry William "Lee" Croft, who survived his brothers Sydney, Edmund J. "Miccie," and Jeremiah "Jerry" to pass away on December 15th of 1951, when I was five years old. It took three years for Grandpa Lee's Tacoma lawyer, Elizabeth Shackleford, to distribute the proceeds of Ted Croft to the EIGHT grandchildren from his four deceased sons: (Sydney had no issue); (Miccie's children) Marshall (1919-1990) and Geraldine Croft Ketel Robben (1922-2004); (Lee's children): William Sydney "Bill" (1919-2003), Bliss Henry (1921-2009) and Gloria Rose Croft Wise Peterson Dickerson Jones (1926-1979); (and Jeremiah's children) Edmund "Doyle" (1914-1994), Jerry, Jr. (1916-1971) and Alice Patricia "Pat" Croft Kasseroff Burla (1917-2005).

Each of the eight final heirs, essentially of their great grandfather John Croft's money, passing on to them through their grandfather Edmund "Ted" Croft's will, consisted of: 607 shares of Southern California Edison common stock, 176 shares of General Motors common stock, and 6 shares of Lion Oil common stock, plus $504.80 in cash. At the time of the distribution on January 2, 1952 the stocks and the cash totaled $4,440.80 in taxable value. My mother, Norma Rose Dingeldein Croft (1927-2022, cf. p. 283) insisted that my Dad, Bill Croft, not spend any of this money on oil wells in Montana where they were living…that the stock be left as is in the market, hopefully to grow in value for the "benefit of our children current and future." As it turned out, the Lion oil company was purchased by another oil company, whose stock they then came to own…and both General Motors and Southern California Edison split a time or two and made some changes (e.g. SCE becomes Pacific Gas and Electric as it grew well).

After the death of my father in 2003, I asked my mother, Norma Croft, how receiving the 1952 bequest from my great grandfather Edmund "Ted" Croft had benefitted them, she answered, "YOU were the primary beneficiary. That money grew by my management and it paid for two years of your college expenses (both tuition and board) in the 1964-5 academic year at Montana State University in Bozeman and the more expensive 1966-7 term of you and wife Betty (cf. pp. 279, 282) and baby daughter Cathy when you attended Arizona State University in Tempe in 1966-7…as well as a year of your brother Jerry's tuition and board in that same 1966-7 year at Montana State University before he went to Vietnam in the Navy."

As I thought about the financial troubles I had to get through my university years, I realized that my great great grandfather John Croft's body had been in a grave in England for 120 years, but his financial legacy had helped me, in his fifth generation of issue, afford a higher education in the United States…in places he could scarce have imagined. That's why I've written my three books about his life and times.

The End

Special Dedication

I dedicate this book to my cousin Margaret Craig Young (b. 1936-) of the Woodburn estate in Kesgrave, Nr. Ipswich, Suffolk, UK, and to her husband, Dr. Stewart Young. Margaret and I are both in John Croft's fifth generation of issue. Margaret is the leading family genealogist and I am her admiring apprentice. —Lee B. Croft, December 15, 2023.

TABLE OF CONTENTS

LIST OF ILLUSTRATIONS

And now to the READERS…Thanks so much for your patience.

This is now REALLY the END….**КОНЕЦ**

Made in the USA
Columbia, SC
16 January 2024

29430019R00237